The Search for

Editor: Harry Tomlinson

In association with
The British Educational Management and Administration Society

THE SEARCH FOR STANDARDS

Longman Group UK Limited
Westgate House, The High, Harlow, Essex, CM20 1YR
Telephone Harlow (0279) 442601
Telex 81491 Padlog
Facsimile (0279) 444501

© BEMAS British Educational Management and Administration Society, 1992

All rights reserved; no part of this publication may be reproduced, stored in a retrieval system, or transmitted in any form or by any means, electronic, mechanical, photocopying, recording, or otherwise, without either the prior written permission of the Publishers or a licence permitting restricted copying issued by the Copyright Licensing Agency Ltd, 90 Tottenham Court Road, London W1P 9HE

ISBN 0-582-07116-X

A catalogue record for this publication is available from the British Library

Typeset in Plantin 10 on 11pt by
Communitype Communications Ltd, Leicester

Printed in Malaysia by TCP

Contents

Contributors v

Foreword x

Preface xi

PART I THE BROADER CONTEXT

1 An overview of ERA + 3 *Duncan Graham* 1

2 Evaluating standards in education *Bert Benham* 15

3 Industry, politics and the search for standards *Harry Tomlinson* 28

PART II THE INTERNATIONAL CONTEXT

4 Standards or standardisation: school reform in the United States and Great Britain *Bruce Cooper and Wayne Shute* 45

5 Quality in education: standards in Europe *Joanna Le Métais* 68

PART III THE PROFESSIONAL CONTEXT

6 The implications for the Examination Boards of the *Education Reform Act* of 1988 *Kathleen Tattersall* 89

7 The changing perception of standards in the independent sector: the impact of ERA *Vivian Anthony* 105

8 To lever up educational standards? *John Horn* 125

9 Choice or chaos? *Peter Smith* 136

PART IV PARTNERSHIPS

10 Captive audience *Joan Sallis* 147

11 Developing school governor effectiveness in the 1990s *Mike Kelly* 155

PART V QUALITY AND STANDARDS

12 Total Quality Management and standards in further education *Edward Sallis* — 169

13 In the pursuit of quality *Mike Ash* — 189

14 Improving schools: an approach to quality in Birmingham *Peter Ribbins and Elizabeth Burridge* — 198

Index — 221

Contributors

Vivian Anthony is the Secretary of the Headmasters' Conference. He was Headmaster of Colfe's School in London from 1976–1990 and has been the Chief Examiner (Awards) in A Level Economics for the Oxford & Cambridge Board for nearly 20 years. He has written or contributed to many books and articles on Economics and Education.

He was educated at Cardiff High and LSE, Cambridge, Oxford and Leeds Universities. Apart from lecturing in education at Leeds University he has also taught at Leeds Grammar School, Tonbridge and the King's School, Macclesfield. He has chaired the Academic Policy Sub-Committee of the Headmasters' Conference 1988–90 and served on the Professional Development Committee.

Michael Ash started teaching in 1967. His teaching career included experience in secondary modern, grammar and comprehensive schools, and finally as Deputy Head and Acting Head at Fairham Community School, Nottingham. He has been General Education Inspector in Ealing and Senior General Adviser in Suffolk. More recently he has been Principal Advisory Officer and the Assistant Director in Bradford, and is now seconded to Bradford and District Training and Enterprise Council as Education Initiatives Manager. In 1988/89 he was adviser to the management side for the National Steering Group for Teacher Appraisal. From 1990 he has been Education Officer for the National Association of Inspectors and Education Advisers (NAIEA).

Bert Benham is an independent consultant in public service management. When the Audit Commission began operation in 1983 he was invited to join it from HM Treasury where, as an operational research scientist, he co-ordinated work on performance measurement in government departments. Until September 1989 he managed the Audit Commission's special studies in education. He is a Visiting Fellow at the University of London's Institute of Education.

Elizabeth Burridge is Policy Adviser for Monitoring and Evaluation for the LEA in Birmingham. As such she has carried day-to-day responsibility for the city's initiative in quality development. Before that she was Co-ordinator of Quality Development in the Continuing Education Division. She has also taught in further education and in primary school. She has written extensively on a wide range of aspects of Monitoring and Evaluation in Education.

Bruce S. Cooper Ph.D., is professor of Educational Administration, Policy and Urban Education at Fordham University, School of Education, New York City. He is a graduate of the University of Chicago, and has authored the following books: *Federal Aid for the Disadvantaged: What Future Chapter?; Taking Charge; State Actions for School Reform in the 1980s* with Denis Doyle and Roberta Trachtman; *Labor Relations in Education: International Perspectives; Training for School Management,* with R. Wayne Shute; and *The Graying of America's Teachers: Retirement and Early Retirement Incentives* with Frank V. Auriemma. Dr Cooper is currently examining the micro-finances of eight school districts, with Robert Sarrel.

After a career in teaching and local government administration, **Duncan Graham** became Chief Education Officer for Suffolk in 1979. He developed the National Scheme for Teacher Appraisal and brought about considerable curriculum change in Suffolk. He served on the Burnham Committee and chaired the National Mathematics Working Party. He was Chief Executive of Humberside County Council for a short period and then Chairman and Chief Executive of the National Curriculum Council from 1988 until 1991. He is now an Educational Consultant and is working on projects with Birmingham and Manchester Universities.

John Horn has been Head of Ossett School since 1979. He previously taught at Lee School, Cambridge and Millham School, Cumbria, before becoming Head of Aireborough Grammar School, Leeds in 1973. As a member of the SHA Education Committee he was involved in responses to Better Schools, the Higginson Committee, the Arts in Schools and Lower Attaining Pupils' Project. He was Chair of the SHA's Education Committee, and as Honorary Secretary from 1986 to 1988 involved in writing SHA's response to the Education Bill. As the Act has been implemented he has been for 3 years a member of SHA's presidential trio, serving as President in 1989–90, taking as his theme 'One Purpose – the Best for All'.

Mike Kelly is Head of the Education Management Centre at Manchester Polytechnic, and is currently chair of governors at a Manchester primary school, and deputy chair of governors at a secondary school in the city. As part of his professional work on management training and development in educational organisations, his research and consultancy work focuses upon occupational stress among head teachers and principals, the development of appropriate mentoring arrangements for newly appointed heads, under the School Management Task Force initiative, and the effectiveness of school governance.

Since 1984 **Joanna Le Métais** has been Head of EPIC Europe (Education Policy Information Centre) and National Head of the EURYDICE education policy information network for England, Wales and Northern Ireland. EPIC provides an information service to senior policy-makers and in other member states of the EC through the EURYDICE network. She was educated in the Netherlands, Australia, England and France and has been Head of the Foreign Languages Department in a comprehensive school before working in local authority administration. Now a member of the Institute of Directors, she has published numerous papers on education policy and carried out research on the impact of teacher mobility (Association of Education Committees Trust), and factors affecting mobility within the EC, sponsored by the Commission of the EC and the NFER.

Peter Ribbins is Reader in Educational Management in the School of Education, University of Birmingham. Before this he worked in public sector higher education, as an education officer and as a teacher in two secondary schools in London. He has spent many years as Consultant to the Quality Development in Colleges and Schools Projects in Birmingham. Currently he is Editor for BEMAS of *Educational Management and Administration* journal.

Edward Sallis is the Associate Principal at Brunel College of Technology, Bristol. He has experience in further education working in six colleges, where he has taught management and public administration. His current research interest is in quality assurance and in particular the application of Total Quality Management to education. He has published widely in the field, including *The National Quality Survey* (1991), *College Quality Assurance Systems* with Peter Hingley (1991), and *Total Quality*

Management and Further Education, also with Peter Hingley of Bristol Polytechnic (1992).

Joan Sallis is a miner's daughter from Wales who obtained a first class honours degree and worked for 10 years in the administrative civil service. She resigned to have her family and it was concern about the poor image of, and low level of public participation in, the state education system which led her to become involved in home/school issues and the reform of governing bodies. She served on the Taylor Committee in 1975–7 and has since worked almost full-time lecturing, writing and campaigning, throughout this time being deeply involved in CASE, the Campaign for State Education, of which she is National President. Joan writes weekly for the *Times Educational Supplement* and has written several successful books about parents and governors, guides to the law and much governor training material. She has visited Australia as a Commonwealth Fellow, is a special professor in Nottingham University and an associate fellow in the Educational Management Unit of Leicester University. In 1989 she won a Jerwood Award for CASE, given for a 'distinguished contribution to the theory and practice of education'. She lectures in over 70 LEAs and has spoken to over half the state school heads in England and Wales.

R. Wayne Shute, Ed.D. is professor of Educational Leadership, College of Education, Brigham Young University, Provo, Utah, and Director of Doctoral Programs and a graduate of the University of Southern California. He has written numerous books and articles, including recently *Training for School Management: Lessons from the American Experience*, with Bruce Cooper (1988), *British Columbia's 'Year 2000': A Plan in Jeopardy*, with N.A. Muhtadi in *The Canadian School Executive*, 11:1 & 2, (May–June 1991), and 'Standardele Educatieri Americane,' *Revista de Pedagogie* (May 1991).

After he came down from Oxford, **Peter Smith**, an English graduate started his career as a city banker. After three years, however, he succumbed to his family's destiny by entering the teaching profession, first teaching in a grammar school in London, but later moving to a direct grant school (which subsequently went independent) in Croydon.

He joined the staff of the Assistant Masters Association in 1974. After the Assistant Masters and Mistresses Association came into being in 1978 he was appointed Deputy General Secretary and, since 1988 has been the Association's General Secretary. Described by *Education* as possessing '*an original and analytic mind with a caustic vein of humour'*, Peter Smith now leads a teachers' association which has more than doubled its size in the last 10 years and is the leading teachers' union in the independent sector.

Kathleen Tattersall, a former teacher with both secondary and primary school experience, had been Secretary to two CSE examination boards, ALSEB and NWREB, and to one of the foremost GCE boards, the JMB. She has been a researcher with the Schools Council and is the author of *Differentiated examinations; a strategy for assessment at 16+?* Kathleen was a member of the first Council of the SEAC from 1988 to 1990. She is now Chief Executive Designate to the Northern Examinations and Assessment Board (NEAB), which is being formed from a merger between the JMB, ALSEB, NREB, NWREB and YHREB. It will become operational in September 1992.

Harry Tomlinson is Principal of Margaret Danyers College, Stockport. After working abroad and in Lincolnshire, Essex and Walsall he has been headteacher and principal of three other institutions in Manchester and Stockport all of which have closed due to reorganisations. He is Treasurer of the Secondary Heads Association (SHA) and Chair of their Equal Opportunities Working Party, Chair of the Manchester Branch of the British Institute of Management (BIM), and National Chair of the British Educational Management and Administration Society (BEMAS). He has recently edited *Performance Related Pay in Education*.

Foreword

As we move into the 1990s with the Conservative government having achieved a renewed mandate and a new Secretary of State it is a sensible time to look back at the impact of the Education Reform Act. BEMAS has published a series of books on the implications of ERA and this one provides an opportunity for a review of what has been achieved and, unsurprisingly, to consider whether any inadequacies in the legislation have been revealed.

Harry Tomlinson has persuaded many of those who have played significant roles in the education service in the last four years to consider the impact of ERA. There has been a shriller and more insistent emphasis on improving standards since the Callaghan Ruskin speech. This book provides an opportunity for the reader to consider the impact of ERA on quality and standards in a deliberately rather wider context.

The initial overview is presented by Duncan Graham who was central in the development of the National Curriculum, as the curriculum is the major issue in improving standards. The context requires clarification of the meaning of standards and also the relationship between business and politics. The international dimension involves a consideration of both European and US perspectives. Leading members of teacher associations consider the impact on pupils and teachers. The changes in testing and examinations inevitably perhaps need to be understood. The roles of parents and governors in the new dispensation provide a framework for a final consideration of issues relating to quality in further education, but also the future of the advisory/inspectorate services and LEAs and their role in improving standards and quality.

This issue of standards is complex, but it is important that standards improve. This book provides a thorough analysis of where we are, how we have reached this situation and the significance of ERA in this, and by implication provides an opportunity for a consideration of how the new government might be advised to develop policy. BEMAS, like the government, can now look forward to the 1990s and further challenges. It is hoped that serious analysis of 'the story so far' will inform future developments.

Derek Esp

Preface

Part I puts the search for standards in context. As former Chairman and Chief Executive of the National Curriculum Council, Duncan Graham is in an ideal position to present an overview of the effects of the *Education Reform Act*. His main emphasis is on curriculum improvement and he deliberately places teaching and learning at the centre. The broader aspects and consequences of *ERA* he evaluates in terms of their contributions to learning. Bert Benham examines what we actually mean by standards. It is important to ensure that the debate about standards is clear conceptually, and that the technical issues are understood. Further scientific research and operational work on monitoring standards are required if we are to find acceptable evidence to make meaningful judgements. Harry Tomlinson attempts to put *ERA* in its historical and political context. He examines how the supposed needs of industry, the nature of the enterprise culture and the forms the new vocationalism takes distort, for political reasons, the debate about standards.

In Part II the British experience is placed in the wider international context. Bruce Cooper and Wayne Shute examine the differences between US and British experience. The most obvious contrast they explore is between a country with a common national curriculum which is heavily tested in Britain, and a highly decentralised curriculum in the USA with the testing system not aligned at all with the curriculum. Joanna Le Métais examines the issues which are seen as significant in Europe in secondary and higher education in particular. Resources are only made available when there is evidence they will produce improved standards. The solutions, across the range of issues dealt with in this book, vary greatly in different parts of Europe.

In Part III the meaning of standards in examinations and schools is the main focus. Kathleen Tattersall discusses the role of examinations and the examination boards in assessment, but also the impact of the new relationships on the curriculum and teaching methodology. The tensions between Key Stage 4 assessment and GCSE is one area where the boards may be able to assist in ensuring a consistent, reliable and coherent set of national standards. Vivian Anthony questions whether the introduction of GCSE has not led to a decline in standards, which he suggests may also be the case at A-level. He is concerned that standards for those of highest ability should not decline as a consequence of *ERA*. John Horn considers the ragbag of the parts of *ERA* and questions fundamentally the whole market approach to raising standards. He suggests that the effect of raising standards for some has been calculated to lower standards for others, particularly with the distortions of funding reinforcing this trend. The politicians who carried this through are ignorant of the maintained system. Peter Smith examines the history of choice in the educational system and the political context in which *ERA* emerged. Looking forward he makes the case for a nationwide strategic plan with clearly focussed additional resources if we are to achieve genuine fundamental change.

Part IV presents views from the two groups empowered by the Act to improve standards, parents and governing bodies. Joan Sallis looks at *ERA* as it affects parents and schools. She does not underestimate the failure of schools to take parents sufficiently seriously in the past. However she recognises how the Act has changed relationships between teachers and parents, not always helpfully. Parents still may not have all the information they need to work with teachers to make schools better. Mike Kelly provides a model for increasing school governor effectiveness. His three key results areas are organisational focus and direction, organisational productivity and review of progress. The model provides a framework of planning for those trying to ensure that governing bodies produce the improvements in school performance that they were established to achieve.

Part V clarifies the meaning of the concept of quality, in practice the central issue if the search for higher standards is to be achieved despite or alongside government policies. Edward Sallis provides a consideration of Total Quality Management (TQM) in practice. The particular context is further education and the relationship of TQM to BS5750. Mike Ash examines the history of inspection by both HMI and LEA, and the implications of current developments. Quality assurance is his major focus and this arises from quality processes. He suggests that validation and accreditation procedures like those in higher education would be appropriate for individual institutions. The role of the LEA he suggests is not essential. Peter Ribbins and Elizabeth Burridge however demonstrate how one LEA which takes quality seriously can create a purposeful role for itself and improvement for its schools. Birmingham is certainly one of the most successful LEAs in quality development with its comprehensive training package. The model developed could be replicated elsewhere. Standards are being improved in Birmingham by taking quality assurance seriously.

The search for higher standards is crucial and complex. It is obviously a matter of international importance. Those working in the educational system in Britain are clearly aware of the danger of oversimplifying the issues, but also recognise that quality developments may provide the way to achieve improved standards. This book demonstrates that three years after *ERA* the evidence for higher standards is uncertain. If standards are higher the contribution of *ERA* is equally questionable. This book provides a full opportunity to consider the evidence.

PART I: THE BROADER CONTEXT

1 An overview of ERA + 3

Duncan Graham

The National Curriculum in its early days had about it an aura of revolution, reflected to a lesser extent in changes to management and control of schools. The meat may have been too strong for the English palate and there is a post-convulsionary retreat to the more familiar compromise and muddle, initiated by politicians and seized on for different reasons by opposing sections of the educational establishment, professional and lay. As pillars of the past such as LEAs and HMI are toppled, there is a seeming paradox – is this being done to promote changes which they have resisted or to enable a smoother reversion to what preceded them – the traditional 'golden age' values? It looks as if their achievements are to be thrown out with their perceived excesses. We are witnessing the eclipse of the expert – 'educationist' being for the present a pejorative appellation: it is a matter of debate as to how far this is justified – and further, what will be the consequences of the populist approach to management and policy formulation. If it is a howling success – and it could be, what will that say for the establishment over the last 20 years?

It may assist an objective evaluation in due time, if we review the causes of such rapid change, progress, and the possible outcomes. A clearer understanding might enable us to mitigate heartache and tears, and to take heart from the more solid achievements. It might help towards a more balanced approach to complicated issues which deserve more than the black/white 'yah-boo' treatment which often passes for debate in our political system. Perhaps we could forget about unrelieved gloom and national self-flagellation about standards and inject some morale-boosting optimism instead. At least, education is for the moment at the top of the political agenda.

The yardsticks for measuring success to date and in the future derive from the past. It is necessary, perhaps painful, to reflect on why change was inevitable. The decade following the Ruskin speech has seen heated debate. Some of it has reflected international concerns. A common theme is that of Economic Competitiveness – or the lack of it in the 'old' industrial world. By 1985 the signs of being beaten at their own game by emergent Eastern nations was too worrying to be ignored in the USA: it was concluded in the White House that even if no more mistakes were made, it could be too late – hence a series of initiatives. As here, the link was made with education – and with the 'bottom 40 per cent' where the UK does pretty abysmally. If education is economically and commercially significant then inexorably education and its link with training is highlighted, as it has been in Europe, the USA and New Zealand. In these places, but especially here, this has led to shooting from the hip at the pianist, before listening to the tune. To be fair the melody has been cacophonous rather than euphonic: the education establishment, in failing to justify and explain what it was about, may seem to have gone out of its way to court disaster.

A volatile combination of professional reticence by the many, and extremist talk from the few has dented public confidence more than most teachers realise. In the last year or two I have been all too often cross-examined by well-meaning anxious parents about their unshakeable conviction that the basics (whatever they are) are no longer taught (if they ever were!). Common sense tells us that children need a bit of old-fashioned discipline as well as mastering self-discipline, that not everything a child learns can be enjoyable, that slog is a part of learning (and life), and 'learning by doing' can be usefully augmented by learning by rote. Parents are dubious that long-division no longer matters, or that reading can be acquired by osmosis. Ninety-nine per cent of teachers agree, and teach accordingly but are not perceived to be doing so. This is fertile ground for those who want change to their own agenda and are not encumbered by facts or evidence but fuelled by conviction. The debate becomes polarised and confrontationalist, lacking in objective analysis. A group of parents handed a questionnaire with blanks to be filled, went to town on 'All teachers are . . .', 'Standards have gone . . .', 'Basics are not . . .'. Whatever research has been going on in recent years, it has not been able to furnish evidence objective enough to raise and inform the quality of the debate.

Some longer standing weaknesses in our system are unique to it – for example the 'Romantic Flaw' or 'Matthew Arnoldism'. Technology passed us by to the extent that by 1939, as Corelli Barnett points out, Britain had 200 technology colleges, Germany 3,000, while our universities preferred pure to applied science. Much of our curriculum has been, to be charitable, ill-suited to most youngsters, particularly as they approach the end of compulsory schooling. The accusation of 'watered-down academic' holds water still: our examination system does not help. Not surprisingly therefore, and despite substantial improvement in the last three years, tradition is strong and many have opted out physically or mentally before 16. We should worry as much about the staying *in* rate as about the staying *on* rate. Making the work enjoyable or less demanding does not seem to have helped. Polls have shown that many recent leavers have considered their last years at school as wasted, with as many as a third confessing to doing 'not much or nothing at all'. They would have preferred more vocational education, more relevance, and more discipline. Their view is reinforced by the 1991 British Social Attitudes Survey – more training and more discipline are the things which parents want.

This fact is hardly surprising when the diet offered for examination as recently as 1988 is considered. Fifteen per cent of pupils were studying no English or mathematics, only 15 per cent took a balanced science course, with boys taking physics and girls biology. Almost none took three sciences – an interesting thought for the independent schools lobby to ponder! Less than 40 per cent tackled a foreign language, less than 60 per cent history or geography, less than a third any of the creative arts. The premature slamming of doors echoed throughout the land. The National Curriculum should in time remedy this, although the retreat from an entitlement to balance to age 16, and seeing 'vocational slants' as add-on extras gives cause for concern.

Behind everything lies the intractable standards argument. However we twist and weave over international comparisons, there is no evidence which suggests that ours are too high; likewise with expectations where the contrast with emerging nations is stark. The public perception is pessimistic – perhaps unjustifiably so. Teachers are pilloried, without objective evidence. HMI talk of excessive concentration on 'the basics', the public perception is to the contrary.

In looking at the last three years, tentative yardsticks (or perhaps metresticks?) begin to emerge. Have standards improved since *ERA,* or at least is there evidence that they will? Is the curriculum now more relevant to the needs of youngsters and of the country? Are the 'basics' more clearly identified and addressed? Is there meaningful dialogue between professional and consumer – stimulated by changes in management, governing bodies, parental reports and so on? Has or will teacher appraisal improve classroom performance and teacher image? Has local management contributed to improved performance in the classroom or merely served as a distraction? Are examinations at

16 and 18 better geared to the country's needs? and has the academic/vocational divide been narrowed at all? Most importantly has a broad balanced curriculum been preserved – or is that an outmoded uncommercial concept in itself? Has methodology changed for the better, particularly in relation to progression and differentiation?

It is worth considering how the reform initiatives which have poured forth in a torrent relate, if at all, to each other? How much thought went in to absorption and assimilation rates? Where was the Business Plan so dear to the hearts of the private sector? Were the resource implications costed – people and material? Was a break-even point identified? Cynics might wish to know how much of it was the result of prejudice, how much of a compulsive desire to rearrange deck-chairs to distract from the leaks below the waterline of the good school Titanic, not to mention its flat roof!

History is the record of conflict. No analysis of success and failure can be made other than on this basis. The conflicts which lie behind the period since 1988 inevitably involve power-groups and issues. As far as the former are concerned, key groupings were at the centre – Ministers, the DES, other government departments, and the new boys – NCC and SEAC. Ministers tend to have a profound distrust of the professionals, of the education establishment. Change was not in their view going to come from that stable. One only has to look at the concepts, the language, and impracticalities of the master-plan to see this – at once its strength and its weakness. Teachers were not to be trusted, with standards, expectations, content, and especially not with testing. Researchers were not to be entrusted with investigating or validating: in some ways this was the most profound change of all. I recall when invited to chair the Mathematics Working Party that the emphasis was on a group of people from experts to laymen, taking soundings, harnessing common sense and working to impossible deadlines. It was the first indication of the changed order. It must give pause for a great deal of establishment heart-searching that they succeeded at least in the sense that the content of the National Curriculum mathematics syllabus (and that of other subjects) was and is widely accepted. The challenges merely reinforced the ministerial view that they were right – it could have taken 10 years and have omitted tables and long division! As a non-mathematician I saw striking evidence of the gulf between what the 'expert' wanted and what society expected. There is a case that the political thrust was not misplaced. Where it went too far was in over prescription and in the testing saga where the narrow three subject National Curriculum tested by

The Broader Context

short sharp tests concept was rejected with a vengeance. It is intriguing to speculate how much of what was enacted stemmed from the panache of the then Secretary of State and how much flowed from the pens of the civil servants.

The National Curriculum gave an unprecedented opportunity to the DES, for years stung by the jibes of other departments, that they ran nothing, and bypassed by the (then!) all-powerful, richly-resourced MSC. Certainly much of the detailed groundwork and thinking was theirs based on impressive intellectual prowess and little class-room experience. Although NCC and SEAC were later and conveniently to shoulder the blame for over ambition and over elaboration, the Act was set in tablets of stone some time before they put up their plates in York and Notting Hill Gate. In the gentlemanly punch up lasting 150 years between DES (and its predecessors) and HMI, advantage in the curriculum area passed to the former with the latter reacting where previously they had initiated.

The stresses here were to have their impact on the newcomers. NCC was a threat to a DES already under pressure, and might wrest the prize so newly won. SEAC might gain everything from its remit – we all know that what you test is what you get. Apart from facing the problems of establishing organisations and reputations NCC and SEAC were quangos – not things ever favoured by the mandarin establishment. Later they were to find that what is set up by one minister, can be anathema to another! Their greatest problem was to be, and is, to retain an independence which could make their views valuable and respected – mouthpieces of neither politician nor professional. There is, to compound their problems, the view of the recently retired HMCI, that independence equates to impotence in the great power-games.

Equally imponderable was to be their role in supporting change and disseminating information. Having been specifically charged to do this, the central rivalries soon ensured a massively increased output from DES and HMI as well! There then ensued the 'great communications wrangle' which ministers 'solved' by so drastically reducing circulation that the only people who got everything required by all were the Independent schools. The endemic anecdotal approach was applied. It is hardly surprising that Heads assured ministers that they were 'inundated' while almost every major NCC document was sold out and reprinted!

It is too soon to place bets, but how the non-political groups at the centre fare will be increasingly worth the watching. Ironically the reward of the DES for entry into the direct curricular and extracurricular battleground may well be to have become just as suspect as the 'traditional' educationists. What is undoubtedly true is that all at the centre were united in recognising the importance of turning an exciting but unwieldy brute, the national curriculum, into a mechanism for change and improvement. They were conscious of its role as a compensating factor to the decentralising impetus of LMS, opting out, CTCs and so on. We may have to wait 30 years to find out if there was a 'plan' to achieve balance through a localised control of a national curriculum. There was unanimity too in the view that *ERA* having wrested the initiative from the establishment the ball must be handed back to a partnership with teachers and academics if enduring change is to be brought about. It is not clear if that lesson has been absorbed by ministers. Enduring change comes from partnerships and consensus: shock treatment is not a way of life.

The other players had peripheral roles in policy formulation. Lest that be misinterpreted it is vital to emphasise that in implementation, the teaching profession performed miracles – as usual unrecognised and unacknowledged. The evidence from HMI and from NCC is that improvements have been marked, significant, and encouraging, particularly in primary schools. The pace was deliberately unrelenting as politicians need quick results; delay might allow for a successful rearguard action. The unions fought manfully and from my viewpoint, constructively. They predicted the great testing confusion, but were not heard. LEAs and their advisors for the most part, carried through the training and supporting roles with distinction in the face of open hostility bordering on contempt. Some of those in higher education took longer to come round: perhaps now they recognise how vital their role will be in ensuring that the future is one of measured change, rather than the inveterate tinkering which is now the norm – inspired or otherwise.

The support of parents and industry was instant and constant, especially after they began to understand it. It would be hard to abolish the National Curriculum now. Their contribution has been more significant in working out the other consequences; not least resources and management ones. They have detected the incompatibilities of a prescriptive curriculum, no attempt at costing and financing it, and the management of it thrust upon governing bodies. Accountants have been hired to do the sums.

There were conflicts of substance which it was not safe to speak of out loud in the early days. The almost new GCSE was not really compatible with the brand new National Curriculum. One could go so far as to say that they might have been deliberately devised to give the maximum heartache all round. Politically

GCSE had to be supported (even though it was suspected of being a downmarket GCE with too much coursework): reconciling it with Attainment Targets and Programmes of Study was and is a major problem, and a distracting one. There is a good case for seeing the GCSE as anachronistic – why should the UK alone have 'terminal' examinations at 16 when the whole thrust is to improve staying on rates and to give 16 year olds adaptable modules to add to a personalised post 16 programme? Sadly the whisper of the word 'module' could bring forth wrath. How quaint that the services and industry recognise their merit, as do the Scots, but nowhere in Elizabeth House . . .. What the national curriculum and GCSE had in common was their suitability for a course work/modular approach. It is tragic that to put it charitably a misunderstanding of their potential has led to their virtual proscription. The problem of maintaining standards is not presented by the principle of course work, but the practice. It has been cracked in many places, particularly in vocational courses post 16. The work of BTEC in this respect is exemplary.

Had it been possible to base a certificate on the National Curriculum Attainment Targets, delivered in modules, how much easier it would have been to bridge the academic vocational divide and blend school curriculum and NVQ. Everything was and is of course bedevilled by the perverse choice of the 'A' levels as the Gold Standard. It is actually possible to believe in standards and in academic prowess and not to have 'A' levels in their present form and in their narrow focus! Imagine what would happen to innovation of any kind if it was attacked on the premise that 'what we have is so good that we cannot change it for fear of diluting it'! It is tiresome to see overdue change opposed as a threat to standards.

The mess is compounded by the polarisation of testing into the course work versus traditional written exam. Neither is morally superior: both have their place. It is hard to see a higher level qualification in English based solely on course work; it is equally difficult to see technology and practical science tackled on high stools with quill pens. The arguments are developed in other contributions to the book. The argument must not be lost for lack of debate. There is evidence that the public preference for formal testing is growing – more rapidly amongst those with no formal qualifications.

Yet another implicit conflict has been that over the narrow ten subject (to 14 at least) curriculum and the Whole Curriculum. In this respect the Act itself was generous; perhaps surprisingly so in something so prescriptive. It did ensure breadth and balance, accepting the total as more than the sum of the parts. Perhaps because teachers had always seen the curriculum as broad and liberal, with non-examinable, non-vocational, value laden features, the view from the centre was immediately one of suspicion leading to a desire for a narrow 'basics' diet. There was justification of a sort for concerns about standards: less worthy was suspicion that teachers might work to dilute and possibly to subvert. Predictably polarisation set in – not 'both and' but 'either or'. This was NCC's finest hour; even its detractors might concede that the battle for the whole curriculum was waged and won, if only for the time being. It is a fact that after 120 years of State education there was no consensus as to what its overall shape, philosophy, or purpose should be. Treatises abounded, consensus did not. In the seminal Curriculum Guidance Three NCC suggested something rough-hewn but practical – a diet of core and foundation subjects (not immutable) – the statutory base, complemented by *dimensions* which must pervade all that is taught (equal opportunities, multi-cultural education *et al*), *skills* which would be transferable post 16, and *themes* which might be within the subjects or free-standing. NCC identified five which are accepted as a minimum sine quo non: Health Education, Environmental Education, Careers Education, Citizenship and Economic and Industrial Understanding. Who would gainsay their importance? There is real evidence of a levelling up of standards: good practice abounds and curriculum plans are more coherent. Eternal vigilance and the highest of standards in delivery will be required to protect what has been achieved. So will the continued support of industry and commerce whose leaders proved to be enlightened supporters. They accepted that it is quite feasible to make a curriculum more practical and relevant and at the same time to produce good citizens.

A conflict where the judgement of history will be interesting was over multi-cultural education and equal opportunities. NCC did its best to ensure that as dimensions they did pervade all aspects of the curriculum. The accusation that they failed to produce specific guidance documents must be examined both in the light of the professional fear that that could lead to them being pigeon-holed and peripheralised, and of heavy political pressures. Whether the National Curriculum will in time bring about a better deal for the deprived and underprivileged remains to be seen. Tom Sobell the visionary Chief of the New York Education system said chillingly when last in the UK that in spite of everything poverty still equals underachievement. Have the last three years done much to close the gap? The National Curriculum is there to be harnessed. Other changes have probably

The Broader Context

exacerbated the situation and increased inequalities. Choice must be balanced by opportunities.

Conflicts are complex – none more so than those embracing choice and consumerism. The movement has its origins in at least two stables. The more respectable is the response to the exclusion over the years of parents and governors from decision taking. LEAs in the post-war era were no more responsive to public pressure than other bureaucracies. On matters of catchment areas, school choice, reorganisation, and closure, little apparent heed was paid. This is possibly unfair to an extent, and problems were undoubtedly exacerbated by the constraints increasingly placed upon LEAs. Nonetheless the public perception was of big brother imposing: not for the first time, the establishment failed to justify or explain what it was about. Schools followed suit: we can all remember the signs at the door, indicating that any parent bold enough to appear had better report forthwith to the Head . . . . Some of them are still there! Too often it appeared as if the parent was a peripheral adjunct to the business of formal education albeit it consumed only 1,000 or so of the 8,760 hours in a non-leap year. Parents did not have access to the Secret Garden – never mind a hoe or a rake! Schools tended to be defensive in the face of attack underrating the validity of some criticisms; not providing information to refute others. Much has changed, but not in time to halt the movement for greater involvement and choice.

Probably none of this mattered much as the wider political thrust of choice, consumer rights and participation was applied to education. Certainly it did not come as a result of research least of all of what parents actually wanted. The evidence is that parents want involvement rather than having management thrust upon them. Look north of the border to see how an imposed school governor system can result in waves of apathy and an unlikely but effective alliance between parents and teacher unions.

Choice and freedom where schools are concerned are difficult concepts. The results of bestowing it on one group can often be detrimental to another: those in the 'good school' which expands beyond its resources or who are locked into the death throes of a 'poor school'. The struggle between the 'raw results' faction and the 'sociological background' group illustrate graphically the problem both of definition and of choice. The tax and charge-payer who forks out for an under used plant in one school and simultaneously new building down the road has cause to ponder the cost of choice, and of opting out. Local authorities with some justification claim that in fact the changes have resulted in less freedom not more, as their discretion has been whittled away by over regulation.

Although local management of schools may well have its origins in a combination of LEA-bashing and a sound business principle of devolving power to the most effective level, it has become inextricably intermingled with the choice movement. Its benefits seem to be solid in terms of increased managerial discretion. The question is whose? Is it the Head's? It is the Governors'? Whose should it be? Intriguing questions remain to be answered about the effect on the role of the Head. In the longer term will it have been seen to raise the standards of management and educational standards, or one at the expense of the other? How will that be measured and by whom? If competition and a consumer-led philosophy shape curriculum, it will be interesting to see if it is broader or narrower, more or less relevant, more or less vocationally orientated. It may well turn out to be different in different places, which may sit uncomfortably with a National Curriculum. There seems to be looming a conflict between National Standards, on the one hand and consumer-led choice on the other. This may in part explain the trend towards reducing the scope and content of the National Curriculum. There badly needs to be a reasoned case developed for what needs to be the irreducibly essential national entitlement and what is discretionary. The big step forward is that we are examining these problems from quite a different perspective now, a statutory basis for debate.

Equally interesting will be the effect on teaching methodology. One of the great merits of the Act was that it did not prescribe teaching methods – the birthright of the profession. The evidence of the first three years is that the impact has been beneficial. There is no evidence that the wide range employed by schools has been narrowed. Instead they have been critically re-examined and significantly sharpened. Where project methods are used, for example, particular care has to be taken to ensure that the statutory is covered within it or systematically in addition to it. It appears that a balance is being more surely struck between the modern and the more traditional methods. All this is in imminent danger of being swept aside by a tide of romantic traditionalism – gut response to one's own school days, over reaction to anecdotes of widespread trendyism. It is not difficult to call the National Curriculum in aid as a pretext for streaming and serried ranks. This may well be right, for some, but the pressure comes for the wrong reasons. Legitimate and good innovation may become a covert and risky exercise. There is much talk in the USA of the need to step outside existing teaching methods and look for completely fresh alternatives: project 2061 in science is a good example of this. Could the English system be precluded from

The Broader Context

doing the same? Traditionalists will say that is a good thing. The proposition that what was largely founded in the 19th Century is in the right mould for the 21st must be tested by validly researched informed debate.

It is possible for the optimist to see hope in the extent of the debate about education and about standards, however ill-informed about it many of the participants appear to be. Some impartial research might not go amiss, bringing light where there is only heat. The starting point might be quality 'Control' or 'Assurance' or 'Development' as one's semantics dictate. It must be common ground that that is the key to positive change, and that there is at present something of a black hole. The traditional custodians of quality, however imperfectly they are believed to have been performed, are no longer there. HMI are in the process of change and some might say dismantling. LEA advisory services are under political and financial attack, the potential of NCC and SEAC has been limited in many eyes by their increasing politicisation. Can populism and the market place do better? It is an open question – the more so when an attempt has to be made to clarify what quality is.

My views have been shaped by 30 odd years of experience – some of it bitter. My conclusion is that it can be left neither to one group or interest nor to a chance amalgam of all or some of them.

It cannot be left to individual institutions. These lack perspective and comparative experience, and internal mechanisms in any field are open to criticism. Credibility and praise where it is due come better from outside, as do warnings about complacency. Having said that, it is equally true that the best and most effective change comes from within, as long as it is externally moderated, and backed by long-term support.

It cannot be left solely to parents and the community. Their innate common sense is constant. They can see (where politicians can't or won't) cause and effect. That is why they consistently place smaller classes, more books and equipment, better paid teachers above the more fashionable nostrums. Nonetheless, the evidence is that left to it in curricular and standard terms, they discourage change, settle for a norm, and narrow the curriculum. We may need some but not all of this.

It cannot be done by testing and league tables. How convenient – and cheap – if it could be. It is the kind of thing that people believe should be done to others. Many derived quiet amusement from the reaction of the private sector to crude tables compiled by a newspaper. The air was thick with codicils, appendices, and explanations required to give a 'true picture' of selective catchment areas. Some argue for market forces and consumerism based on these tables as 'Evidence'. Those who do, and they include Ministers diminish their own arguments for choice. No one would buy a family car on evidence as flimsy and one-dimensional as that. There are some things which just cannot be made simple for the convenience of political dogma.

Quality cannot be guaranteed by four yearly inspections by outside agencies. Of the many flaws in this I shall let two suffice. To be effective inspection and monitoring need to be part of a continuous process, based on knowledge of the track record of the school and an awareness of change and evolution within it. Snapshots are useful but can be misleading. Visions of itinerant and motley bands of inspectors culled from the 'dispossessed experts' and those industrial consultants who cannot make lucrative pickings elsewhere descending briefly on schools after a good lunch and a glass of mead in the local hostelry are amusing, frightening, and an insult to those who have brought about vast seemingly unrecognised improvements in this area over the years. There could be several thousand of these strolling minstrels, inspired by the profit motive. *'Quis custodiet custodes?'* The system required to control and monitor them properly might cost more than the inspections themselves.

The job might well be done, subject to qualifications, by LEAs. Quite the best work in quality assurance has come from the majority which have worked with schools and teachers, combining a constructive approach with sufficient rigour to ensure change and improvement where necessary, and usually by agreement. It is ten years now since Suffolk for one set up a system based on a curriculum resulting from wide consultation and consensus, and which embodied elements of self-appraisal, external inspection and follow up support. It worked and Suffolk was not alone. In this book there is a contribution from Elizabeth Burridge and Peter Ribbins on a case study in Birmingham which speaks for itself.

LEAs, in my judgement could and should be the basis for the future, but although there are many good LEAs, some are not so good. Sadly, their image has been severely if unjustifiably compromised; their life expectancy is perhaps limited. Alone in any case, they are suspiciously 'expert'. Two things could put them at the epicentre of Assurance. One would be a formalised, structured relationship with a credible professional National Inspectorate. Those of us who have laboured in vain to overcome the prejudices and vested interests which have so far prevented this happening must hope for a rethink. The other is teacher appraisal. Delayed and nibbled round the edges the national system may be but its essential integrity remains intact, its

The Broader Context

benefits clear, its positive powers to improve demonstrated in the pilot studies. It is tempting to believe that a combination of teacher appraisal and a National Curriculum might do the trick on its own. Certainly appraisal touches many hitherto unreached parts of the system.

There is a view in some quarters that all our woes stem from teacher training – 'if that were put right, we should soon have standards, basics and relevance'. These views have been arguably the most uninformed of all. While there is always room for improvement the remarkable changes in training over the last decade have been virtually unremarked by those who prefer to deploy the odd aberration as sufficient grounds for mass condemnation – the ultimate triumph of prejudice over reality. Improvements in training have already occurred. There is more to be done as the National Curriculum beds in. The teacher training institutions have much to offer in consolidating the National Curriculum provided their case is cogently expressed. How tired the clichés are about teacher training, how quick the fixes.

There is no single panacea. There is a yawning gap at the very heart of the nation's concerns. Many groups have something to contribute, but not exclusively, and certainly not at random. There appears to be no agenda for a planned approach to the right blend – the ingredients but not the recipe. We would do well to explore further the accreditation of individual schools as I have seen in California. The model of BS5750 for quality assurance in industry has something to commend it. A process must be devised which brings all the interested parties into play, is consistently applied, and which furnished valid comparative material. It could in time be singularly reassuring to the nation as well as meeting the EEC standards already envisaged.

However defined, the search for standards, is top of everyone's agenda, and has been since the Act of 1988 was enshrined in statute. How does the balance sheet read? On the positive side the National Curriculum, based on such reliable evidence as is available, is beginning to bring about improvements in the curriculum in its planning and in standards. According to the 1991 SCPR Survey there is growing support for a centrally delivered curriculum – almost twice as many as in 1987 support the concept – now a clear majority. The questions arise not about having a National Curriculum but about its scope and specificity, about its breadth and balance and about its testing. Fundamentally they are about whose hand is on the tiller and why. There is a danger that the long thorough preparation will be jeopardised by modifying in haste, if not by whim. While Secretaries of State for Health have not yet performed brain surgery themselves, their counterparts in Education have been less reticent about the detail of education – by ministerial decree history ceased in 1962! There are unresolved power struggles, unresolved debates about testing and external examination at 16 and 18, and unresolved questions about the purpose, nature and emphasis of education.

The expert in education is in danger of extinction. This may not matter, particularly if all that has happened so far is thought to be the result of a conspiracy. On the other hand it is worrying if those who exercise power no longer hear the pros and cons, or are reminded of the financial and human costs. It can be tiresome to be encumbered with facts and practicalities. It can be dangerous not to be. The 'new experts' may have a fairly bumpy learning experience; so might those who teach and learn. In the meantime while the nostrums are peddled, and the fixes are instant and zero cost, parents continue to worry about their own child, about class-sizes, about the shortage of books, and even about teachers pay. They exercise choice by exception and show a healthy disinclination to manage and to run schools. What's new?

2 Evaluating standards in education

Bert Benham

Kinds of standard

It seems sensible to start with some definitions of what we mean by standards. *Collins English Dictionary* (Collins, 1985) is most helpful. Two of the 19 meanings listed there are relevant, and there is even a clue to an issue which warrants, I believe, detailed discussion:

(1) An accepted or approved example of something against which others are judged or measured;
(2) A level of excellence or quality: *a low standard of living*.

Congratulations to the compilers! They are much clearer in their minds, it seems, than many people who are concerned with, and about, standards in education.

First they make the distinction between, on the one hand, a goal, aim, target, objective or budget and, on the other hand, a result, level, or out-turn.

Second they distinguish in one of the entries between a thing being *judged* against a standard and being *measured* against a standard. The main thrust of this chapter will be to draw some conclusions about where we stand in applying this distinction to standards in education.

We might note in passing that the second meaning of the term can imply comparison just as much as the first meaning: one level can be compared with another.

The user of standards

Discussing standards is not a simple matter, not least because what we know about them, what we would like to know and how we define them all depend on who we are. The engineer's idea of a standard, or even the computer programmer's idea, seems rather remote from that of the educationalist. American Standards Association 200 film – ASA 200 – is well known to the camera wielding public and even better known to film manufacturers the world over. Similarly, one does not have to be a computer buff to have heard of ASCII – the American Standard Code for Information Interchange. But IBM know much more about it, and need to know much more, than most users.

It seems, then, that BS, ASA and the like are not at all the kind of thing we are talking about here. The world of education is large, confusing and frequently confused, and lessons drawn from other spheres may on occasion be illuminating.

Take the question of knowledge about standards. Clients or receivers of goods and services need to understand what they are getting. But the providers usually need to know much more than the clients, otherwise they would not be capable of producing the good or service. I myself am very careful to buy electrical goods that conform to British Standards, but I have not the faintest idea about the detailed specifications that allow goods to qualify for the BS mark. I am not even clear about how many BS marks there are. It could just be that I am the victim of an enormous confidence trick. Well, I just feel better that way. Nonetheless I am not so gullible as to be taken in by some manufacturers' claims, BS goods or not.

Now drawing the analogy with education, parents and students need to understand what they are getting, or are offered, in the way of education. But it is quite reasonable to expect that the educationalists need to know more. (And it is no more sensible to attack educationalists for using technical terms or trying to develop new techniques than it is to attack engineers or doctors for doing the same.)

Of course, there is the matter of communication between providers and clients. Sensible providers keep clients happy not only by providing items of high quality but also by making sure the client realises that this is so. Educationalists tend not to be quite as expert as commercial people at this, partly because they are worried lest scarce resources be wasted.

If one looks at, say, *Standards in Education* by HMI, one may be enlightened about the state of education but will not get a very clear idea of how standards are defined. Take, for example, a passage from the 1988–89 publication:

> Standards of work within schools are a continuing worry. While in 90 per cent or so of primary schools basic work in mathematics and

English is satisfactory or better . . . . (Department of Education and Science, 1991)

My own impressions from this are first that these are professional inspectors who really do know what they are talking about, and secondly that things are satisfactory in the areas mentioned. But I am none the wiser about the measures taken to assess the standard. It looks as though there is some kind of scale, because HMI use a fixed set of expressions like 'inadequate', 'poor', 'very poor' and 'satisfactory'. But the 'satisfactory' does not have a detailed specification. Not in *Standards in Education* anyway. I am unclear too about the place of the other kind of standard – the desired position, goal or objective as embodied in ASA 200 film.

Perhaps it would be better if HMI gave a much clearer picture in each one of its reports about how it went about a particular job and how it came to conclusions – not just for the benefit of Heads and teachers but so that the public at large can appreciate the considerable professional expertise that has been applied. Certainly LEA inspectors and advisers could do more to convince the outside world of the value of their contribution. I shall come back to them later.

Measurement and modelling

Educational inspectorates, both local and national, have a particular specialist interest in standards. There is another group of people who have a particular interest: educational investigators and researchers.

The Audit Commission has recently put out a Working Paper, *Two Bs or Not . . . ? Schools and Colleges A-level Performance* (Audit Commission, 1991). Personally I do not approve of dots in titles, but in this case they at least signify there is more to follow. And rightly so. In the business of standards there is always more to follow because nobody ever solves the problems to the satisfaction of others.

The Commission paper is all about value added in education. It states that:

> 'Education is about more than examination results, but examination achievements are one of the primary outputs of education.'

The authors go on to argue that examination results do not necessarily indicate the effectiveness of schools and colleges. The different attainments of students at the time they enter a school or college must be taken into account.

The argument is familiar and has much to commend it. It applies with equal force to other phases of education. But the analysis for those other phases is likely to be more problematic: work on 'A' levels only has to cover a time lag of two years, whereas other phases have much longer lags.

The paper goes on to say 'no generally accepted robust methods for measuring value added have as yet been established'. To use the language of the modern set book: you can say that again. Or, more elegantly, what a masterly understatement!

In this chapter, I am concerned with two elements of the Commission's understatement: 'generally accepted' and 'robust'. My interest is not in splitting hairs but to see what is practical. If we agree, as I do, that no generally accepted robust methods are available, what are we – parents, pupils, teachers, governors, LEAs – to do about standards?

Part of my answer is that it is all much more about 'generally accepted' than appears at first glance. And, to a lesser extent perhaps, it is about robustness.

The Working Paper is one of a number which has reported research into value added in education. Much of the research applies one statistical model or another to a particular set of data to see whether value added can be assessed; and getting some data to work on can be a major problem in itself. In the Audit Commission case the data is from the Youth Cohort Study of England and Wales and it is analysed with a view to establishing methods of 'comparing courses, whole institutions and types of institution'.

The plain fact is that all of these approaches are riddled with assumptions. It is unavoidable that assumptions have to be made and I do not mean to criticise the Commission Paper on that count. Indeed, the authors recognise some of the assumptions explicitly, and they would probably agree that there are many implicit assumptions as I shall mention below. But results are frequently quoted without proper reference to the assumptions, particularly when there is an axe to grind and the results happen to assist in the grinding.

Worse still, there are some, perhaps many, who will uncritically place great weight on the results when they come to make educational choices for their children or their clients on the supposition that something has been 'proved'.

To start with, there is the question of scoring. Ideas on truly multi-dimensional decision-making are still too rudimentary for many practical purposes. One difficulty is that numerical modelling which deals in many decision variables (rather than a single score) will in general come up with multiple conclusions.

The Broader Context

Consequently the judgement of someone or other will be needed to sort them out. It is, then, not surprising that the multi-dimensional picture provided by exam results in various subjects is condensed into a single score for each pupil.

Researchers recognise the problem well. But those who follow the path of using a single score then tend to brush the issue aside and concentrate instead on the statistical analysis which forms the main body of their work. Some may even feel that unless they do *something* to bring the various examination results onto a single scale their analysis will come to a stop very soon after it starts.

Two Bs or Not...? says of the weighting given to Year 11 (i.e. GCSE, CSE and 'O' level) results 'it is only one of a number of possible ways of measuring Y11 examination achievement'. On 'A' levels it says 'there are several ways in which success at 'A' level can be measured, none of which is universally recognised'. That again is understatement. For 'a number of ways' or 'several ways' read an infinity of ways.

What really counts is the *recognition* of the device adopted. If the universal recognition so patently lacking were there, discussion on that particular point could end and we could get on with making decisions and acting on them. But the recognition is not there and we are still in the position of either discussing weightings at length or ignoring the problem.

The Commission's research makes use of the UCCA points score system which is based on aggregating points on the following scale:

Grade:	A	B	C	D	E	O	U
Points:	5	4	3	2	1	0	0

I might, for argument's sake, suggest the following scale instead:

Grade:	A	B	C	D	E	O	U
Points:	64	32	16	8	4	2	1

If I were to do that, we could have endless discussion on the relative merits of the two scales. Depending on the context of the discussion and the way it went we might reach a conclusion because:

(1) we saw a logical advantage of one scale over the other; or
(2) we could not really argue the merits, but were obliged to agree so that we could move on to actually apply the chosen scale.

For those who might think my choice of scale is in some way more arbitrary or less believable than the UCCA scale, let me start with the latter and discuss one feature of it. In the UCCA scheme there is a difference in kind between an A grade and the others. The fact is that the A score is the best you can get, and there is always the possibility that if there were something better like A+ or A++ you would have got that too. The sky is the limit: perhaps you are really an A+++ person – the human counterpart of a first rate hotel or an Australian beer.

The other grades are not like that. If you were that much better than a B you would have got an A. So why have the same difference in score between A and B as between B and C? Would it not be more reasonable, keeping other scores the same, to score six for A? Or seven? Or 64?

Unless their underlying logic is clearly displayed, scoring schemes of this kind may really be entirely arbitrary. In that case, they will only be of real use in one of two situations. The first is where they are generally (or universally) recognised like cash or temperature quantities. The second is where it can be shown that the values adopted do not really matter.

The question of recognition is very important and I shall return to it. But to show that the values adopted do not really matter, i.e. that the conclusions or actions based on the analysis would be the same whatever the scale, the researchers would have to demonstrate the robustness of their conclusions. Some attempt this through a sensitivity analysis.

The Commission's *Working Paper* does do a little sensitivity analysis. It looks at 'A' level success in three ways: (i) the total number of UCCA points a young person obtained; (ii) the number of 'A' level passes; and (iii) the average number of UCCA points achieved for each subject entered. Even so, the results are heavily dependent on the acceptability of the UCCA scale, since two of the three ways of looking at success use it. The third way, the number of 'A' level passes, is equivalent to the following scale:

Grade:	A	B	C	D	E	O	U
Points:	1	1	1	1	1	0	0

The researchers' hope is that, if the results are broadly the same when based on the two rather different looking scales, our choice of scale does not really matter. But how many scales does one have to try and how different must they look before the reader is convinced?

Even if we assume, however reluctantly, that a particular scale is appropriate, that is by no means the end of the assumptions.

The Broader Context

Mathematical models of all kinds, including statistical models, are what their name implies. They are but models of the real world, and we need to satisfy ourselves that they are faithful to it, at least for our purposes.

Regression analysis is frequently used in value added research. The authors of *Two Bs or Not...* use stepwise multiple regression:

> The statistical procedure first identifies which of various *postulated* factors is the best predictor of 'A' level performance; it also considers each of the others, in turn, to see whether they improve the prediction of 'A' level performance still further. When the procedure has chosen a second predictor it looks at all the remaining factors to see if they, in turn, can contribute to the prediction further still. It goes on selecting factors in this way until the last chosen factor fails to make a *statistically significant contribution* to improving the prediction. (Italics are mine.)

Note first that the factors are postulated. That is a matter of judgement, not on the part of parents, teachers or governors but on the part of the researchers. I would not dare criticise the judgements themselves. I simply point out that they *are* judgements. I also point out that they are not made by parents, say, or by others who might want to apply the results of the research. They are made by the researchers themselves.

Note, secondly, that statistical significance tests are used. The choice of significance level is also a matter of judgement, although conventions with no particularly firm base seem to have grown up. And even the statistical tests themselves involve assumptions about the form of the underlying distribution, uniformity of variance and the like.

Now all of this technical stuff may be an awful bore for the parent, governor or teacher who just wants to use the results. But the results will depend on the judgements used by researchers in formulating their models, on the assumptions they are obliged to incorporate and on their skill and judgement in interpreting the output of their models. Consequently, it is of some importance for parents, governors, teachers and others to appreciate how all these things influence conclusions they might adopt. I make no mention of politicians: there are some who, I suspect, will adopt whatever conclusion is convenient.

Many of those who use the products of research into value added are unaware of the precise assumptions that have contributed to those products. Some, I suspect are not even aware that assumptions have been made. They have a touching faith that science does not need any. They are people who make statements like, 'It has been *proved* that the level of resources makes no difference to educational results'.

Those who do appreciate the position on research into value added can follow a variety of courses in deciding if and how they apply the results. If they possess the technical equipment (in this case mostly a knowledge of mathematical statistics) they can follow the arguments in the research carefully and make up their own minds on the logic, assumptions and judgements that have gone into it. If their equipment does not stretch that far, they may be able to examine some assumptions like scoring schemes but take others like the statistical ones on trust. Some people may decide to use the Guru approach: faith in the actual researchers who have never so far let them down. And of course there are those who accept results because they have always known in their bones that this was the truth.

In summary, there is a tendency to treat numerical approaches to problems of educational standards as 'black boxes'. A black box in this context has nothing to do with airlines: it is a process which can only be described in terms of its inputs and outputs. What goes on in between – the mechanism or logic – is unknown. There are drivers who treat their cars as black boxes. You can recognise them from the way they poke aimlessly inside the bonnet when the car breaks down.

Statistical black boxes invariably contain sets of assumptions. There is no avoiding that. But although black boxes come in all shapes and sizes they have only one colour. That ensures that the assumptions are invisible.

Kinds of model

As we all know, attainments of students and pupils on entry to a phase of education are by no means the only determinants of their educational attainments on leaving – however assessed.

As well as comparing students' certified achievements before and after their post–16 courses, the Audit Commission study team which prepared *Two Bs or Not* is looking at management arrangements, costs, and the quality and standards of teaching. It is absolutely right that it should do that. Standards, even if assessed only in terms of UCCA points, are dependent on all of these things and more.

These are early days in the Commission's initiative in this area. It is not clear from the Working Paper how much of the work will turn out to be based on modelling of relationships, like regression of output scores on various components of cost, and how much will turn out to be based on the team's judgements following fieldwork. The paper does say, however,

The intention is that "value added" should only be one of a number of indicators used to assess an institution, since it is acknowledged that any assessment defined in terms of quantifications is constrained by the scope of the quantifications themselves.

Whatever turns out to be the balance of the work, it will not be a matter of more or less assumption or more or less judgement. Rather it will be a matter of different kinds of assumption and judgement.

Let us look at the issue of just one factor apart from previous attainment: the resources factor. The *Education Guardian* recently published an article by Wendy Berliner called 'Piggy-banks can't fly' (Berliner, 1991). It is about the shortage of teachers in Cambridgeshire and other LEAs. According to the council's own study, Cambridgeshire needs more than 500 extra primary school teachers and over 100 extra secondary school teachers to make the National Curriculum work. It has as much chance of providing extra teachers as pigs have of flying.

One paragraph of great significance reads:

> Cambridgeshire has reacted to the staffing report by looking for a second opinion. It is now poised to choose outside management consultants who will test the accuracy of the assumptions made in the survey.

That small paragraph could provide a field day for cynics. If the results had been more to the council's liking would it have brought in consultants to check the assumptions? There is an important issue here and it is not one of politics. Models are frequently tested by looking at results and deciding whether they look reasonable (or acceptable). That can involve as much judgement and creativity as the original construction. One is entering the realm of the scientist who accepts a theory for working purposes until an observation pops up to disprove it. Or perhaps until it is no longer convenient because the results are not pleasing.

Another paragraph of the article reads:

> Across the country the staffing implications of the National Curriculum are setting in as local education authorities abandon crude methods of determining teacher numbers in favour of sophisticated ones based on the work teachers now actually do.

Perhaps the Audit Commission was ahead of its time. As long ago as 1986 it published *Towards Better Management of Secondary Education* (Audit Commission, 1986) which formulated and recommended a scheme of activity led staffing. Activity led staffing is as applicable to primary schools as it is to secondary schools because it recognises differences in activities. And it is as applicable today as it was in 1986 because it recognises changes in activity.

Activity led staffing is also a model. It differs in kind from the points score regression model. In the first place it is not aimed at producing research results which may later be applied to practice. It itself is the proposed practice: the proposed way in which LEAs will decide on how many teachers they need. Not that they will necessarily be able to get those teachers, either for lack of money or for lack of teachers with the necessary expertise.

More significantly for the present discussion, the activity led model is not concerned with estimating the value of parameters. All it does is provide an algorithm for calculating teacher requirements once parameter values have been established. The parameter values might relate to how long a teacher needs to spend on an assessment or to how many children can be accommodated in a PE class.

Furthermore, the model itself is easily understood by its users. It takes no more than a few minutes' reading to understand what it is all about. There is no need, for example, to know what homoscedasticity means!

Recognition

Another feature of the activity led model stems in part from the fact that it *is* easily understood. It is what one might call a widely recognised model in the sense that there is little argument about its appropriateness. LEAs (when they had more control over their own fate in the pre-*ERA* days) may or may not have decided to use it or its sister curriculum led model, but there were few who would have maintained that there was a flaw in its formulation.

Regression analysis for value added and similar purposes is not like that. There is a whole body of literature which debates the merits of various versions. This is the point I had mentioned above and had promised to return to. General acceptance, or better still, universal recognition, can save enormous hassle. That applies to models, to scales and to expertise. People accept in general that a medical GP, backed – one hopes – by his training and experience, will be using his judgement in dealing with a patient. We ought really to be in that position in relation to educational inspectors and advisers in dealing with a school.

Assessment and experts

The *Collins English Dictionary* wisely distinguishes between judgement and measurement. I hope I have shown, in relation to educational standards at least, that judgements are contained in what we call measurement. I shall therefore change the Collins' wording slightly. There is a useful distinction, I suggest, between numerical measurement and non-numerical assessment. This distinction can be blurred by all sorts of ifs and buts, but I leave those aside. They do not materially affect the present argument and the issues are complex enough as it is.

It is, of course open to anyone to assess standards in education. But the judgements involved will depend on the use to which the assessments are put. Just as one would expect a producer of goods to know much more about standards than the general run of customers, so one would expect people who produce an educational service to know much more about them than the general run of parents, pupils or students. That does not mean that parents are necessarily undiscriminating, any more than a Marks and Spencer customer is undiscriminating. It is simply that within M & S there will be experts on standards of various products. The experts will include professional buyers and investigators as well as quality assurance staff.

Quality assurance people within a retail organisation and quality control people within a producer's organisation are employees with the interests of their employers at heart. Nonetheless their job is to counterbalance the tendency to produce goods as cheaply as possible by ensuring that those goods are produced to a certain standard of quality. In an indirect way they are acting in the interests of the customer.

Any customer who has doubts about the quality of some item or service can seek advice from a range of possible experts. In the case of a building, it may be a chartered surveyor, in the case of a car, an AA inspector, in the case of a whole range of goods and services, a local government trading standards officer.

The educational equivalent of quality assurance staff is the LEA inspection and advisory service. So much so that 'quality assurance' is now one of a welter of 'OK' words in the business.

At present, it is fashionable to denigrate the efforts of inspectors and advisers. They are criticised on at least four counts.

First, they are accused of being ineffective and/or inefficient. That may well be true. The Audit Commission report *Assuring Quality in Education* (Audit Commission, 1989) points to:

> ... poorly defined purposes and weak links with LEA priorities; lack of leadership from inspection and advisory service management, leaving advisers working in isolation, both from their colleagues and from the general purposes of the LEA; lack of leadership of advisory

teachers by inspectors and advisers; inadequate monitoring, with poor documentation of such monitoring as there is.

The Commission team observed that: 'The tasks on which individual members of inspection and advisory services use their time were often selected haphazardly.'

None of these criticisms, however well-founded, implies that a good inspection and advisory service is unnecessary.

Secondly, it is suggested that they protect the interests of the educational establishment rather than those of parents and pupils. The idea seems to me to be almost wilful misunderstanding. They do indeed represent the education establishment in the form of the local education authority, but that authority exists to serve parents and pupils and to have stewardship of the resources provided for that purpose. Inspectors and advisers serve parents and pupils much as quality assurance teams serve customers. They hold the ground of quality against the encroachment of economy.

Thirdly, parents' representatives have put the view that parents themselves know who are the better teachers. That is a reasonable claim for some, though not all, parents. There are politicians who go further. They suggest that inspectors and advisers may not be needed at all or, if needed, can be bought in as required. But the professionals make – or rather should make as *Assuring Quality in Education* points out – a number of particular contributions to ensuring high standards in education. They observe teaching and learning in class; they record their observations so as to keep track of variations in a school's or individual teacher's circumstances and performance; they advise on how to secure improvement; and they give support with practice and training.

Finally, examination results are said to speak for themselves. Speak they may, but who will understand? The day to day educational interpretation that is essential to the understanding of crude examination results or their more refined counterparts, measures of value added, can only be provided by skilled professionals in education. These are, almost by definition, inspectors and advisers.

Two kinds of work on standards are needed: scientific research work, mainly for defining and establishing standards, and operational work, mainly for defining (again), maintaining and monitoring standards. Both kinds necessarily use expert assumptions and judgements. Research can help practice through models; practice can help research by providing data and giving information on what is 'generally accepted'. The sharp end of all this work is with pupils and students. At the sharp end we need experts who can critically scan research assumptions, determine what is 'generally accepted', observe what actually goes on and give considered opinions on what action should be taken.

When we need to consult a doctor, lawyer, accountant or any other expert, we must first make sure that the expert is the right one for us. We engage a specialist only when we are convinced he is good at his work and right for the job we have in mind. After that we accept the expert's view, tempering it with our own common sense and critical faculties.

We should do the same in education.

References

The Audit Commission (1986) *Towards Better Management of Secondary Education* (London: HMSO).
The Audit Commission (1989) *Assuring Quality in Education* (London: The Audit Commission).
The Audit Commission (1991) *Two Bs or Not ...? Schools and Colleges A-level Performance*, (London: Audit Commission).
Berliner, W. (1991) 'Piggy-banks can't fly' in *Education Guardian*, 3 December 1991.
The Collins English Dictionary William Collins & Co Ltd (1985).
DES (Jan 1991) *Standards in Education 1988-1989 The Annual Report of HM Senior Chief Inspector of Schools*, London: DES.

3 Industry, politics and the search for standards

Harry Tomlinson

Britain's economy has been thought to be failing for at least a hundred years. There has been a parallel and equally unclearly defined belief about the weakness of the education system for about 150 years. The possible conflation of these two over the last 100 years has meant that it is easy for politicians, seeking a scapegoat for industrial decline throughout the period, to find an explanation for the failure of its own industrial policies in the education system. Hence the apparently continuously falling standards. The evidence for this is actually very difficult to find, and indeed is suspect. There are of course several more soundly based alternative explanations for the 'failing economy'. These include analyses based on our national attitudes and identity and the consequential perpetuation of the class system, the legacy of the overprotected markets of the empire, high levels of military research and development, tensions between the needs of manufacturing industry and the short termism of the city, and finally perhaps, even the absence of a coherent government industrial policy.

The inadequacies in planning strategically of the banking system, manifested in their ill-timed investments in the 1970s property boom, the Third World, and some of the grubbier figures of the Thatcher years, and their behaviour in the current recession, suggests that their understanding of their own world is, one might argue, somewhat limited. Their presence as representatives of the supposedly more real world on our governing bodies to offer us guidance in raising standards, or even managing the money effectively under LMS, is something we should be wary of. Their own managerial and planning standards and expertise are clearly at least suspect. There is nevertheless underlying government policy, with its almost obsessional commitment to the City rather than manufacturing industry, the apparently contradictory belief that we can also become a high technology, high skills, high value added economy, presumably not only in the service sector. This implies a consequential recognition that we have a low skills, low quality, low wage equilibrium at present – low standards, for which someone has to be responsible.

The industrial language of cost-benefit analysis, performance indicators, outcome related funding, inputs and outputs, is well known to our industrial governors from the manufacturing sector. This is presumably why it is thought that applying these ideas will lead to improved educational standards. This language might be more acceptable if one could accept that British industrial management was itself able to use these concepts successfully. British managers are, by international standards, relatively uneducated and untrained, the former presumably the consequence of teachers encouraging the wrong people to go into industry. However the poor economic performance and low productivity of capital and labour in Britain is by no means always the fault of our managers – according to the DTI. For the DTI it is a consequence of the poor image of industry combined with a relative lack of incentives to accept the risk of an industrial career. There is still less risk and more money perhaps in accountancy. There is however also, as an explanation, the alleged academic bias of much of the education system. This academic bias relates partially perhaps to exploring seriously, possibly even in sociology, the causes of labour disputes, of exploitative working conditions, the problems of environmental damage and conspicuous consumption, as central aspects of environmental education and economic awareness. Possibly an analysis of contemporary exemplars of deadly sins like greed might enliven religious education.

The service society, jobless growth, post-Fordism, flexible specialisation, and the enterprise culture are, nevertheless, apparently the culture of our new world. Enterprise in this context, however, ought to mean the opposite of massive profits at privatisation and increasing dividends for those with money to invest in the continuingly scarcely controlled former state monopolies. Given this experience, even the alleged belief in enterprise appears somewhat superficial. When subjected to even a less than rigorous critical analysis the clutch of values such as individualism, self-reliance, competition, self employment, profitability, minimal government and unfettered capitalism emerge as having little content. It ought to be possible to take 'Investors in People' and 'World Class Targets' more seriously. The hysterical pace of educational policy change in the last 10 years demonstrates that there has been no clear long term thinking about raising standards.

The enterprise culture, in theory characterised by competitive, self-advancing individualism, in practice also appears to be about controlling the wealth and income of the less well off by unemployment following de-industrialisation, or deskilling and reskilling. For those in work there is the growing casualisation of employment with the creation of peripheral workers. Wages for this group are now increasing at the rate of inflation in order to control those in employment building on the anti-trade union legislation. For the wealthy however it implies rewarding each other with large salary increases and large tax cuts in order to motivate them, even when profits fall substantially. Money motivates the rich to work harder but not the poor. It nevertheless continues to be asserted that class is an inappropriate concept for analysing society. We are now supposedly heading for the Conservative classless society. The education service is no doubt to play its part in facilitating the achievement of this challenging endeavour. Whether this implies that education might be understood as investment in the future rather than consumption remains uncertain. Perhaps the language of human capital theory is not an accepted part of improving standards. This world only makes it possible for some to have high standards of living and educational achievement, at the expense of others.

It is not entirely clear who schools ought to be encouraging to go into manufacturing industry. A substantial proportion of physics graduates head for accountancy related professions where they are paid more. Those who leave school earlier might be considered unwise to enter manufacturing if they have a choice. Government policies very clearly focus on sustaining the City as a financial centre at the expense of manufacturing industry and service industries, with the present high interest rates (February, 1922) being a most obvious example of this priority. Young people recognise that attempts to persuade them to go into manufacturing industry when the real rewards are elsewhere are unworthy. There really will be no shortage of engineers when they are paid as much as accountants, or of those seeking work in industry if it is a challenging experience. Young people have a clear recognition of the double edged nature of technological change which includes its capacity to inflict social, environmental and individual damage, most crudely in manufacturing industry. Those leaving school now know that the demographic trough was going to guarantee them employment. However unemployment like that in the late 1970s and early 1980s is returning, and may be even more persistent. Even a major improvement in standards will have little impact on these structural issues.

The economic and cultural character of Britain has been

changed by the financial measures to limit the money supply, the labour and employment policies intended to reduce the power of trade unions, and fiscal measures to reduce direct taxation and expenditure on public services. All of this in order to improve standards throughout the economy. Ironically the highly skilled labour force will be smaller in size and therefore a high quality education service for the majority for work in the emerging finance dominated high tech service economy will be less necessary. Even teachers are now to be trained increasingly as mere technicians. The inculcation of the self-concept of failure is consistent with the preponderance of jobs in the labour market requiring only low or modest levels of skill. A learning society may be essential if we are to be a healthy society, but this has little priority since too many even of the highly skilled may have no jobs. Hence perhaps the need to significantly reduce the course work proportion in GCSEs and the exploration of the possibility of splitting the grade A in order to build back in more failure and alienation, and carry out the rationing function more effectively.

The *Education Reform Act* and the apparent search for improved standards needs to be placed in its historical context. *ERA* was about redefining the aims of education and restructuring the processes through which it is controlled. The tripartite system essentially held sway for 20 years from 1944. This was thought to be the way to provide the highest possible achievement, high standards, for all pupils across the ability range. There never was of course parity of esteem because there was never equality of investment in the education of grammar school and secondary modern school pupils. It is also true that technical education, intended for the middle ability group, was never seriously developed. The class system was perpetuated by the tripartite system.

By 1964, if a date has to be selected, it was widely accepted that comprehensivisation was to be the means of raising standards by ensuring that there could be made available a grammar school education for all. There never was quite the same consensus over this new system, though Margaret Thatcher, as Secretary of State, presided over the disappearance of more grammar schools than any other Secretary of State. The examination system ensured that comprehensive schools often contained grammar and secondary modern schools within the same institution. The *Black Papers* in the 1970s did raise the issue of standards in comprehensive schools, and attacked the growing Plowden orthodoxy in a way which foreshadowed *ERA*, and as exemplified more crudely by the present Secretary of State (1991). The *Black Papers* were about a return to greater investment in the elite which was thought to be in some danger of losing its excessive advantages. It is their standards which count.

Callaghan's Ruskin speech in 1976 established the pattern for the third post-war phase, that of an increased emphasis on vocationalism, particularly for the least able 80 per cent. This language is not frequently openly applied to such a large percentage of the age group below the age of 16, but the implication of the continued commitment to Advanced levels demonstrates that this has been the real message. An issue to be considered is whether the underlying model providing the basis for government policy making is 20 per cent, 40 per cent, 40 per cent of the tripartite ability range as perhaps TVEI implied, or 20 per cent, 80 per cent. With this alternative the 80 per cent would be trained for intermittent semi-skilled, peripheral working which requires little more than functional literacy, numeracy and routine skills. This has implications for standards in education also. The alternative, a highly unlikely eventuality, would be a serious attempt to change the nature of work relationships in Britain. The government response to the *Social Charter* demonstrates just how unlikely this is.

It would appear that the right attitudes not abilities are essential for an increasingly large proportion of young people for successful functioning at work in the post-industrial society. The education system is a preparation for this. A personality that can survive by conforming is valued more than the quickly obsolescent skills which it has been alleged industry requires. Real skills inevitably are knowledge and context dependent. Before the National Curriculum was implemented education appeared to be being emptied of actual substance for the majority. The National Curriculum is however a fascinating development as a response to claims that irrelevant academicism needed to be replaced by a more work-relevant curriculum. The 10 subjects are very much the curriculum of the academic 1960s grammar school. Perhaps the new reforms are designed for the middle classes who cannot quite afford public school education. That the National Curriculum is fraying at the edges already may demonstrate this.

There is developing again however, partially through the cross curricular themes, concepts and dimensions, in themselves of potentially immense real value, a growing demand for technical education for the 80 per cent, with thinking often based on the German model. The problem here would appear to be that German employers work with trade unions, see the *Social Charter* as giving rights to employees, and welcome employee representatives onto boards, whereas in Britain government, even more strongly than major employers, see trade unions and indeed employees as the enemy rather than partners and high standards not relating to the whole cohort. Hence the emphasis is on routine training rather than technical education.

It might also be argued, despite the assertions of teachers and employers, that for those leaving secondary modern schools or the lower streams of comprehensive schools, the problem never was the transition from school to work. For these pupils in particular, the problem was the transition into the secondary grammar school culture, even in comprehensive schools. The curriculum was unsuitable for them and the National Curriculum is perhaps still unsuitable. Education for the working class has rarely been genuinely exciting and challenging, and certainly not the top priority.

The problem for this group, certainly from the mid 1970s, has been that even training in skills cannot produce jobs or even practice in the real skills required if a recovery ever develops. It can be argued that there has not been any significant attempt to provide real education for work because there never will be the jobs for this group which will require high level skills. British companies do not sufficiently believe in investment in capital or labour. Adaptability, flexibility, and being compliant towards the working conditions and economic thrust of contemporary capitalism are what is expected of young people. This is the opposite of real creativity. Words like adaptability and flexibility do require analysis. There are both positive and negative connotations, and the different meanings may be used to confuse.

Modernising apprenticeships by abolishing time serving and training for flexible working simply added to the problem of surplus labour. Training measures have been confused with attempts to meet the threat to social order posed by unemployment. All this has washed back into schools with consequences for standards. Adjustments to the unemployment statistics have served a similar purpose. Training became about exercising control over the negative attitudes of young people who reject the exploitative disciplines of the workplace. Their academic standards may be in practice too high. Certainly the messages from life at work about the importance of standards affect schools. Schools were criticised in reality not because they had failed, but because they allowed young people to acquire unrealistically high expectations of the nature of work.

A more rational approach to raising standards would be to lengthen learning times, to increase real adaptability and transform work into open ended education, rather than narrowing education into routine work. Industry, in a recession, and there have been several, ensures that there is a massive decline in the number of jobs, and seeks cheaper labour, as well as more efficient production methods. YOP and YTS were in reality predominantly about reducing unemployment and providing cheap labour. YT seems not to be significantly different but will have to be if training of high quality is ever to emerge. In the language of the market place, the customers are extremely suspicious about training schemes after their experience of the last 15 years, and hence about education.

The economic crises of the 1970s led to rising inflation and the recession, the collapse of industry and increasingly high levels of unemployment accelerated by extreme monetarism in the early 1980s. The same process is being repeated now in the early 1990s as a result of mismanagement of the economy in the mid 1980s. Responsibility for this recession also has had to be allocated if the government and industry are not be be held accountable. From the mid 1970s educational institutions have been singled out for criticism as employers and government attacked what they saw as the source of anti-industrial and anti-capitalist culture. This displacement of responsibility for economic failure and decline, from the political and economic areas to educational institutions and teachers, had as intended, the effect of distorting the public policy debate about the relationship between economic change, education and employment. The debate about standards is now fulfilling the same function.

In the 1980s again the Treasury and the Department of Trade and Industry became increasingly exasperated by the educational priorities of the professionals which were based on social and personal development, entitlement, the disinterested pursuit of truth and academic freedom – education. This real education was perhaps achieved for the elite only. The consequential government concentration on changing the content of education, occasionally in mutually contradictory directions, and on the allegedly negative attitudes of teachers and learners, has in practice again led to the neglect of the part played by political and economic factors. A similar process is occurring now with the issue of standards, particularly relating to the teaching of reading and SAT scores in primary schools. There could be an intelligent debate about how we could improve standards if the government's priorities were not so insistently to blame the victims, both children and teachers. The implementation of the National Curriculum in primary schools will provide a broader more balanced curriculum, but it will certainly leave less time for concentration on reading. One is driven to the conclusion that this debate is again being manipulated for political reasons. There is no real interest in improving standards for the majority of the population, since this would require a demonstrable commitment of resources to teachers and education and social justice.

The absurd Assisted Places Scheme, based on no evidence whatsoever that the standards of performance for individuals will improve if they receive an independent school education, demonstrates that standards are not the real issue. Similarly the massive injection of resources into City Technology Colleges and the bribes which have been necessary to persuade schools which would often otherwise have been closed to opt out of local authority systems into grant maintained status, shows that the government is not really interested in standards, particularly for the bottom 40 per cent, but merely in using the rhetoric of the market place when the market is so clearly rigged. Yet these developments are amazingly said to be about raising standards.

The Callaghan Ruskin speech in 1976 was originally interpreted as an expression of mild prime ministerial censure of the professional priorities and the methods used in schools by teachers. The country was in economic crisis, youth unemployment was rising rapidly and the education system needed to be reminded of its responsibilities towards young people in preparing them for work in a rapidly changing economy. During the subsequent period in office of the Labour government there appeared to be merely loosely co-ordinated pressures for a greater emphasis on economic awareness and education for employment within the curriculum. However it was in reality intended as the opening shot of a protracted political struggle for control over an education service perceived as being too autonomous, and opposed to the national interest, perceived as such by Labour and Conservative governments. This led inevitably to *ERA* and the search for control, not standards.

VET (Vocational Education and Training) has been about economic instrumentalism rather than the liberal–humanist concept of education. Even TVEI has become part of the process of the educational colonisation of everyday life, partly precisely because teachers have concentrated on process rather than content. Training schemes following on have become increasingly about social control because the affective aspects of the curriculum are being redefined as instrumental. The hidden curriculum of student behaviour and attitudes is becoming a central part of the manifest curriculum. Teachers would want to pay more than lip service to the principles of negotiation and learner autonomy, but real autonomy is not what the 'new vocationalism' is about. Indeed it is perhaps the opposite of this. High standards should imply in Britain that 90 per cent of young people are in full time highly structured education and training until 19 or 20, as in

Korea. This would have a powerful impact on schools and standards here.

ERA and VET are about dependency, despite the attack on the concept. Dependency must be in a form which is acceptable to the government. This means dependency on employers for those in employment and dependency on schemes which give the illusion of the possibility of a real job for the others for whom the prospect of employment is actually unlikely. Even training credits, with the large variations in allowance, will only provide the illusion of individual control over training. Guidance within training schemes may well involve a more sophisticated form of control. The present forms of VET trivialise the curriculum, patronise the learner and have little bearing on the occupational skills they are allegedly a preparation for.

The credentials which schools do provide demonstrate that the students have a capacity for learning, but also for responding to instruction and training. They indicate possession of the appropriate habits of order and discipline required by the labour sector. More directly and importantly they provide an apparently objective means of career grading. This is why, despite all the rhetoric about the dissatisfaction of employers with the school curriculum and assessment, they rely so largely on it as a means of selection. Employers demand an attitude of co-operative common sense with an acceptance of any cultural norms of behaviour associated with the occupation. These desirable qualities are only indirectly related to academic ability though schools sometimes spend much effort in linking them together, conniving with employers in order to motivate those for whom the curriculum is not sufficiently relevant. It is also easier for employers than becoming involved in the complexities of the competence based, learner centred development of NVQs. Even when these are used the distinction between NVQ levels 1 and 2 may be interpreted by employers in traditional pass fail terms.

The government continues to insist that academic and vocational qualifications deserve equal recognition, but makes no proposals which would help in achieving this. Standards are asserted as equivalent with no evidence or argument at all. The Advanced and Ordinary Diplomas and GNVQs are massively irrelevant because their purpose has not been thought through. The consultation documents give the impression that 'A' levels are for the elite, and certainly for those in the independent sector. BTEC National qualifications provide progression from TVEI for the middle ability level, possibly into higher education. The rest of the cohort will only be allowed access to training of frankly doubtful educational value, certainly in terms of the opportunities it is claimed it will open up. NVQ levels 1 and 2 will not lead to employment with two or even three million unemployed. Indeed had the demographic trough not coincided with another recession there may not have been the concentration on training the 16–19 age group which is now emerging as the new policy.

In the credentialling business we should now be able to distinguish in schools between core skills, generic competences, transferable skills and the CBI's common learning outcomes before we can begin to evaluate them. Problem solving, communication and personal skills genuinely could have real value for work preparation and personal development and do appear on several of the lists of skills, but a thorough analysis finds little which can be measured, or even evaluated. This would appear to be essential if they are to be taken seriously as central to learning. The Secretary of State, of course, dismissed core skills as irrelevant for the academically able at the North of England Conference in 1991. The link with standards pre–16 is unclear.

The vigour of the Manpower Services Commission (MSC) in extending the age of dependency, to the age of 19 had the effects both of depressing young people's wages and removing half a million people from the unemployment register. This policy has shaped the economic environment for those implementing policy making at schools also. The reflection of the class structure in the education system was evident in the grammar schools. It is returning again with increasing strength in the 'new vocationalism' initiatives which have characterised the last 15 years. The MSC in its myriad forms, has really not been about training in high level skills because the investment of government has been inadequate and that of employers derisory.

It is important to place education in other political contexts. Education policies inevitably reflect the political structures of the society. The democratic aims of promoting equality of opportunity and of education for empowerment – raising standards – clearly conflict with the economic imperative of allocating individuals to unequal economic positions and life chances. In a capitalist society such as Britain the alleged meritocratic and egalitarian goals are merely formal and rhetorical because the social structure will by design reproduce inequality. The education system is part of this process even though some schools may be more successful than others at the margin. Hence standards in Britain are largely predetermined and reinforced.

The state and political institutions in relation to the 'race question' over the last three decades for example cannot possibly be interpreted as neutral. The political system is no more separate from racial structures than from class structures. In order for equality, including standards in education, to be on the agenda the relative powerlessness of blacks as a political force would have to be overcome. The evidence of underachievement in education and discrimination in employment is overwhelming. More obviously John Major's public campaign to get some women into some top jobs, Opportunity 2,000, will not only be ineffective in dealing with the causes of sex discrimination, it may legitimate, by sleight of hand, holding the majority of women in the unequal position which structural inequality perpetuates. The deeply embedded nature of gender inequality in school and work cultures will not be changed by the promoting the presence of some middle class women.

The struggle against sexism and racism is centrally about improving standards. These will not be achieved through platitudes about equal opportunities and compensatory training, but by effective measures to tackle sexism and racism and underemployment and unemployment as they affect young women and blacks. These two issues, if not high on the political agenda, are increasingly recognised by many women and blacks as about educational achievement as a prerequisite for further action. They are about standards.

It is difficult to demonstrate the immense significance of class issues in the education debate at present, because Mrs Thatcher has so successfully altered the terms of the debate. The changes which are occurring are apparently contradictory; most obviously exemplified by the real differences in emphasis of TVEI and the National Curriculum. These tensions are undoubtedly due to the political ideologies of different groups within the Conservative Party. The 'Industrial Trainers' are part of the pragmatic reaction to the evils and inefficiencies of the welfare state. The 'Old Tories' exude their benevolent paternalism. The 'Populists', perhaps most notably exemplified by Rhodes Boyson in education, concentrate on the betrayal of the people by the experts, the educational professionals. The 'Moral Entrepreneurs' seek self-discipline, the traditional family and national moral regeneration. The 'Privatisers' provide the intellectual and economic case for the market. In view of these varied perspectives it is unsurprising that there are contradictory policies with different perceptions of standards.

The search for better standards should be about improving the standards of those whom the social structures most clearly deprive of the opportunity of achieving what they are capable of. They can most obviously achieve considerably more. Government policy appears to be about improving the standards of wealthy and the academically able, who are already particularly well resourced and achieving nearer their potential.

TVEI was imposed without consultation in November 1982, the year after *A New Training Initiative: a consultative document* and a year before YTS with its 103 generic and transferable skills. There was at the time generally a low level of teacher morale following years of declining funding of the education service, falling rolls, and apparently declining public esteem fomented by the government for its own ideological reasons described above.

Inevitably therefore this meant a warm welcome for anything that promised extra funding and the possibility of professional development. There was nevertheless considerable resistance to a narrowly defined vocational education – the preparation of factory fodder, and anything which threatened the principles of comprehensive education. Though these principles, as I have suggested earlier, may have been rather different from the practice in many schools. There was a heightening of resistance as a result of the apparent attribution to teachers of the blame for the national decline in the debates that prefigured TVEI, where teachers appeared as the major part of the problem, rather than the solution. Though standards may have been inadequate there was no evidence that they were falling.

Despite all this and the development of a growing pressure towards some kind of differential reward for performance in the payment of teachers, the possibility that some subjects might disappear from the curriculum because of declining staffing levels, a heightened awareness of competition between secondary schools possibly involving their very survival as a result of falling rolls, TVEI was welcomed by teachers and made into a successful curriculum development, though not without disadvantageous implications. Its success in raising standards was never evaluated, though it was the most evaluated project ever.

TVEI, whatever the social function it might eventually serve, encouraged us to take more seriously processes through which education takes place. It facilitated the development of new teaching styles and increased the experiential and practical in the curriculum. There was a reconsideration of the role of assessment. Equal opportunities was at least put on the agenda. The degree of idiosyncratic autonomy of institutions which resulted in little curriculum progression was recognised. TVEI genuinely gave importance to technology as a tool of communication and of enquiry, in the way which has subsequently been developed in the National Curriculum. Within five years however TVEI was transformed from a cohort led and lavishly resourced curriculum experiment piloted in selected schools and regarded with some suspicion by educationists to a scarcely adequately funded compulsory core curriculum involving all 14–18 year olds. It is supported by an increasing number of teachers and administrators who have vested interests in the project. This perhaps contrasts with an almost unfunded massive National Curriculum change. Although an educational success it appears to be unrelated to any improvement in performance. There will shortly be no more money with inevitable consequences for standards.

There is a basic flaw in much of the thinking about how to improve the standards of education and the related quality of training. Questions are rarely asked about the quality of work itself, its structure, design and organisation. Extending training for existing forms of monotonous and humdrum work is likely in the end to increase the conflict between trainers, teachers and employers when expectations are frustrated. The nature of work has been taken as given by educationists and others and therefore there have been few attempts to combine improved work design with policies for training. Trade unions and employers have shown remarkably little interest in the need for workers to participate in well designed jobs, or even to reduce working hours. A central difficulty has been that the debate about whether we can move from the low skills low quality equilibrium, and whether the new high technology era will require more or fewer highly skilled jobs, has not taken place. Assertions have been made but there has been no serious analysis. In other words is there evidence that we need to raise standards?

The *Education Reform Act* was allegedly centrally about raising standards. In 1988 there was also the DTI *Enterprise and Education Initiative*, the CBI *Building a Stronger Partnership between Business and Education*, and the *White Paper* 'Employment for the 1990s' which led to the establishment of TECs and of Youth Training with the expectation that all those on the scheme would work towards NVQ level 2. Though this could in theory lead to improved standards to build on those expected in the education service, the system remains increasingly divided. The early selection, low participation system remains since NVQs are essentially work based and the GNVQ and Advanced and Ordinary Diploma proposals promulgate the academic vocational divide.

The weakness of YTS was that it was about confirming the collective fate of the young unemployed with its curriculum arrangements rooted in personality structure and the assumed personal and social inadequacies of the young unemployed themselves. The YT claim to be about equipping young people with the knowledge and skills which they really need to have successful rewarding and productive careers at work already seems absurd. The demographic trough, which was to ensure work, has ceased to be significant with the expectation of two million unemployed as a permanent feature of the 1990s. It does also depend on a much more serious and rigorous analysis of what this knowledge and these skills are.

One can question the lead body model for determining strategic national planning. The TECs, with their apparent obsession with quality and particularly BS5750, are free to arrange payments directly related to output and performance so the fate of those with special needs or those just without special needs may be uncertain. It is really most peculiar that, having finally created a national system of education, the government has finally abdicated all responsibility for the training of school leavers, and both in the interests of raising standards. The transfer of some three billion pounds from central to local control and the ability of TECs to reach down into schools via control of the education–industry partnership monies is clearly a high risk strategy. This is more clearly the case if one is sceptical about the supposedly measurable objectives for securing quality training and enterprise development. Most British companies still appear to cut back on training when times are difficult, rather than investing in the future. Their industrial restructuring policies rely heavily on redundancies, the subcontracting of skilled work, and deskilling strategies, rather than upgrading through improved product development and internal training.

There remains a real doubt, after considering government policies in the areas of training as briefly outlined here, which have supposedly complemented those in education, whether the government is really about improving performance through high quality training. Equally, but perhaps more obviously, it is not about raising standards through high quality education, because there is no real commitment to investment. In the area of training they have certainly not been able to persuade industry to invest. The TECs have been ineffective in encouraging industry to invest in training. The intention was that the TECs themselves should seek determined imaginative leaders with the power to effect positive change, men and women of prestige, energy and expertise. It is not yet possible to make a fair judgement, but the civil servants who have been appointed to some senior executive positions are not stereotypical entrepreneurs. The board members who are not required full time by their own companies and often do not have a training background may not be ideal for the apparent role.

The *Education Reform Act* was in practice about a centralised, doctrinaire, anti-pluralist form of education policy making. I note that the *Guardian* for February 25, 1992 contained perhaps the ultimate comment on standards in advertisements from SEAC for the assessment of seven and 11 year olds in 1994,:

> No one should feel hampered by lack of knowledge of SEAC's requirements and procedures as SEAC's staff will be happy to explain more about the work.

In the end one has to ask whether the government is really determined to improve standards. After examining the evidence I suggest not.

PART II: THE INTERNATIONAL CONTEXT

4 Standardisation or standards

School reform in the USA and England

Bruce S. Cooper and R. Wayne Shute

> We want our students – whatever their plans for the future – to take from high school a shared body of knowledge and skills, a common language of ideas, a common moral and intellectual discipline. We want them to know math and science, history and literature. We want them to know how to think for themselves, to respond to important questions, to solve problems, to pursue an argument, to defend a point, to understand its opposite and to weigh alternatives. We want them to develop through example and experience, those habits of mind and traits of character properly prized by our society. We want them to prepare for entry into the community of responsible adults.
>
> (US Secretary William J. Bennett, *James Madison High Schools: A Curriculum for American Students* (1987))

> These grammatical and literary failings among young people are evidence that, in most schools today, English is badly taught, and that it used to be taught better. But English teachers themselves would not agree. Nor would the official body responsible for their activities – Her Majesty's Inspectors. The HMI does not blame schools for producing pupils unable to write standard English grammatically and ignorant of the literary classics . . . .
>
> (John Marenbon, *English Our English*, (1987), p. 8.)

Introduction

Standards are easily 'raised', in fact, perhaps too easily. Governments have only to require students to take more course work, for longer periods of time, with more rigorous examinations, and teachers to have more extensive training and higher quality of performance – and everyone can claim that education standards are improved. It's much like the expression: 'Giving up smoking is easy. I've done it hundreds of times'. So, too, raising standards is simple; we've done it numerous times, and we keep doing it.

In the mid 1980s, the United States, during the so-called 'first wave' of school reform, raised its standards, with 40 states requiring more academic work for students, done to higher levels (*see* Doyle, Cooper, and Trachtman, 1991; Fuhrman and Malen, 1991; Blank and Schilder, 1991). And 45 out of the 50 states increased their students' high school graduation requirements, perhaps the most popular (and easiest) means to 'improve' standards. As the Education Commission of the States reported (1989, page 6):

> Most of the changes accomplished in the first wave of reform were directed to improvements in student achievement, often in the form of strengthened graduation requirements, college admission standards, testing, competency statesments, no-pass/no-play for interschool athletics, attendance rules, etc., and to the education profession, as salaries increases, strengthened certification requirements, and in some cases, differentiate salary systems.

But the net improvements, what few were seen, have not been encouraging. SAT scores, one of the few national tests (given by a private agency) taken by about 35 per cent of eligible high school students all across the nation, have diminished significantly over the last 40 years, though some 'recovery' has emerged in the 1980s. As Figure 4.1 shows, both the Verbal and Mathematical, dipped dramatically through the 1960s and 1970s, and showed some modest improvements since 1987. Figure 4.2 compares the national SAT scores with those of students in the state of Utah, indicating the range among the states and just how low the 'average scores' really are.

Perhaps, the most troublesome news was that the SAT scores of the very top students admitted to the nation's most elite universities, such as Harvard, Yale, Stanford, and Dartmouth, had dropped by 60 points on average in under two decades, indicating an erosion of quality for students from the best secondary schools, affluent homes, and the 'best' communities. Drop-out rates have risen too, and incidences of violence and misconduct have mounted.

And on most indicators of achievement domestically and internationally (Corbett and Wilson, 1989; Cibulka, 1991), American children come out low among the industrialised nations, behind Japan and most European nations. The most

Figure 4.1: Trends of SAT Scores 1952—1988

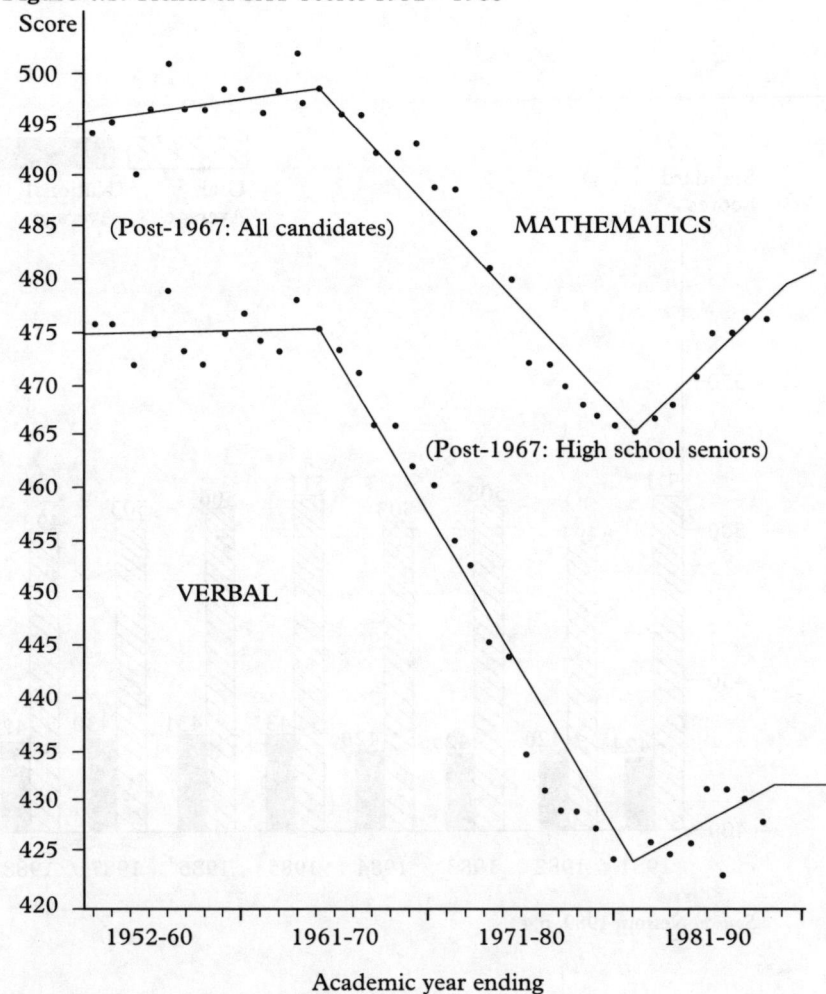

Source: Wirtz, 1977, p.6; Nelson, 1983, p.47; 1989, p.44.

Figure 4.2: Utah versus National SAT Average Verbal Scores

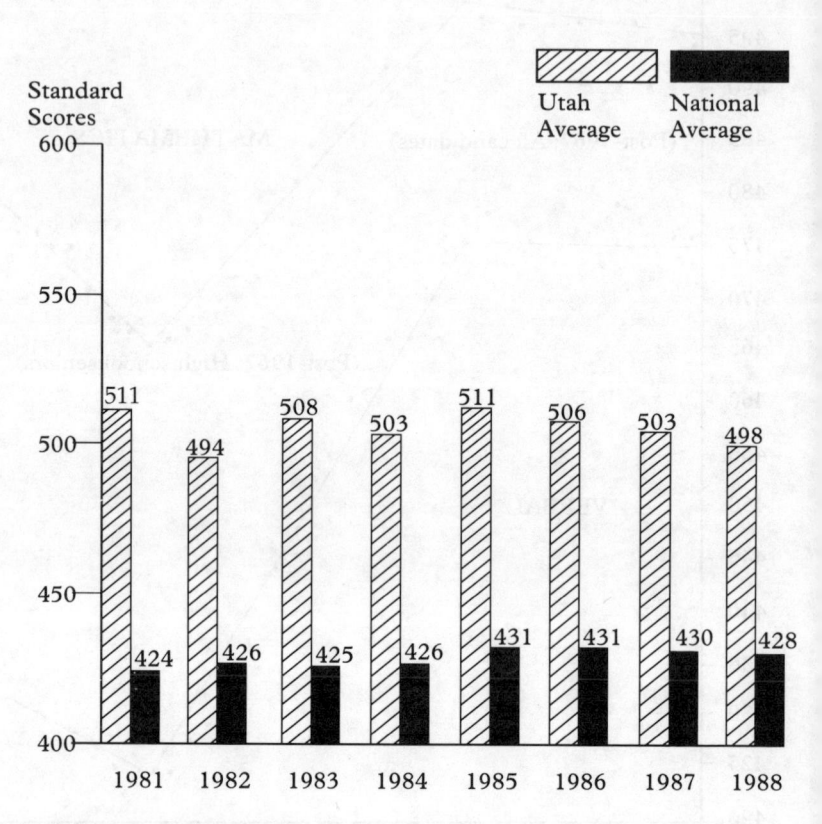

Year	Utah Average	National Average
1981	511	424
1982	494	426
1983	508	425
1984	503	426
1985	511	431
1986	506	431
1987	503	430
1988	498	428

Source: Nelson, 1989, p.43.

recent international comparisons (Education Testing Service, 1992) found the USA was outperformed by all the industrial nations, testing ahead of 13 year old students only from Jordan, Portugal, Brazil, and Mozambique in mathematics and (add Ireland) in science. In response, Education Secretary, Lamar Alexander, said that the nation should set higher standards for students and 'encourage them to reach those standards' (Rothman, 1992, p. 13).

Ironically, in fact, raising standards can actually appear to 'lower' achievement by setting more unattainable goals which greater numbers of students fail to reach – allowing critics to blame children, their parents, and the schools. Often governments, intent on staying in office, can finesse the issue by keeping standards down or constant, thus giving the appearance of improvement on tests. International comparisons temporarily remove the parochial view of student growth, when American students fare very badly, far behind Japan, Europe (particularly Germany) and even Israel and Sweden on many measures. These external standards give pause to those who use narrow criteria.

Also, complaints from businesses about nearly illiterate, ill-mannered, unpunctual, and uncaring high school graduates also take the blush off the rose, exposing the failure of schools and the ineffectiveness of simply raising standards on paper without a wider understanding of the difficulty of improving standards in modern democratic societies.

Hence, while improving standards is among society's most arduous tasks, the process itself may be essential if school productivity is to be improved. Thus, standards, properly measured, provide the following:

(1) *Bench-marks:* Systems have great difficulty getting a fix on how well they are doing. Standards allow participants, leaders, and consumers to judge the activities and outcomes against some norm of quality and efficiency.

(2) *Minimum standards:* All systems are concerned about producing defective products. Standards help to set a 'floor' under the efforts of members. Schools 'retain' certain students, refer others for additional help, and devote extra resources to students – all based on some sense of when students are reaching the boundary of acceptability.

(3) *Vision and direction:* Standards help members to direct their energies, set their priorities, and operate effectively. If a school system sets a reading standard (literacy) for all students, then staff know how to devote their time and whom to help.

(4) *Conditions of excellence:* Standards and test results can indicate not only the minimum level of attainment but also the highest levels as well. Britain, it seems, tests for both minimums and maximums ('A' levels for college admissions), while the United States seems to favour minimum competencies testing (most high school graduation standards are minimums).

(5) *Staffing and programme decisions:* Finally, standards assist decision makers in determining who should be working in the organisation, what criteria to use for hiring, and what level to expect from programmes. Without standards, a common basis of action is lost, making reform, improvement, and transformation all but impossible.

Conditions of standard setting

Setting standards may be relatively easy, while actually *raising* them appears difficult for large scale education systems. It is somewhat like trying to encourage athletes to jump higher. Simply raise the bar, some might argue, and contestants will leap higher and reach greater levels of accomplishment. But at least three conditions pertain to improving performance on the high jump. First, why should contestants even try, unless the goal is somehow attainable; and they recognise the value of the event and see the benefit in doing it better? Consensus, agreement, and recognition pertain.

Second, athletes must be trained, enabled, and encouraged to jump better through better conditioning, diet, skill building and lots of practice. Just raising the bar, without the support system to help jumpers to accomplish greater feats, may in fact frustrate contestants, causing them to try less hard, even quit the event, unless some evidence of support and recognition are available. And third, a mechanism is required that will measure their attempts, explain their shortcomings, correct their errors, and calibrate their accomplishments. Methods of accurate, prompt and reliable assessment and feedback are central or athletes will have no way of knowing their improvement.

Hence, raising standards sets in motion an organisational dynamic that can be beneficial or harmful, depending on the context and results. We shall argue in this essay that certain 'traps' appear when nations attempt to raise standards in education. Currently, the United States is discovering what Britain learned a few years ago: that efforts to change the stakes of education, to make demands, increase requirements, and institute testing, all exacerbate the divisions in society. As recently as 29

The International Context

January 1992, a *New York Times* headline announced: 'Prominent Educators Oppose National Tests' (Chira, 1992). Fifty well-known educators and testing experts publicly criticised a proposal by the bipartisan National Council on Education Standards and Testing to establish a national curriculum and national tests, an all too familiar argument in England and Wales which now have both.

The Council's proposal flies in the face of a revered American tradition: of letting states and local education authorities determine school goals, curriculum, and examinations. 'This would be a radical departure,' Susan Chira of the *New York Times* explained, 'from the long standing American tradition of local control of curriculums that has led to a patchwork of uneven course requirements, tests, and school results' (*New York Times*, 29 January 1992, p. B-9). Reactions to the belated effort in the United States to institute standards and testing illustrate the difficulties, permitting us to compare the USA which is just embarking on this kind of standard setting and raising, with England and Wales which has begun the process. We shall argue that though many of the problems and pitfalls are the same, the solutions are somewhat different, given the cultural, political, and historical differences between the UK and the USA – three interrelated conditions in whatever nation they are attempted.

Although the process of national curriculum and national testing is not the only means for raising standards, this level of analysis permits us to examine the conditions necessary for improving academic standards at any level in any nation. As shown in Table 4.1, a dynamic of consensus on outcomes, a clear relationship between priorities, teaching, and testing must occur, if improvement is to occur. Third, nations must have the skills and capacity to assess academic improvement, to gather accurate information, and to make these data readily available to schools, parents, and policy makers.

Common purposes

Societies must generally agree with the basis of setting standards; otherwise, they contest the type, purposes, and level of standards. In the United States and Great Britain, basic conflicts arose about the very purpose of schooling, not to mention the appropriateness of standards and testing.

Alignment of goals, curriculum, activities, and testing

Once nations generally accept the aims of education, the next difficulty is to 'align' the levels of the education system – its goals,

Table 4.1: Relationship between Curricular Design and Outcomes

	England and Wales	United States
1. Demands: Consensus on the 'good society', 'good citizen', and the 'educated person'.	Focused; Set at national level.	Fractured, divided; Divided among federal, state, and local levels.
2. Programme: Alignment of goals, curriculum, teaching, and testing.	Set curriculum in eleven areas with national tests at ages 7, 11, 14, 16, and 18.	No national curriculum, no tests given across the country. Few states require curriculum and testing.
3. Methods: Means of testing students regularly, reliably, and efficiently.	Struggling to implement 'democratic', universal testing, using methods that teachers can handle.	Mostly machine tests for aptitude and intelligence, not real subject based achievement tests.

activities, programmes and pedagogy – with the appraisal system. The United States has a long history of tests which relate to pupil aptitude and ability (SATs, PSATs, CATs) but have little to do with the *curriculum* of the American school. Thus, when scores on SATs drop, high schools wonder what this has to do with them.

Implement a reliable testing system

When the curriculum is aligned, then some means for assessing the progress and outcomes are required. In large nations, the logistics of operating the testing system are staggering, taxing resources for assessing students, and analysing the results by child, classroom, school, local education authority, state, and even nation, and making results available to communities, political leaders, educators, and parents.

This chapter examines the 'standards movement' in the United States in comparison to England and Wales. The purpose is to leap to the heart of school reform: the perverse problems of trying to reform education through improved standards and testing, in a society without common agreement about the means and ends of education, without common definitions of success and failure, without a willingness to face the consequences of real test results and comparisons between students, schools, communities, and states (not to mention nations).

The dynamics of standard-raising

Mixed missions – cross purposes

Nothing can be more volatile than a debate about what our children should learn and be able to do. At root, national values are exposed and contested, and the purposes of child rearing, educating, and preparing children for adulthood are at stake. The dialogue over educational purposes, levels of attainment, and means for assessment can divide along a number of dichotomies, all of which play a role in determining standards. Without some consensus about the mission of schooling, the nature of learning and curriculum, and appropriate pedagogy, real national or even regional standards are difficult to establish and carry out. Take these divisions, for example:

Excellence versus equity

In both Britain and United States, reformers argued bitterly about the mission of education, whether to promote excellence and exceptional ability, or to offer a chance to those least able to make it on their own: the poor, immigrants, handicapped, children of colour, children of the inner cities. While such debate sounds academic, even ideological, it becomes crucial when determining the purpose of the curriculum, the standards of attainment, and the way resources are to be spent in society.

If standards are set to separate the 'brightest and best' from the 'rest', then schooling is highly divisive, competitive, and elite. If the 'standard' is inclusion, with a desire to improve each student *on his or her own terms*, then a different philosophy is involved, different standards are set, and even different tests are given. In Britain, the first set of *Black Papers* (Cox and Dyson, 1971) raised the issue of whether the curriculum should be traditional or progressive, elite or inclusive, rigorous or accessible to all children.

These kinds of discussions strike at the very heart of the purpose of the educational system: whether to separate the most academic from the rest, or to offer an experience in which all students can readily share. Also, some have seen attempts to impose a national curriculum as a form of 'mind control', ideological indoctrination, and social domination. Ivor Goodson (1991), for example, wrote about the British national curriculum as a means to create subjects, not citizens, as people controlled by government, not controlling their political leaders. He wrote:

Seen in this light the political project underpinning the National Curriculum assumes a further dimension for the hidden curriculum of the National Curriculum is a reassertion of the power of the state in nation-building. This project is diametrically opposed to the alternative project of educating students, from a plurality of cultures, for active citizenship in a democracy. The history of mass mechanical obedience as a bedrock for nation-building is well known, but it leads not to democracy but to totalitarianism.

(Goodson, 1991, p. 230).

Basic skills, versus high-order thinking

Establishing academic standards raises the question: standards in what? Some have argued that students need to learn the basics, the 'facts', and be literate in the 'Trivial Pursuit' sense of knowing what happens on which date, where Somalia is, and who chaired the Second Continental Congress. Former US Education Secretary William Bennett, for example, lamented that 'two-thirds of American eleventh graders did not know that the [American] Civil War happened between 1850 and 1900. Half were unaware that the First World War happened between 1900 and 1950' (Bennett, 1987, p. 20).

Others speak vociferously for advancing students well beyond formal skills to critical thinking, to help them through their own learning. Here the content of the curriculum is less important than empowering and motivating students to take control over their own learning and apply higher-order thinking to problems that they, the students, select. While it may be possible to teach facts and concepts, using memorisation and analysis, the debates over standards often focuses on either one or the other. When it comes to testing in particular, will the examination evaluate the students' ability to recall facts and figures, or the ability to think and reason?

Centralised control versus local autonomy

A set curriculum, standard testing, and unitary standards of performance, some argue, are antithetical to the very purposes of education reform. As early as 1985, Iannaconne presciently alerted policy makers to the dilemma of legislating learning, of standardised curricula, and pre-established standards, and the possibility of vouchers being instituted if the states (California was his example) instituted strict, centralised standards and controls. Iannaconne (1985, p.8) explained:

> The state centralization of educational control is setting the stage for the next conflict in the politics of education .... The specific nature

of the battles ahead is becoming clear. The absurd attempts to produce effective schools by state standardization, increased state centralization of education, fiscal controls and regulations requiring the imposition from the top of effective school characteristics may be the greatest policy contradiction we have seen in public education in two decades. That contradiction could be leading to a new public education system. To illustrate using California: were the recentralizers to win the battles ahead in my state [and they have], they would lose the war given the continuation of present, well established, ideological drift among voters. The success of centralist officials in Sacramento [the state capital] would, I predict, finally place educational vouchers on the state ballot [which may be happening in 1992].

Multi-culturalism versus a mainstream curriculum

Another hot issue, one that emotionally divides the efforts to set a standard, is whether the curriculum should teach the history, art, music, culture, and literature of a range of peoples or primarily the white, European-based, 'high culture' of Shakespeare, Milton, and Hardy, 'American' and European history, and ignore the role and contribution of African–Americans, Armenian–Americans, Asian–Americans, Jewish–Americans. Attempts to compromise have sometimes offended everyone and pleased no one. In Britain, as the National Curriculum was formulated, the combatants reached the point where they battled over the actual percentage of the curriculum that would be devoted to British history, versus the rest of the world. The then Secretary of State for Education and Science, John MacGregor, MP, was reported as follows:

> The issue which has hitherto aroused the most controversy is the Minister's insistence that the group [drafting the curriculum] should increase the proportion of British history for secondary school pupils. At the moment, the group is planning to devote only one third of the syllabus to British history as a compulsory subject for 11 to 14 year olds. This figure rises slightly to two-fifths for 14 to 16 year olds. Mr MacGregor wants British history to be taught for at least 50 per cent of the time devoted to history in secondary schools.
>
> (*Times Educational Supplement*, 1989, p. 4)

Both Britain and the United States have debated the nature of education – whether for personal fulfilment or national (even international competition and development), whether for the average or the gifted, whether standard or individualistic. Issues of curriculum will never be resolved: whether to teach and test for the top of the class or the bottom, whether to teach thinking or facts, the mainstream culture or all cultures, in the main language or the tongue of newcomers. Yet, governments must decide and some have. Tentatively what appears from an international comparison is the following: that the system of standards, curriculum, and testing are a reflection of the education system itself. That is, education in the USA is highly fractured, differentiated, and complex, as is the system of standards, while Britain has greater coherence to both the intent of education and its accountability.

Under the Socialist government in the 1960s, for example, many of the elite British grammar schools were closed and with it the highly necessary system of testing (the notorious 11-plus test). With 'comprehensivisation' came more 'democratic' tests, the changing of the old 'O' levels (which were essay style tests, normed, and fairly rigorous), to the GCSE, based greatly on the students regular class work. Now, with the return of the Conservatives, a national set of standards and tests, with the reintroduction of support for elite education (Assisted Places Scheme, CTCs, and the possibilities of new grammars).

Britain has forced the issue of national curricular goals, in part by finessing the various opinions and imposing a solution over the objections of the educators, the opposition parties, and others. It is not that England and Wales now agree on what standards to set, the nature of the curriculum (or even whether to have one), and the means for assessing it. We found great division within Great Britain over, firstly, whether the nation should even have a national curriculum, secondly the size and expanses of this curriculum – whether a few really key subjects or many, and thirdly the nature of the curriculum, and lastly the assessment process. The Thatcher Government simply pushed the National Curriculum through, with the attitude that the details would be worked out by the curriculum writers and testing experts at the appropriate time.

To some large extent, this strategy of making bold, general policies, and letting the specialist work out the details, has been working. Britain does have a national curriculum in eleven areas (maths, science, history, English, languages, geography, music, art, religious education etc.) which is adjusted to various age-grades, and is building tests for ages 7, 11, 14, on top of the existing 16 year old GCSE (formerly the 'O' levels) and 'A' levels for age 18. How was Britain able to overcome all the antipathy to a national curriculum?

Perhaps because of Britain's small size, relative homogeneity compared to the USA, and the working relationship between educators, politicians, and others serving on the curriculum development and testing groups, the process was possible. Or, perhaps the willingness of the Conservative government to plunge ahead, regardless of objection from the 'education community', best explains the developments. Once, determined, the structure of British school governance made implementation possible. After all, education in Britain is a *national* matter: shires, boroughs, and other units of government look to the national Department of Education and Science the way American schools look to their state education departments.

The United States is a long way from this point. First, the national government hardly has the power to force a national curriculum; instead, Washington under President Bush has sought to build a head of steam for improvement by holding the nation's first Education Summit meeting in Charlottesville, Virginia, attended by the nation's governors. From that grew pressure for national standards in maths and science, and for some way of assessing the outcomes, though the USA, unlike Britain, stopped short of a national curriculum. The US settled for 'national standards' and a voluntary national (but not necessarily federal) test – and not a national curriculum and universal testing as in Britain.

Thus, it appears that liberal democratic states have great difficulty accepting that some children will indeed 'fail' and that the poor, minority, and non-native speakers of the national language will be among the most likely to underachieve. Yet, both Britain now and the United States in the future, are trying to overcome the resistance to national standards, national curricula, and national testing. Britain's recent experience is informative.

Somehow, Britain introduced the most elaborate national curriculum in the world, with 11 'essential' subjects across the age levels, being prescribed, detailed, and tested. So far, only the first test for seven year olds has actually been administered, with some negative reports of children unprepared and unable to handle the stress of such formal examinations at such an early age. Teachers, too, complained that the testing itself was overly elaborate, tedious, and time consuming. But, it is likely that over time Britain will work out its national set of standards, curriculum, and tests, while the United States fights over who should set what and how.

Aligning the system

A second barrier to the setting of national standards, curriculum, and testing is the difficulty in many nations of bringing coherence to what to teach, teaching it, and then testing it. The United States probably leads the world in having the most non-aligned curriculum/testing system. That is, while the nation can agree on the need for literacy, numeracy, basic competency, and even higher-order thinking skills, the difficulty comes in imposing a curriculum to carry out these goals, and then testing to see if the alignment is working.

Instead, the United States appeals for one set of goals, say a high achievement in technology, mathematics and science (note President Bush's 'America 2000' goals of world leadership in maths and science); then recall that the majority of American children escape high school with two years or less of mathematics; and when tested, these same students take such nonspecific tests as the Scholastic Aptitude Test (SAT) which does not even evaluate learning in science, mathematics, and technology but rather general aptitude in vocabulary (which American schools fail to teach), grammar (a lost art in most schools), reading (which is not part of the high school curriculum) and 'math reasoning' which is really tricky middle-school mathematics and has no algebra, geometry, trigonometry, and calculus on it.

When American students do poorly on the SATs, it is not because the high schools curriculum is failing (because the SATs do not test the secondary school work) but because American children have stopped reading, watch too much television with its restricted, low level language, and do not learn vocabulary on their own. Furthermore, the test makers are very careful to norm the examination as low as possible, to make only the weakest students fail. Thus, the school district will continue to buy the test, the company can make a profit, and the children can feel 'good about themselves'.

Only two regularly given tests are truly rigorous and based on high school curriculum: the Achievement tests of the SATs and the Advancement Placement (AP) tests in particular subjects. The latter, the AP exam, is really a university level test of a course taken for university credit. Hence, students taking AP courses are college bound, academic, and high powered; the exam is geared for the true contents of the course, and passage of the test (graded on a 1 to 5) with a three or better grants university credit at whatever university the student may attend. Great idea, it is not unlike the Oxbridge tests given for university admissions by Oxford and Cambridge in England.

Hence, a real barrier to standards in the United States is the absence of any real alignment between goals, course, and test, making it difficult to improve any of the above. American children are not doing well on tests like the SAT, CAT (California Achievement Test), and others because these instruments have little to do with what is taught. How can the test makers, whether working for commercial testing firms or for the states' test-making offices, know what's being taught in the thousands of LEAs that may elect to buy or use them. So questions are general, curriculum inclusive and general, appealing to basic ability, intelligence, and exposure, not to learning, grit, hard work, and the school curriculum.

Thus, on a technical level, standards require the ability to test and demonstrate progress and failure. Such standards rest on a careful alignment between the goals of education, the school's curriculum, testing, and instructional programme, and the content and method of the tests. American tests have always been 'out of line' with what is theoretically being taught. In fact, testing companies gave up years ago even trying to second guess what children were learning in schools and gave instead non-specific, subject free, skills based, aptitude tests, which can be easily and inexpensively written and scored, can be universal and non-dependent on the idiosyncrasies of local textbook choice, programme, teaching sequences. Why not give a 'reading test' instead of a course specific examination of *Moby Dick* or the 'nations of the Mediterranean Sea'?

If it moves, test it

Finally, raising standards requires systematic feedback on students' progress and a willingness to alter the curriculum, programme, instruction, and homework to address the problems on the test. In effect, societies cannot easily raise school standards without a whole set of changes in purpose, programme, assessment, and practices.

Yet, even if the United States decided to set a national curriculum and standards, would it be able to test and assess nearly 46 million school children on a regular, reliable, and useful way? So far, no. At present, the United States has no national tests at all; instead, it has scores of state-specific tests and some national longitudinal samples of students (the National Educational Longitudinal Sample, NELS, and High School and Beyond, HS & B), both of which have selected between 50,000 and 77,000 children to represent the rest, and then follows them over five to 10 years, or more.

The few truly national examinations, such as ACT (American College Testing) and SATs are just that, aptitude tests of just those students seeking entry into university. But, these tests do not relate directly to the schools' curriculum and are virtually useless to schools to help them improve their curriculum and standards. While more and more secondary schools are offering 'cram courses' for the SAT, these are an afterthought and are done with some guilt, since the schools have failed miserably over 12 or more years to teach basic vocabulary, mathematics, reading, and grammar.

Also, a number of districts (LEAs) are moving away from standardised tests altogether, assessing children instead by the 'quality of the year's work'. Called 'portfolio analysis', this more totalistic (holistic) approach to assessment is preferable, since proponents claim that paper and pencil tests using multiple choice methods, for example, penalise children who may otherwise be bright, talented, and original. Using portfolios, the teacher would keep a file of the student's work during the year, much like an artist's collected works, and evaluation would be based on the best work of many months, not a single test taken in an hour or so. This attempt to use more realistic, naturalistic, and individualistic approaches to testing is commendable, but it negates the move toward more valid and reliable national examinations for all children. How can a society sustain the effort to build a porfolio on 45 million children in five to eight subjects, evaluate these products, store them, norm them, and build a curriculum around them? How can children, schools, LEAs, and ultimately nations be evaluated and compared, based on subject evaluations of a child's 'output' during a whole year?

Hence, in the United States, the problems of a national curriculum and testing are monumental and solutions seem a long way off. Britain has created just such a system, among the world's most complex, and we must wait to see the outcomes. While schools in England and Wales are struggling to carry out the national effort, American educators are struggling even to agree whether to set national standards, which kinds and in what subjects, evaluated how.

Conclusion

Great Britain is rapidly aligning its total system of standards, which have always been tightly related to the curriculum in the upper grades (6th forms) where students literally practised using old tests for their coming Advanced Levels ('A' level), Oxbridge, University of London, and other tests. The 'set pieces' (assignments) are practice runs (called 'revisions' because students do them over and over again), using the real questions on actual topics (*Macbeth* in literature, the Boer War in history, theories of Marx and Keynes in economics). The curriculum and the test are so tightly in line that they squeak, as the examinations dominate the curriculum of the entire sixth form (ages 17 and 18). Students often become so familiar with the curriculum, and the test, that they can present the answer in flawless prose in ink without mistakes (even mathematics is sometimes done in ink).

Whether the National Curriculum in the lower grades is able to attain this level of quality and alignment remains to be seen, since Britain is democratising its testing for the first time. Previously, only a relatively small number of the elite students took 'O' levels, 'A' levels, and Oxbridge. It was proposed that all seven, 11, and 14 year olds would take tests in 10 or 11 subject areas, seriously overloading the ability of teachers and other graders to handle the load. Even with the reductions, Britain will face the effects of mass education on setting standards for the first time, as it attempts to assess all children regularly and in every subject area.

In comparison to Great Britain, school reform in the United States in the 1980s and early 1990s has been a long road with few clear trail markers: a great deal of talk about 'excellence', improving standards, and better education but with virtually no tangible results. In fact, the 50 states did raise standards following the publication of *A Nation at Risk* (National Commission on Excellence in Education, 1983), the national study that rang the alarm bell concerning poor quality education, a 'tide of mediocrity', and national crisis. But these 'higher standards' have not demonstrably improved results; in fact, in many areas the quality has dropped while expectations, costs, and concern have increased.

The US Department of Education reports, for example, that between 1965 and 1989, the costs per pupil rose from $2,800 on average to $5,300, while Scholastic Aptitude test scores dropped from an average of 970 (out of a possible 1,400) in 1965 to 903 in 14 years. The National Assessment of Education Progress, NAEP, scores were also appalling, showing a lack of the most rudimentary knowledge of American history, culture, government; 60 per cent of American children at age 16, for example, could not read and summarise relatively complicated reading material; 94 per cent of high school seniors (17 year olds) could not solve a multi-step mathematics problem or do basic algebra.

While the United States has no recognised national tests, the states give a variety of aptitude and some subject matter tests. But the examinations are not given regularly or universally. Instead, states tend either to use 'aptitude' and skills tests, not real examinations of the content of the school curriculum, or tests aimed so low ('minimum competency') that they tell us very little about achievement across the ability groups and signal teachers that little is expected of the students. Furthermore, these low level exams signal teachers that the state's expectations are not very high. Hence when these state wide aptitude and skills tests go up and down over the years, often the reason is familiarity or newness of tests, not a real indicator that academic attainment is improved.

Most states and education authorities (local school districts) cannot even boast much agreement on what schools should teach, children should learn, and governments should assess, much less what real standards to set. Thus, the United States suffers from a three part disease: a lack of a real substantial curriculum across the nation; the absence of agreement on what should be taught and to what standard; and virtually no universal national test standards to assess the progress of the curriculum. Not knowing what to teach, to what quality, and determined by what, the nation can talk much about standards but do little to set and achieve them.

The one exception is the Scholastic Aptitude Test (SAT) which less than half the students ever take; but the SAT is geared for testing reading, vocabulary, 'math skills', not hard academic achievement. It's so sad when students graduate from 12 years of school and do not know the meaning of words, analogies, antonyms; how to read a short passage for content, simple word mathematics problems, and interpreting charts and graphs

In England, in contrast, education for those who stick it out (most leave at age 16 with few awards, diplomas, or much of anything to attest to their accomplishments) is well demarked: GCSE and 'A' level examinations, not to mention a whole battery of new tests under the 1988 *Education Reform Act*, to support the 10 or 11 essential subjects. For all the fighting between 1987 and 1988 about a 'national curriculum' and 'national testing', British educators seem to share a basic view of what should be taught, at what level, and to what standard.

Americans certainly do not. Even feeble attempts to adopt a state wide social studies (history, geography, and political science combined) curriculum have exploded in many states with angry cries from ethnic 'minorities' about the 'Euro-centric', racist, anti-African/Asian/native American bias of government approved textbooks and a rapid abandonment of 'Western' history for a mix of African, Far Eastern, and 'ethnic' history with each ethnic and cultural group getting its moment in the textbooks (e.g., Jews, Armenians, African–Americans, Chinese, Irish). As a result, students may learn nobody's history very well and remain uninformed of all cultures and generally ignorant of the world.

Without a common set of values, beliefs, and experiences, it is nearly impossible to set any real goals for education, much less to assess them. Thus, much of what passes for standards of testing (particularly computer graded SATs, the CATs, MATs, METs tests) are not even vaguely related to what is taught in schools. Rather these examinations tap such non-specific, non-curricular areas as 'aptitude' to learn, 'basic intelligence', 'thinking skills', and vocabulary, not history, literature, algebra, chemistry, physics, foreign languages, arts, music – anything that one might associate with a true school curriculum.

Ironically, too, after nearly 11 years of formal schooling, many middle-class children in the USA then pay fees (around $400) to private tutoring companies (e.g., Stanley Kaplan's Preparation Services) to take a six week course in vocabulary, analogies, 'math concepts', reading and interpretation, and other supposedly unteachable 'aptitudes' to improve their scores on the SATs, so they can gain a seat in a college or university. These institutions of higher learning, aware that American high schools do not conform to any common standard of performance expectations, must rely on SAT scores, letters of recommendation, and interviews to determine quality.

Hence, the 'excellence movement' of the last eight years (1983 to 1991) has been symbolic and structural, not curricular and instructional. It has been a battle of words, not standards and pedagogy. The war has been won: choice, competition, restructuring and empowerment are now widely heard and used. Yet, standards of pupil performance have fallen, and schools of all kinds have basically failed. Inner city schools, with some exceptions, still lose many of their students to drop-outs, drugs, violence, poor standards and low graduation rates. Wealthier suburban and ex-urban schools, even with their resources and better homes, cannot show a great deal of 'value added' from students' experiences. Students are not being pushed; standards are not soaring.

One good indicator of this sad fact is the small number of students across the nation taking 'Advanced Placement' courses in high school – perhaps the one example of academic substance, high standards, and real and absolute tests of achievement. Since high school students can earn university credits if they pass the advanced placement test at the end of their high school AP course, the qualities of real standards are present:

(1) *A complete, rich curriculum in a substantive subject or discipline:* Advanced Placement Calculus is perhaps the toughest mathematics course offered in the USA; Advanced Placement History is real history, without all the ideology and rhetoric that accompanies some 'social

studies' courses of study; and Advanced Placement Chemistry is laboratory and classroom based with solid content on a par with college freshmen science. These courses, because of the impending examination, accept no excuses for poor work. Since the courses are voluntary, students who cannot or will not work can leave – or complete the course work and opt out of the qualifying examination.

(2) *A high level of expectations and teaching:* These AP courses are taught in a substantive and fast paced manner, since during the term students must cover the course of study prescribed by the national syllabus. Often, AP courses get the best, most expert teachers with a solid grounding in their discipline and a willingness to teach to the 'top' not the bottom of the class.

(3) *A high level, demanding examination system:* The AP tests are set at a very high standard – equivalent to university levels – and are national in scope. Such as in 'A' levels in Britain, the AP tests are graded or marked on an absolute scale by national graders, not by teachers for their own students. Grades or marks run from 1 to 5, with a 3 or better necessary for receiving university credit.

Yet, for all the value of AP courses, painfully *few* American students even take one AP course, and even fewer actually take the AP examinations (they are optional at the end of the AP course). Doyle, Cooper and Trachtman in *Taking Charge: State Action on School Reform in the 1980s* (1991), found that in 1981, only 2.9 per cent of American high school students had taken an AP course; and after nearly a decade of 'raising standards', 'excellence', and a massive discourse on the needs to beat the Japanese and improve schools, less than seven per cent of eligible American students by 1990 took even one such course, much less to take and pass the rigorous examination in each subject administered nationally by the College Board Advanced Placement Program. Utah led the nation in the percentage of students taking Advanced Placement courses, with 15 per cent of high school pupils enrolled in an AP subject; schools in some states offer virtually no AP courses at all.

Short of these few truly national, standardised, and high quality tests, however, American children never take a real subject based test with national norms and standards. Instead, they sit for a plethora of 'reading', 'math', and general tests which are avowedly designed to set a *minimum* standard (NY State Regents test, for example), not to set a high standard and raise student and teachers' expectations. One analyst estimated that American children spend about 20 per cent of their focused classroom time 'being tested' on something by someone. But for all that time and energy, we have no national standard or bench-marks in education. Most states have some assessment 'instrument', usually a commercial, computer marked aptitude test of 'basic skills', such as the Metropolitan Achievement Test and California Achievement Test which are not specific to any course or discipline, are not real summative evaluations of standards in particular subjects (though they have verbal and quantitative scales).

And the United States, unlike Britain, is only barely closer to obtaining a national set of standards in education. President Bush has made national standards and performance a goal for the country, and the panel on student curriculum and performance have gone to work defining national goals, standards, and perhaps even a curriculum and tests. But, such national efforts take years and ultimately depend on state and local jurisdictions. With the lowest quarter of American students doing worse and worse on most measures of learning, much energy is focused on 'pulling up the bottom' and the middle and top are ignored. Setting a truly high standard would only make the system 'fail' to an even greater extent than it is now, a fact that most politicians and educators could not bear.

Changing standards does not change educational practices. If the nation cannot agree on a curriculum, all the tests in the world will not work. If students get by with low level work for 11 years, setting a tough test in the twelfth year will only punish students for the weaknesses of their schools. For the schools themselves are hardly challenging, and teachers are unwilling or unable to raise the standard of each course to a level that makes real demands on students. While television watching and socialising increase yearly, reading, writing, studying, and learning have not. Schools are losing out to the electronic media and other competing 'curricula'. As Larry Cuban explains:

> The bulk of instructional time finds students listening to teachers talk, working on tasks that require little application of concepts, imagination or serious inquiry. Description after description documents the Sahara of instruction demanding little thought from students beyond information already learned. What emerges unblurred in what Theodore Sizer calls a 'conspiracy of the least, a tacit agreement between teachers and students to do just enough to get by' (Cuban, 1984, p. 661).

Raising standards in education appears so simple: just require more, and more learning will occur. But until the society agrees that higher standards are essential and which standards to raise, little will be done. Some have argued against tougher standards for fear that more children will 'fail' and be dropped or pushed out of the education system. Others believe that until basic services – health, housing, nutrition, family support, welfare, transportation, and jobs – are improved, the schools may fail many children who come to school sick, abused, hungry, anxious, disturbed, and ill-suited to academic improvement.

Whatever the conditions of society, higher standards without educational consensus, curricular testing alignment, and hard work seem quite futile. Education systems, then, seem able to standardise their procedures, requiring this and that. But doing things just alike does not amount to standards, nor the means for reaching them. Recording a dying patient's temperature will hardly save his or her life.

References:

Blank, R. K. and Schilder, D. (1991) 'State Policies and State Role in Curriculum', in *The Politics of Curriculum and Testing*, Fuhrman, S. H. and Malen, B., Eds., pp. 37–62, (London: Falmer Press).

Chira, S. (1992) 'Prominent Educators Oppose National Tests', in *New York Times* (January 29 p. B9).

Cibulka, J. G. (1991) 'Educational Accountability Reforms: Performance Information and Political Power', in *The Politics of Curriculum and Testing*, Fuhrman, S. H. and Malen, B. Eds., pp. 181–201, (New York: Falmer Press).

Corbett, H. D. and Wilson, B. L. (1989) 'Raising the Stakes on State wide Mandatory Testing Programs', in *The Politics of Reforming School Administration*, Hannaway, J. and Crowson, R. Eds., (London: Falmer Press).

Cox, C. and Dyson, A. E. (eds.) (1971) *The Black Papers on Education*, (London: Davis Poynter).

Cuban, L. (1984) 'Policy and Research Dilemmas in the Teaching of Reasoning: Unplanned Design', *Review of Educational Research*, Winter, Vol. 54, No. 4, pp. 655–681.

Doyle, D. P., Cooper, B. S., and Trachtman, R. (1991) *Taking Charge: State Action on School Reform in the 1980s*, (Indianapolis: Hudson Institute).

Education Commission of the States (1989) *School Reform in Ten States*, (Denver, COL: ECS).

Education Testing Service (1992) 'Learning Mathematics', 'Learning Science', Education Testing Service, Center for Assessment of Educational Progress.

Fuhrman, S. H. and Malen, B. (Eds.) (1991) *The Politics of Curriculum and Testing*, (New York: Falmer Press).
Fowler, W. S. (1988) *Towards the National Curriculum*, (London: Kogan Page Ltd).
Goodson, I. F. (1991) '"Nation at Risk" and "National Curriculum": Ideology and Identity', *The Politics of Curriculum and Testing*, Fuhrman, S. H. and Malen, B. Eds., pp. 219–232. (New York: Falmer Press).
Goodson, I. F. (1988) *The Making of Curriculum*, (London: Falmer Press).
Goodson, I. F. (1987) *School Subjects and Curriculum Change*. (London: Falmer Press).
Goodson, I. F. (forthcoming) *Subjects and Schooling: the Social Construction of Curriculum*, (London: Routledge).
Iannacconne, L. (1985) 'Excellence: An Emergent Educational Issue', in *Politics of Education Bulletin*, vol. 12, pp. 1, 3–8.
Moon, B. and Mortomore, P. (1989) *The National Curriculum: Straitjacket or Safety Net?*, (London: Colophon Press).
Rothman, R. (1992) 'Council Calls for a New System of Standards, Tests', in *Education Week*, 19: 21 (January 29, 1992): 1, 30.
Rothman, R. (1992) 'Twenty-Nation Study Shows U.S. Lags in Math, Science', in *Education Week*, Vol. 11, No. 21 (February 12, 1992), pp. 1, 13.

5 Quality in education
Standards in Europe
Joanna Le Métais

Introduction

Whilst the concern for quality is shared by educationists and others throughout the European Community (EC) and beyond, there are no easy definitions or indicators whereby educational quality may be measured. This arises, in part, because of a lack of consensus concerning both the general expectations and the specific objectives of education.

The quality of education may be defined as the extent to which the service as a whole succeeds in accomplishing the objectives which have been set. The selection of goals, the definition of their scope and the weight given to their relative importance are complex matters which depend, to a considerable extent, on the values of those involved (Barroso, Sjorslev *et al*, 1990, p. 133). Specific objectives for educational establishments may be further refined according to the contribution which this phase is expected to make to the lifelong educational process. Comparisons may be made between institutions if their objectives and input factors are the same. However, emphasis on measurement by input–output criteria frequently ignores important parts of the aims and goals of education which are not easily measurable, leading to narrow, unproductive evaluation.

Educational objectives must meet the expectations of parents, students, employers, tax payers and others, including the providers. These expectations vary, reflecting the different values and interests espoused by the groups and by individuals within them. In most countries, it is recognised that there is only a loose consensus among these groups in the area of education and training. However, in certain Member States (e.g. Denmark, Spain), the lack of consensus is seen to be off-set by the representation of all parties in the educational–political structure and control.

The devolution of education management to the level of individual institutions is discernible in Denmark, England and Wales, France, the Netherlands, Portugal and Spain. Whilst such delegation may deflect criticism from central authorities, the latter are ultimately held responsible through the ballot box. For this reason, and to safeguard mobility and recognition of qualifications nationally and within the wider Community of the EC, an agreed framework and a credible system of evaluation have been deemed essential by all the Member States.

This chapter does not allow for detailed values analysis and will therefore restrict itself to the identification of five contextual elements which have stimulated the 'quality' debate and then look at how a number of criteria have been applied in selected Member States. Finally, it will draw on the findings of some surveys which have attempted to measure the levels of satisfaction or dissatisfaction with 'the education system' in different countries.

Context

The debate around the quality of education may be traced back to sources inside and outside the system. Internal sources include the structure, content and the participants. Among the influences underlying the expansion and development which have characterised Member States of the EC since the 1960s are the growing economic competition and interdependence of nations, and the gradual spread of a homogenous worldwide culture. In Western societies, competitiveness has been the main thrust for economic, technological, social and cultural development (Bottani, 1990). One of the principal objectives for education is therefore to prepare individuals for a life which will involve frequent adaptation to changing demands and circumstances. These changes in turn shape public opinion on fundamental economic concepts such as labour and currency, because of the correlation between levels of education and social and professional mobility, human capital and gross national product (Walberg, 1990). In terms of objectives, this raises questions of minimal levels of competence and the relevance of learning to future economic activity.

A second dimension is the necessity, at a time of demographic decline, to use all the available human capital, not merely the most able (Bottani, 1990). A common response has been to raise the school leaving age and to open access to post-statutory education. This approach, which is intended to realise the potential available throughout the population and to satisfy the ideology of equality of opportunity, has brought with it concerns about quality of education versus quantity.

A third element is financial. Bottani has found that 'many countries are no longer willing to approve on trust expenditure on schools without any satisfactory returns in the form of tangible results' (Bottani 1990 p. 338). This has introduced a concept of productivity, more commonly expressed as a measure of the efficiency or cost effectiveness of education.

A fourth factor is the tendency for schools to become the central unit of educational administration, especially through different models of delegated authority. This has been accompanied by increasing levels of participation by parents and others in policy setting as well as in the evaluation and control of performance and outcomes, which has resulted in a search for a clear system of evaluation and of accountability to the users of education on the one hand, and to those who fund education on the other. This manifests itself in pupil testing, staff appraisal and the evaluation of education systems. Thus, the last decade has seen a growth industry in performance indicators and other evaluative mechanisms.

The fifth element follows from the preceding two. The allocation of resources is increasingly tied to student numbers and institutions have to compete with one another for funding by attracting students. The policy of competition between schools is nowhere as overtly expressed as in England and Wales, but the exercise of parental choice in Belgium, France and the Netherlands is beginning to affect both the composition of schools and attitudes towards marketing schools. At university level, competition is an acknowledged fact not only at national but, increasingly, at European level. Thus establishments have to consider their 'unique selling point', which may be expressed in terms of examination passes, staying on and truancy rates and the destination of ex-students, or in wider terms such as a reputation for pastoral care, extra-curricular activities or good discipline.

Criteria

Competence and relevance

In all countries, parents expect the education system to help their child secure a 'good job'. In most countries, and especially where there is a choice between academic, technical and vocational schools at secondary level, they seek to get their child into the most prestigious school or course which will give access to the highest level of academic education. It should be remembered that the professional and chartered institutes which accredit the professional competence of doctors, lawyers, architects, engineers etc. in this country do not exist elsewhere and professional qualifications are awarded by universities or other establishments of higher education. Increasingly, however, it is becoming recognised that academic school and university qualifications do not guarantee employment and greater stress is being laid on the development of relevant knowledge and skills, expressed in terms of competencies.

The respect for competence, whatever the field, is strong in Germany. This may be one reason why German parents differ from their counterparts in other Member States in their choice of school for their children. A recent survey (IFS 1989) showed that in 1981, only 45 per cent of parents wanted their child to achieve the *Abitur*, the school leaving qualification which grants access to university. Of the remaining parents, 38 per cent opted for the *mittlere Reife* which would grant access to further technical and vocational education and 17 per cent aspired to the lowest level school leaving certificate. Eight years later, in 1989, the aspirations had risen so that 56 per cent named the *Abitur*, 34 per cent the *mittlere Reife* and only 10 per cent the basic school leaving certificate. These expectations may, in part, reflect what parents themselves had achieved and their perception of their child's competence. The upward drift may also be attributed to the higher levels of education received by later generations. However, what is significant here is that many parents opt for non-university vocational training for their child and that non-university training also enjoys a high level of prestige in Germany. This is confirmed in the findings in the 1989 survey that nearly three-quarters of the parents sought non-university vocational qualifications for their children (42 per cent *Berufschule*, 15 per cent *Fachschule*, 17 per cent *Fachhochschule*) as compared with 26 per cent of parents who hoped their children would obtain a university qualification. One of the contributory factors may be that unemployment amongst graduates was taken by one quarter of the respondents to indicate that university studies no longer paid off.

The concept of 'competence' goes beyond factual knowledge and the development of skills. Thus, in Nordrhein-Westfalia it is argued that all school types must address changing social influences by promoting attitudes and personal characteristics such as adaptability, team spirit, independent thinking as well as conveying knowledge and developing skills (OECD 1990). The training undertaken by French young people in the *lycée technique et professionnel* seeks to develop appropriate attitudes and expectations by increasingly mirroring the pattern of working life. Students therefore carry out projects in collaboration with local industries to the standards required by real customers and their school day, like the working day, runs from eight a.m. to six p.m. with a two hour lunch break.

The pursuit of relevance is also at the basis of educational reforms in Spain. Criticism was expressed at the early choice between general and vocational routes in secondary education and at the overloaded curricula, unsuitable for age motivation and aptitude of students, especially in the upper cycle of general education. This resulted in a considerable dropout level at the end of primary (age 12+) and lower secondary education (14+). The reforms which are being implemented between 1992–1998 are addressing this challenge by extending the period of compulsory education to age 16 and by adapting the curricula to pupil needs. Vocational courses, which did not motivate students and provided poor links to working life, are being revised and elements will be compulsory for all secondary school students, to provide an essential knowledge base for all and to raise the status of vocational education.

Spain is proud of the high participation rate in higher education (30 per cent of the age group) but the relevance of some university level courses remains a matter for concern. Although the unemployment rate of graduates at 10–11 per cent is lower than the average (16 per cent), it represents a considerable waste of human talent and educational investment, arising from disparities between supply and demand. First, there is a shortage of graduates from short cycle courses (e.g. paramedical staff, technicians) but a surplus of long cycle graduates (doctors, architects) as compared with demand. The largest proportion of the student body opts for arts and humanities courses and many suffer unemployment, whilst there is a shortage of engineers and applied scientists. Finally, some engineering courses concentrate on complex theoretical knowledge which enhances the status of the course, its teachers and graduates, but at the expense of some of the practical and managerial issues which students will face on employment. The Council of Universities is reviewing the curricula with a view to making them more relevant to employment needs.

Quantity versus quality

The length of statutory education, and the participation rates in post-statutory education, are commonly quoted as positive indicators. In recent years, the Netherlands has lowered the compulsory starting age from six to five years and Portugal and Spain have raised the school leaving age from 12 to 15 years and 14 to 16 years respectively. Proposals to raise the school leaving age from 14 to 16 are before parliament in Italy. The proportion of young people aged 15–24 engaged in full or part-time study has grown continuously in France since the end of 1960s, in Germany from 1976 and, in the Netherlands full-time participation has increased by 30 per cent between 1971–1986. Similarly, access to higher education has been broadened in most Member States.

Nevertheless, quantity is not in itself an indication of higher quality. The higher participation rates in some Member States may be partly explained by the custom of requiring students who have not achieved appropriate levels of achievement to repeat a school year and the age span of pupils in a secondary school can therefore range two or even three years beyond the norm. This procedure allows students who learn more slowly still to achieve higher level qualifications. An alternative procedure in the Netherlands allows students to transfer from the final class in one school type to the penultimate class of the next highest, thereby working their way up to the highest qualifications. This option is also catered for at higher education level, whereby those who have not achieved the certificate necessary for university entrance may, by completing the first cycle of certain higher vocational education courses, transfer to the first year of a relevant university course. These mechanisms are intended to enable all to benefit from the highest level of education of which they are capable but the cost of such provision is increasingly being questioned.

Concern with the situation where some pupils leave school without any formal qualifications led the French inspectorate to conduct an analysis into variations in the staying on rates in a sample of 10 academies. Effectiveness was measured in terms of the percentage of the age group which stays on to the *baccalauréat* (18+ school leaving certificate). This criterion differs from the more usual criterion of percentage of entrants who pass at the *baccalauréat*. Considerable progress has been made between 1985–1990 in staying on rates. Lille adopted a specific policy of entering as many students as possible for the *baccalauréat*, on the principle that even if mass entry entails a risk of failure, it also increases the chance of success. As a result, Lille has seen an increase of 8.3 per cent in the proportion of the age group who pass the general or technological *baccalauréat* between 1982–1987 (TGV 72).

This successful approach is reflected in the *Loi d'orientation*, which seeks to raise the participation rate of 18 year olds in full-time education to 80 per cent of the age group by 2000. New streams and special vocational *baccalauréats* have been developed to provide education and accreditation for all young people, adapting the curriculum to suit the different aptitudes and interests of students, whilst still meeting the needs of employers. This represents a significant quantitative shift, but does not necessarily entail a corresponding qualitative rise in the level of individual achievement. Some confusion between the quantitative and qualitative objective has arisen among English speakers due to the similarity between the French *passer le baccalauréat*, i.e. to take the *baccalauréat*, and the English to pass, i.e. *être reçu au baccalauréat*. Whilst retaining the prestigious title of *baccalauréat*, not all such certificates will represent the same level of achievement, nor will they all grant access to the same forms of higher education or employment. As the general level of education rises, it may well be that the qualifications required for different forms of employment rises correspondingly.

One of the major obstacles remains the perceived status of academic as compared with vocational courses. This is not the case in Germany, where vocational courses enjoy high prestige amongst parents, students and employers and are not seen as a second rate option for post-statutory education. This may explain why the achievement of the *Abitur* diploma by 30 per cent of the age group is seen as success why this level is carefully maintained by variations in the selection procedure of 10 year olds.

Productivity or cost-effectiveness

The desire to raise the standard and to improve educational opportunities for all young people lies at the basis of many reforms. These have affected the structure and content of education and, more particularly, the formal training of teachers to meet the demands of diverse pupil groups. However, given the considerable expenditure involved, schools and institutions of higher education are being subjected to measurements of 'productivity'. Common indicators include participation rates, attendance rates and the number and level of qualifications achieved. Those countries in which pupils transfer from one class to the next on the basis of performance, rather than chronological age, use the number of 'failures' at each stage as a key indicator of school effectiveness.

Before the implementation of the reforms, Portugal experienced high rates of truancy amongst pupils aged 10–12 (the last two years of compulsory schooling) and a high proportion of pupils needing to repeat a grade. The failure rate in the first phase of primary school was 41 per cent and pupil dropout in Grades 5 and 6 (age 10+ and 11+ years) reached 22 per cent. These weaknesses were due to a shortage of schools and of qualified teachers, linked to a high staff turnover and a highly centralised system with insufficient school autonomy. Failures at secondary level were ascribed to theoretical, academic and ambitious curricula which offered little scope for vertical and horizontal transfer. A major interministerial programme was launched in December 1987, to reduce the failure rate by 5 per cent in the first year and 10 per cent in the two following years. Complementary measures to improve the quality of education include the extension of compulsory schooling from six to nine years (age six to 15 years) and curricular reforms.

The high financial and personal cost has led to the adoption of different strategies to reduce the numbers of pupils repeating a grade. In France, additional classes in French, mathematics and English are available for one hour each week, to help secondary school pupils experiencing difficulties in these key areas to keep up with their peers. Greater emphasis on individual pupil needs has reduced the staying-down rates in French primary schools from 9.2 per cent to 5.1 per cent between 1981 and 1990 (TGV 70).

In the Netherlands, better guidance at age 12 is intended to channel pupils into the most suitable secondary school type. However, these efforts may be frustrated by some parents who want their child to attend the most prestigious school type, and who only accept a transfer to another school type when there is proof of the child's inability to make the grade. This contrasts with the situation in Germany, already mentioned above, where there is only a very small drop-out rate as almost all pupils leave with a certificate of some kind.

At higher education level, the United Kingdom stands out as a model of efficiency in contrast to its European partners, where the time taken to complete a course of study frequently exceeds that originally planned. This concern is shared to a greater or lesser extent by France, Italy, the Netherlands, Portugal and Spain and involves the conflict between two values, namely the freedom to pursue personal and professional development and the need to contain the costs of supporting 'perpetual students'. There appears to be considerable tolerance of and respect for long-term studies which are seen as conferring a high level of specialist competence leading to high status employment. This approach has three main consequences. First, people may be qualified beyond the level required and follow their lengthy studies by periods of unemployment. Second, the level of maturity of those who have remained in a dependent relationship and deferred the start of employment to their late twenties, may lag behind that of non-students. Third, this lengthy initial training is seen to equip the professional for life, without the need for continual professional updating which characterises good professional practice in the UK.

The financial constraints, and the fact that comparability between higher education qualifications in the EC is expressed in terms of length and level of study, has resulted in some harmonisation. From 1988, university studies in the Netherlands were formally divided into two phases, but the blow was softened by providing financial support for a period equal to one and a half times the prescribed duration of the course. Thus students have up to six years to complete the four year first degree course leading to the title of *doctorandus*. Even so, a recent survey shows that as many as 40 per cent may leave university without achieving this qualification. It is argued that the curtailment of the courses has not been accompanied by a reduction in the syllabus and that therefore students need the extra time to cover the course. Some students try to improve their employment chances by using the flexibility to take courses in foreign languages, communication and business skills in addition to their basic degree course, reinforcing the assumptions that training should precede, rather than complement, employment. From September 1992, initial teacher training courses at universities will be funded on the basis of the number of students who complete the relevant course within the stipulated time. This may set the pattern for more stringent selection procedures and less tolerance for complementary activities, as establishments will bear the cost of training those students who drop-out or require longer than the set time to complete the course.

In Spain, the time taken to qualify considerably exceeds the 'notional' duration of the course and there is a high drop-out rate. For example, of those completing the three year architectural technicians course in 1989–90, none had completed it within three years, the average student had taken 6.5 years (an improvement from 7.18 years in the previous year) and 40 per cent had taken between eight and nine years to complete the course. Even in technological courses, where students are most efficient and take on average four years to complete the course, the 'output' figures are undermined by those who drop out prematurely to take up employment. Curiously, this problem is aggravated by the pursuit of quality. The high status enjoyed by Spanish university qualifications (especially in engineering) is often linked to the perceived difficulty of the course. Thus professors attempt to raise their status by passing very few students. They are supported by unions and professional associations, for whom a shortage of suitable specialists has financial and negotiating advantages. Thus many students in long cycle engineering courses currently take seven to nine years to complete the course and have asked for a formal lengthening of courses to enable them to cover the syllabus. The Council of Universities is reviewing the length and relevance of curricula which include theory that will never be applied, but fail to include management and other skills. Consideration is also being given to linking cost effectiveness to university funding, without raising student fees (currently at 20 per cent of real cost) as this may debar certain groups of the population.

In Denmark, there is a similar discrepancy between arts/humanities and sciences/engineering, where there is a shortfall of applicants. The level of concern expressed by the Ministry is not yet shared by the general public who see the unemployment of engineers as reducing the appeal of such studies. Attention is also directed to improving the quality of programmes and teaching to overcome the 10–20 per cent of students who fail to pass a single exam at university level.

Accountability

Educational institutions are increasingly held accountable to the users of education on the one hand and to those who fund education on the other. This can range from the right of participation to the wider entitlements accorded under national (e.g. Parents' Charter) or international agreements (e.g. 1989 United Nations Convention on the Rights of the Child). The demand for more cost effective education has given rise to pupil testing, staff appraisal and the evaluation of education systems.

It is here that the most significant difficulties arise for, whilst there is a greater 'customer interest in educational products', expressed by parents, employers and political authorities, 'for the moment there is not even the faintest sign of agreement on the definition of quality' (OECD 1990, p.4). The criteria include: the educational value of individual and cross curricular subjects, cross disciplinary work in schools, professional ethics and qualifications of teachers, the ethos of school life; and the counselling and encouragement of individuals (OECD, 1990). Many of these factors are difficult to measure objectively and given the individual talents and aspirations of pupils and their parents, opposing views may be strongly held and defended.

Nevertheless, since 1976 politicians and lay people have expressed increasing dissatisfaction with the education service and successive legislation has obliged schools to report on the level of pupil, teacher and institutional performance with a view to raising standards. It may be interesting to compare the response in France to similar criticisms during the same period.

The years between 1977–1984 were years of crisis when schools were blamed for unemployment and accused of causing educational levels to fall. The system was evaluated (sometimes severely) from the outside and studies ranking schools according to their performance made their appearance, the first being published in *Figaro* in 1980 (*see* Ballion (1982) *Les consommateurs d'école*, Paris: Seuil). Since 1984 a new consensus has been reached on the central importance of human resources for the economy, on greater independence for schools and on opening up schools to the outside world. Evaluation is omnipresent. It centres on accountability and focuses on the school as a unit. Marchers demonstrated in 1984 to demand recourse against a state system from which they were withdrawing their trust – and their children – by voting with their feet. Parents had been given a limited say in the school councils (*conseils d'établissement*) set up in secondary schools in 1968 and in primary schools in 1977. In 1983, their power with respect to secondary schools was increased. In the face of this challenge to the legitimacy of the educational system, schools had to accept some external control, established procedurally as part of a funding contract and related to responsiveness to local citizens.

The assessment of pupil performance was introduced in 1989. Pupils in primary school class 2CM (age nine) and secondary school Class 6 (age 11+) are assessed in French and mathematics at the beginning of the school year. The tests are devised to allow for immediate use by teachers in their work with individual children and the 'évaluation – formation – réponses' process aims to diagnose the performance and difficulties experienced by individual pupils, to enable teachers to adapt their teaching style to the needs of each child. It requires a considerable amount of teacher time to assess the child, mark the tests and code the answers for computer processing and methods of optical marking of answers are being considered. Teachers have also expressed reservations about the influence of test results on their expectations of pupils' future performance. However, on the positive side, teachers claim that coding the answers provides them with a first contact with pupils and gives a detailed insight into pupil difficulties which cannot be drawn from files. The tests open up routes to varied teaching styles and contribute to more effective teaching by identifying the aspects of the work which need to be revised (TGV 74). In October, parents are informed about their child's performance. Unlike in England and Wales, pupils' test results are not used to identify individual school performance, but a sample of results is sent to the Ministry of Education which draws up a national profile for publication in the following January.

Meuret in 1990 reported on the regular sample national surveys at age 10, 12 and 14 years. The devolution of autonomy has provided scope for innovation, but funding is renewed only if the project is successful. Teacher in-service courses and training opportunities are measured in terms of their impact and effect in the classroom, by user perceptions or by assessing student performance. It is reported that the Ministry would like to establish about 20 national indicators on the state of the educational system, its costs, its activities and its results, which would be published annually, but this work is still only at the planning stage.

Competition

Competition between educational institutions is affected by three factors: a shortage of potential applicants, a free choice and the funding of educational establishments largely on the basis of student numbers. The *Education Reform Act* explicitly introduced competition between schools in England and Wales as a mechanism to improve quality. In several other Member States, a similar effect is arising from the exercise of parental choice. For example, the Netherlands Constitution safeguards the citizen's right to be educated in a school which conforms to the religious or moral principles of the individual. Given that the state is obliged to provide resources at an equivalent level for all approved institutions, this 'pillarisation' results in a duplication of provision at all levels as schools, colleges and even universities have been established on the basis of religious (usually Catholic and Protestant) or ethical allegiances.

Since 1959 successive reforms in French education have brought about a balanced social mix in French schools by the imposition of catchment areas. Ballion (1991) argues that a relaxation of these catchment areas and the encouragement to parents to express a choice between schools are leading to classification of schools by qualities of excellence, measured in terms of the best examination passes in the 'best' *baccalauréat*, i.e. mathematics. Schools are expected to lead to an employment qualification and serve the needs of the users rather than exercising the traditional roles of transmitting a culture and socialisation. School development plans are thus proposals for adaptation of curricula to pupil needs within a specific framework and a good school plan is one which provides the best opportunities for most pupils to secure a pass at the *baccalauréat*. The school which develops a reputation for caring, or for providing for the special educational needs of pupils with physical, social or personal difficulties, is not well served in this culture of an open market because its strength is frequently perceived as a failure to provide an 'efficient' education (Ballion 1991). The competitive environment will result in schools which specialise in high performance on the one hand, and 'caring' schools at the other extreme. A relationship between suppliers and consumers has replaced the relationship between community 'partners'. Ballion suggests as a remedy that parents should not be encouraged to make a choice but should have the right to appeal against the allocation of their child to a school.

Good schools are identified by a combination of measures including examinations, participation rates, youth employment and social behaviour, although the weighting given to the elements varies in different countries. Those parents who express a choice most commonly seek a traditional academic school, often complementing their child's education by means of private music lessons or membership of sporting clubs. Schools, especially in inner city areas, which are unable to attract parents willing and able to provide moral and financial support find themselves progressively slipping down the league tables in an irreversible spiral. The quality of education offered to the pupils remaining in these schools depends on the extent to which the school and higher authorities can compensate for the lack of popular support.

Competition between universities at European level is spurred by the various mobility programmes (ERASMUS, COMETT, LINGUA) which enable students and staff to spend time at one another's institutions. This has given rise to a harmonisation of the length of first degree courses, to the modularisation of courses which will allow students to complete a part of their course in different Member States and to the mutual recognition of qualifications. Courses may be affected in other ways. One proposal from the Netherlands involves the provision of certain lectures in English so as to make courses more accessible to foreign students. More seriously, the criteria determining the provision of university courses may shift from educational to economic, geared to attracting students. This is especially likely where, as in the UK, overseas students meet the full costs of tuition.

Methods

The role of the national inspectorate has been described by the Spanish authorities as the state's responsibility to ensure that legal obligations are met and to guarantee equality for all (*The White Paper*). All Member States have a national inspectorate, except Denmark and Greece, which rely on advisory systems, and Luxembourg, where the scope of the inspectorate is restricted to primary education. The specific responsibilities of national inspectorates vary, but usually include securing legal compliance and monitoring standards, keeping up to date by visiting schools, advising teachers on curricular and didactic development. On the basis of their close contact with schools and other educational establishments, inspectorates have a responsibility for reporting to and advising the Minister. In some cases, inspectors also counsel teachers, administer tests and examinations, conduct interviews for school and run in-service training courses.

In recent years school management has been seen as an essential strategy in the development of the school's organisation, its effectiveness and efficiency. This is reflected in the devolution of responsibility from central authorities to institutions and in a shift away from the inspection of individual teachers to the assessment of institutional effectiveness. School self-evaluation has been introduced as an internal reaction to external criteria, which have been planned to control and compare results between schools. This usage of evaluation has been frequently opposed by teachers, who prefer school specific criteria which concentrate on process rather than outcome. The tradition of internal evaluation is not yet long or strong enough to play a decisive role in school evaluation. As part of an organic teaching–learning process, self-evaluation makes considerable demands on the administration of education systems and results in changes in role relationships between teachers and those within and outside the school. Individual school plans have been introduced in France and the Netherlands as a guidance and evaluation tool. In the latter case, these must be revised biennially and approved by the inspectorate.

Views from the field

There is no comparable information on the level of satisfaction with the education system in different Member States, but the following extracts may give some indication of tendencies.

Parents

In Denmark, there is no overall general satisfaction with the education system and the scope and level of courses of education and training courses can vary a great deal. However, there is a consensus of trust in professionals and the close relationships between parents and teachers are mentioned with pride. Parental participation in school management is restricted to social matters and does not cover the curriculum content and teaching method. At upper secondary level (*gymnasium*) there is little involvement of parents, which is said to be evidence of the high degree of trust which parents have in teachers. This may be partly due to the high level of teacher education which commands general trust and respect. In a survey into satisfaction with public service institutions, the *gymnasium* scored more highly than other institutions.

An enquiry conducted to assess the level of satisfaction amongst parents – and by extension, the general population at large – with the education system or with individual school types in Germany is reported in the sixth *IFS Survey* (1989). According to parents, 51 per cent of children are happy at school, 43 per cent are happy part of the time and only six per cent are not happy. Only three per cent of parents felt that too much work was expected of their child, whilst 17 per cent felt that this was sometimes the case. When it came to the standard of performance expected of the child, 45 per cent of parents felt the school's expectations were too high as compared with 11 per cent who considered them too low. The school's efforts to help children in difficulties were appreciated by 46 per cent of parents but one fifth of parents felt that schools barely made an effort in this respect. The level of confidence which parents had in their child's teachers ranged from a high degree (42 per cent of parents) to little confidence (11 per cent). In general terms, schools were deemed by parents to give insufficient attention to the following aspects: general knowledge (34 per cent), discipline (32), courtesy and good relations (31), writing (20), critical thinking (16), making schoolwork enjoyable (20), craft and manual skills (nine), subject competence (seven) and parental participation (eight). Only five per cent of parents felt there was nothing to complain of in this respect.

These views may be influenced by differences in the expectations of education held by school, parents and pupils, by the perceived relevance of curricula and by personal relationships between teachers and individual parents or pupils. Ulich (Ulich, 1989) points to the potential for conflict induced between the home and the school in Germany by these and other factors, such as homework and the demands which this makes of parents.

Employers

In 1991 the Chairman of the Dutch Union of Christian Employers,

Dr H. O. C. R. Ruding, expressed the view that the quality of education, which has increased markedly since World War 2, compares favourably with education in other countries, despite the existence of a number of bottlenecks and deficiencies. As strong points, he cited the level of education expenditure, which, at over five per cent of GNP is amongst the highest in the world. Among the weaknesses are the reduction in foreign language competence (since some foreign languages have become optional instead of compulsory) and insufficient interest in engineering studies and science as compared with other countries.

There is a need for improved vocational and educational guidance to overcome a tendency of too many students to drop out, to stop after general education without undertaking appropriate vocational education and to choose courses with no regard for employment opportunities. However, the recommendation of the Rauwenhoff Commission to establish closer links between education and local employment needs were rejected by the Cabinet, employers and educators alike as being too narrow. There should, instead, be a framework of national objectives, national syllabi, and national moderation within which schools can exercise their delegated authority.

Students

A poll (Dubet 1991) among students in upper secondary schools, aged 15–18, in France showed that, although 63 per cent of students felt there was a barrier between them and the teachers, the teacher remained the person most frequently approached for personal problems (33 per cent). This compared with social workers (19 per cent), educational guidance officers (13 per cent), class tutors (11 per cent) and head teachers (eight per cent). One quarter of students responded that they did not discuss their personal problems with anyone. Almost three quarters of students (72 per cent) felt that teachers operated on automatic pilot but 68 per cent still felt gratitude towards their teachers for help received. In general terms, students expected their teachers to be professionally competent and to know their subject (46 per cent), to have the ability to transmit their knowledge (45 per cent) and to organise their courses in such a way as to interest the students (43 per cent).

Conclusion

The more closely countries work together, and the greater the degree of professional mobility, the greater is the pressure for comparability of education and qualifications. Despite their different stages of development, Member States of the European Community share common areas of concern. The most pressing of these are matters of balance between educational opportunity and financial constraints, between the free choice of the individual and the manpower needs of the country and between large scale expansion and the maintenance of standards.

It is clear that education, like health, is a service which will never satisfy demands. As the general level of achievement rises, so new targets will be set, reflecting pressure from competing values which are in turn affected by demographic and economic changes.

References

Ballion, R. (1991) *La bonne école*, Paris: Hatier.

Barroso, J. and Sjorslev, S. *et al* (1990) *Administration and evaluation structures for primary and secondary schools in the twelve Member States of the EC*, Brussels: Commission of the European Communities.

Bottani, N. (1990) 'The background of the CERI/OECD project on international educational indicators' in *International Journal of Educational Research*, Vol. 14, No. 4, pp. 335–342.

Dubet, F. (1991) 'Phosphore' in Ministère de l'éducation nationale *La lettre TGF*, No. 68, 9 September 1991.

Gray, J. and Jesson, D. (1990) 'The negotiation and construction of performance indicators: some principles, proposals and problems' in *Evaluation and Research in Education*, Vol. 4, No. 2, 1990.

IFS Survey (1989) *Die Schule im Spiegel der öffentlichen Meinung. Ergebnissen des sechsten IFS-Repräsentativbefragung der bundesdeutschen Bevölkerung* (Public opinions of schools. Findings of the Sixth IFS–Questionnaire to the German people.) Survey conducted by the Max-Traeger-Stiftung and Hans Böckler Stiftung.

Meuret, D. (1990) 'The outlook for educational evaluation in France' in *International Journal of Educational Research*, Vol. 14, No. 4, pp. 395–400.

Ministère de l'éducation nationale (1991) *Des idées*, No. 10, October–November 1991.

Ministère de l'éducation nationale (1991a) *La lettre TGF*, No. 68, 9 September 1991.

Ministère de l'éducation nationale (1991b) *La lettre TGF*, No. 70, 23 September 1991.

Ministère de l'éducation nationale (1991c) *La lettre TGF*, No. 72, 7 October 1991.
Ministère de l'éducation nationale (1991d) *La lettre TGF*, No. 74, 21 October 1991.
OECD Secretariat (1990) *Education evaluation and reform strategies*, Germany.
Ruding, H. (1991) 'Onderwijskwaliteit en aansluiting op de arbeidsmarkt' in *Didaktief*, Vol. 21, No. 10, December 1991. (Chairman of the Dutch Union of Christian Employers).
Ulich, K. (1989) 'Eltern und Schüler: Die Schule als Problem in der Familienerziehung' (Parents and children: school as a problem in family upbringing) in *Zeitschrift für Sozialisationsforschung und Erziehungssoziologie*, Vol. 9, No. 3, 1989.
Walberg, H. (1990) 'Science, mathematics and national welfare, retrospective and prospective achievements' in *International Journal of Educational Research*, Vol. 14, No. 4, pp. 343–351.

Part III: THE PROFESSIONAL CONTEXT

6 The implications for the examination boards of the *Education Reform Act* of 1988

Kathleen Tattersall

The 1988 *Education Reform Act* aims to raise standards. The strategy to achieve this aim relies on the twin pillars of curriculum targets and their assessment. It is a familiar concept to Examination Boards which, since the middle of the 19th Century, have provided targets and benchmarks in the form of syllabuses and examinations against which the attainment of students has been measured. Through this work the Boards have played a central role in the process of setting, maintaining and carrying forward standards.

'Standards' in the context of examinations are not easy to define. In simple terms, they are the current expectation of what students ought to be able to know, understand and do. That should be at least as good as, preferably better than, what the previous generation of students attained. But how can that judgement be made? The practice has been to rely on the public examination system and to compare percentages of candidates attaining key grades in the same subject and across subjects from year to year. Different viewpoints have then been brought to bear: more candidates getting higher grades prove that standards have risen or that the Examination Boards have lowered their standards to make their examinations more attractive. Paradoxically, therefore, examinations cannot win when used to demonstrate the standards of the time.

But the conclusions which are drawn from examination results are superficial. Examinations are not static nor do they exist in a vacuum, oblivious to pedagogical developments and prevailing educational policy. They are evolving constantly to accommodate changes in curriculum or assessment techniques. The population which takes examinations also changes, as in 1974 when the raising of the school leaving age resulted in a new clientele who otherwise would have left school at 15 without any qualifications. Examination structures have also undergone a number of changes, the three most obvious ones being the introduction of the single subject GCE examination in 1951 which replaced the group School Certificate, the CSE examination in the 1960s and the GCSE examination of 1988. Each innovation was different in some way from what had gone before but each was also expected to carry forward the 'standards' of their predecessor. That link with the previous examination was between particular points of the grading scales: the pass standard of the new 'O' level examination of 1951 was linked with the credit standard of School Certificate and that link was maintained in the most recent innovation, the GCSE, through the equation of the Grade C/D boundary with the former 'O' level Grade C/D (CSE Grade 1/2). The same principle applied to the 'A' level examination, while the more recent AS examination – the half 'A' level – is described as being of the same standard 'A' level.

A scrutiny of the curriculum and assessment requirements of each of the 16+ examinations demonstrates the tenuous nature of the formal linkage. Current examinations are more wide-ranging in their demands and more sophisticated than earlier approaches to assessment. Examination Boards are the only constant element in the system. Their experience, built up over many years, has become the guarantor of standards, however loosely defined that concept might be in practice. Their presence has smoothed the way for changes from one system of examination to the next. The quality assurances which the Boards' imprimatur has given have enabled new curriculum requirements to be accepted by the profession and go unnoticed by the public at large. It is more than a presence: the Boards have been instrumental in the creation of the curriculum through their syllabus development. The Boards' syllabuses have been the sole external requirement for students to aim at. Success has opened the door to the next stage of education, failure has closed the door. Examination syllabuses set the scene and are viewed variously as representing the gold standard or exercising a malign influence on the educational system. Wherever the truth lies, the Boards' role in determining the curriculum of secondary schools has been central to the concept of standards.

The 1988 *Education Reform Act* not only challenges that role but makes it almost impossible for the Boards to do what is still expected of them, namely ensure reliability within the system and consistency with the standards of previous examinations. The act does not define a role for the Examination Boards in either curriculum matters or assessment arrangements. The *ERA* creates two new statutory bodies and defines particular roles for the Local Education Authorities to help bring about the National Curriculum which all students in maintained schools must follow and be assessed in. The curriculum starts with students' entry into formal schooling and ends with their exit at the age of 16. It provides, for the first time, a consistent basis for the measurement of students' attainment as they progress through the educational system. The act, therefore, ties the curriculum to an assessment system which will make possible the regular reporting of students' attainment, culminating at the age of 16. The assessment of students at the end of four key stages of their development – at the ages of seven, 11, 14 and 16 – will use a common reporting scale of 10 levels. The act establishes, therefore, a basis for monitoring students' development and attainment. Reliable monitoring requires the consistent definition and interpretation of the curriculum and assessment requirements at each key stage. Central to that process is consistency in the interpretation of levels by all teachers at all key stages. It is in these respects that the Boards could play a useful part but *ERA* has led to a fragmentation of roles and responsibilities which fails to get to grips with these issues.

There are particular problems at Key Stage 4 where a formal examination system already exists. On the one hand there is an expectation of consistency with earlier key stages; on the other, consistency with previous examination requirements. These expectations could prove to be mutually incompatible because of the detailed specification of the curriculum and because the rules governing the reporting requirements of the act – at Attainment Target and Subject – could require a different approach to determining students' levels of attainment. The exclusion of the Boards from the creation of the curriculum and the determination of the assessment rules does not assist in the task of reconciling the different demands.

The interaction of curriculum and assessment is the key to establishing and monitoring standards across the key stages. But the act creates an artificial divide between curriculum and assessment by establishing separate statutory bodies to be responsible for each of these elements. The National Curriculum Council advises the Secretary of State on the content of the Curriculum Orders for each subject. The Council does not have responsibility for the initial drafting of the content of a subject. That work is undertaken by Working Parties to a remit provided by the Secretary of State. It does, however, carry out consultations on the Secretary of State's behalf with the educational world, including Examination Boards, and the advice which it gives is shaped by a wide range of opinion as to what ought to constitute the curriculum requirements for a subject. It is the Secretary of State who then has the ultimate responsibility to determine for each subject the Curriculum Orders which govern what is to be taught.

The curriculum development model is one to which it is difficult to object but it has within it the seeds of failure. On the one hand it relies on subject expertise, is open to consultation and makes the curriculum rather than assessment the dominant aspect. This approach is not inconsistent with current practice where the government of the day has decided the general principles and policy within which the curriculum and the examination system should operate and the subject experts have then determined the detail. On the other hand, however, the act gives greater powers than ever before to the Secretary of State to decide for himself the detail of the curriculum. The subject experts' view can be ignored. Late changes to the history report illustrate the extent of those powers over curriculum matters. Within that process vital assessment issues can be overlooked or ignored. The sorry saga of mathematics and science with major amendments to their requirements within a year of the first Curriculum Orders becoming law demonstrates the folly of ignoring the reality of assessment demands. It should have been obvious from the start that the assessment of 17 science and 14 mathematics Attainment Targets would be unmanageable. The report of TGAT which the Government set up to advise it about assessment issues was clear that it was neither possible nor meaningful to make assessments at such a level of detail. It took the failure of the system during the first Key Stage 1 assessments, and the Boards' efforts to show the impact of too many Attainment Targets on standards at Key Stage 4, to bring that message home to the Government. The two key questions – can it be assessed? does it make impossible demands? – are the last to be asked and the first to be ignored. The development model is, therefore, weak and there is a real possibility that it will take other failures in practice at other Key Stages to demonstrate the impracticality of many of the demands which the Curriculum Orders make.

The act makes provision for the Secretary of State to determine the targets which schools and students should meet. These are described as Attainment Targets, defined in the *ERA* as 'the knowledge, skills and understanding which students are expected to acquire'. It is the detailed definitions of Attainment Targets, their consistency – or otherwise – at each of the 10 levels of the

National Curriculum assessment scale and their specificity which have implications for assessment. Too many Attainment Targets are unmanageable in assessment terms, as the mathematics and science experience shows. Attainment Targets which are not defined consistently across levels – as in the case of English where some requirements disappear and reappear at particular levels – also make for assessment problems. Within the Attainment Targets are Statements of Attainment which focus on more detailed aspects of the subject. Tensions exist between breadth and detail, between curriculum and assessment needs. Traditionally the Boards have provided the means of easing those tensions. Their exclusion from the process of creating the curriculum and expressing the Attainment Targets and Statements of Attainment in language which can be assessed leaves a void which none of the agencies responsible for the National Curriculum is equipped to fill.

The *Education Reform Act* gives to the Secretary of State powers to determine 'the arrangements for assessing pupils at or near the end of each key stage for the purpose of ascertaining what they have achieved in relation to the Attainment Targets for that stage'. The act also creates the School Examinations and Assessment Council whose responsibility it is to advise the Secretary of State on the arrangements to be made and on the detail of the Assessment Orders which are needed for each subject. Unlike the Curriculum Orders which embrace the whole of the curriculum in a subject, the Assessment Orders relate to the requirements for the Key Stage in question. The obvious danger of this piecemeal approach, as the Boards have pointed out, is that the assessment arrangements are so fragmented that it is impossible to ensure consistency across the key stages. Such consistency is essential if the assessment system is to be a reliable means of monitoring standards attained by the individual student and of ascertaining the extent to which curriculum targets have been met. Arrangements which are both Key Stage specific and agency-specific could fail to meet those expectations. On this and other issues the Boards' advice seems to have been given no more weight than that of any other respondent to the consultative process. It is SEAC's failure to recognise the long experience of the Boards in assessment matters and to take heed of their advice that has implications for standards.

The timescale for the introduction of the National Curriculum in English, mathematics and science has brought Key Stage 1 on stream first with Key Stage 3 assessments hard on its heels. What has happened at those key stages both in terms of the provision of assessment materials and responsibility for standards of assessment offers some insights into the problems of consistency and reliability across the key stages.

At both key stages the development of the assessment materials for use at the end of the stage in all schools – the Standard Assessment Tasks – has been subject to tender, the specification for which has been drawn up by SEAC. At Key Stage 1, following trials involving a number of development agencies, a single agency was commissioned to provide the actual materials. At Key Stage 3, again following trials, different agencies were commissioned on a subject basis to produce the materials. It appears to be the intention that, as different subjects come on stream, the same procedures will be followed at Key Stages 1, 2 and 3. The contracts are specified for a period of time and on a periodic basis new tenders will be invited. This model of test construction has characteristics similar to the present examination system, with SEAC playing the role in SAT development which the Boards play in respect of the work of their examiners. SEAC specifies what has to be done, commissions the work and judges the quality of what the development agencies produce.

Unlike the Boards' work, this approach is highly centralised. It has some attractions since it provides the means of developing a truly national standard within a subject and at a key stage. It overcomes the problem of several tests in a subject, namely comparability of both test materials and outcomes. This is, of course, the situation which exists in the present examination system where several development agencies, namely the Boards, provide a range of options in the form of their syllabuses and examinations. Those options in the GCSE examination are restricted by National Criteria, to which all syllabuses in a subject must conform, and by some broad performance criteria. The possibility of different standards being applied within and across GCSE Examining Groups requires them to go to great lengths in their own procedures and in co-operation with each others to minimise those differences. Subject pairs analyses, inter-Board/Group comparability exercises and SEAC's own scrutinies keep the system under constant review.

The credibility of centralising test provision relies on SEAC's own assessment expertise and on its ability to put in place arrangements which will ensure consistency of different agencies' interpretation of the requirements. Arrangements to standardise the marking of students' work to ensure that responses to the assessment materials are interpreted consistently are also needed. The make-up of the Council, whose members are appointed directly by the Secretary of State, is not a guarantee of the necessary assessment expertise. Nor do the arrangements which have been made at Key Stage 1 for the standardisation of assessments give confidence that across schools and authorities the criteria for the award of levels will be applied consistently. The arrangements to train teachers to assess and be able to judge their students' work against the Attainment Targets rest with the Local Authorities which are also responsible for moderation and the collection of the data required under Section 22 of the act.

In a sense, each LEA has become an examination board for the purposes of national curriculum assessment at Key Stage 1. There are no arrangements, other than the initial induction training by SEAC of LEA personnel, which will guarantee a consistent and reliable national standard. If national curriculum assessment were to have a low profile, that would not matter. The publication of the results of National Curriculum assessment, however, focuses attention on schools and LEAs and underlines the need for reliable cross LEA standardisation. Comments made by individual LEAs to explain their place in the 'league tables' published at the end of 1991 underline the point: teachers in some authorities were stringent in their interpretation of the criteria, others in other authorities more lenient. That is not the way to convince the public that a national assessment system can work. Appeals by parents against individual students' assessments to the Independent Appeals Authority for School Examinations, which deals with complaints about GCE and GCSE results, cannot be far away if some more reliable system of standardisation across authorities is not introduced.

At Key Stage 3 the need for structures which will work across authorities has been recognised by bringing in the GCSE Examining Groups to carry out, on a regional basis, and working under the control of SEAC, an audit of the standards of the assessments made by teachers. Unlike their normal examination work, this audit, as it name suggests, is an activity confined to the post examination stage. The Groups' involvement in the process of determining standards is, therefore, very limited. They play no part in the development of test materials (except where they have tendered successfully for a contract) nor are they involved in the training of teachers on the interpretation of marking schemes and in the recognition of levels of performance. The expertise which they bring to the audit is one of making judgements as to whether consistent judgements have been made in each subject within and across schools and, because their work is across regions, across LEAs. In using the Groups' expertise to audit standards, SEAC is able also to tap into an existing network of subject expertise and administrative arrangements for assessment.

Used sensibly, the arrangements for the Key Stage 3 audit could provide an important link with Key Stage 4 assessment arrangements. The contract specific nature of the audit, however, gives no guarantee of a long term involvement of the Examining Groups in making judgements about standards at Key Stage 3, however desirable that might be. Were the contract not to be renewed and were other bodies to be involved at Key Stage 3, the possibility of different interpretations of levels at two crucial key stages would be increased. This would be most unfortunate, given the inevitable comparisons which will be made between, say, Level 8 in a subject at Key Stage 3 and the same level in the same subject at Key Stage 4. That comparison takes on a new importance in those subjects which some students will drop after Key Stage 3. For them, the Key Stage 3 assessments will be the effective summative National Curriculum outcomes. It will not be acceptable in those or other circumstances to say that the standard applied at Key Stage 3 was different from that of Key Stage 4. The fact is that without a guaranteed link between the two key stages the standards will not be the same. The recognition on a more permanent basis of the Boards' traditional role in guaranteeing consistency and reliability of standards would enhance the credibility of both Key Stages 3 and 4.

The arguments for a single agency to be involved across the four key stages but particularly at Key Stages 3 and 4 are valid regardless of the part which public examinations might play in the assessment arrangements at Key Stage 4. The Secretary of State made clear at a very early stage of the National Curriculum development that the GCSE examination should be 'the main means of assessment' at Key Stage 4. That commitment of Government was not surprising: GCSE was new, it was an examination into which a lot of effort and credibility had been invested, it had been heralded by politicians and others as having raised standards and as having brought about beneficial curriculum changes. Without the GCSE, there might have been no National Curriculum: National Criteria opened the curriculum door to the Secretary of State and the success of the examination demonstrated the power of assessment as a change agent. To ditch the GCSE examination in favour of an untried approach to assessment would not have been acceptable. However, if all students at Key Stage 4 were to be assessed through GCSE, changes to either GCSE or to the system of National Curriculum assessment would be needed. GCSE syllabuses had been designed without a national curriculum in mind, the results were published in grades and, generally, at the subject level only, not all students were entered for the examination. To comply with the letter of the law GCSE's syllabuses, grades and the basis of its awarding would have to change. Furthermore, the concept of GCSE as a qualification for some would also need to be rethought to accommodate the concept of assessment for all.

It is the bringing of GCSE into line with National Curriculum requirements at Key Stage 4 which most affects the traditional responsibility which the Boards have exercised over standards. There is, first, the question of syllabus development. Any syllabus which purports to assess a National Curriculum subject at Key Stage 4 must comply with all the requirements of the Curriculum Orders. The syllabus must be consistent with the Programmes of Study, it must address the Attainment Targets, it must provide the necessary information about a student's attainment. The Programmes of Study leave little room for creativity. Indeed, some argue that their existence makes syllabus development work redundant and that the Boards need only provide an assessment package. National Curriculum thus provides a tighter framework for, and introduces a greater degree of control over, the syllabuses of Examination Boards than, for example, the National Criteria which govern the current GCSE examinations. The Boards have little freedom to determine the content of their syllabuses.

The question of standards is linked with the notion of the population for whom an examination is intended. When GCSE was identified as 'the main means' of assessment, the obvious question was, would it be possible to change the examination from one designed for a restricted range of students aiming at a qualification to an examination to meet the needs of all students across the 10 levels? SEAC's original advice in 1989 to the Secretary of State was that the examination should be redesigned to meet the needs of all students and, further, that students at all levels should be awarded a GCSE certificate. The Secretary of State's response was to separate the question of syllabus and examination design from certification: syllabuses and examinations were to accommodate all students but only those students who attained Level 4 or above (equivalent to Grade G and above) would qualify for a certificate. Those who attained Levels 1 to 3 would have their attainment recorded in their Record of Achievement. To widen the certification of the examination to embrace all students would, the Secretary of State believed, undermine the credibility of the examination as a qualification.

Later pronouncements by the Secretary of State have changed the position. What is now being looked for are assessments for Levels 1, 2 and 3 which are separate from but end on with the GCSE system. Furthermore, the involvement of other examining bodies, particularly the vocational examining boards, in the assessment of students at Key Stage 4 is being encouraged, most notably by the Secretary of State in his speech to the 1991 North of England Conference. At that same conference, the Secretary of State relaxed the Key Stage 4 requirements and introduced the concept of the short course – the 'half GCSE'. Unlike the earlier key stages, therefore, where the assessment package is provided by a single agency, under the control of SEAC, the assessment arrangements at Key Stage 4 have been made more complex by the exclusion of some students from the GCSE examination, greater curriculum freedom and the possible increase in the number of bodies providing assessment.

The link between the diverse and possibly incoherent range of assessment provision at Key Stage 4 is the 10 level scale which all examinations at Key Stage 4 must adopt in 1994. In the case of GCSE, attainment in all subjects regardless of links with National Curriculum will be reported on the new scale. Superficially the scale provides the assurance that consistent standards have been applied in different examinations and by different examining bodies but, as already noted, unless there are mechanisms for interpreting the levels consistently, different applications will result. That is a real possibility at Key Stage 4.

The GCSE Examining Groups have other concerns which relate to links between the new scale and the current GCSE grading scale and their responsibility for carrying forward into the new assessment system current GCSE standards. There are several points of equivalence between the new scale and the former scale (the boundaries of levels 9/8, 8/7, 5/4 and 4/3 relate to grades A/B, B/C, F/G and G/U respectively) but there is no equivalence with that key boundary, C/D, whose linkage with previous systems stretches back to School Certificate. On the new scale the C/D boundary falls somewhere within level 7. The fear of the Examination Boards is that the absence of this key link will undermine their ability to ensure that the new system gains public acceptability. Their expectation is that the 7/6 boundary will probably replace the C/D boundary as the effective entry requirement for courses and training. That could be interpreted as a lowering of standards.

The new level scale is also perceived, however, as a means of raising standards by providing at the top end a further distinction between the best candidates. Level 10 is intended to stretch the most able, the implication being that the present GCSE system fails to do this. A greater use of differentiated papers at Key Stages 3 and 4 is envisaged, with limitations built into the revised (December 1991) GCSE criteria for the ranges of levels which examination papers can target. Overlaps between the targeted levels will be built in, complicating even further the already complex task of ensuring comparability and consistency of awards. The assumption is made that tasks can be targeted successfully at particular levels and, further, that candidates respond to those tasks in the manner expected of them. Actual examinations show how ill-founded these assumptions can be. Differentiated papers might seem an easy solution to assessing students of all abilities but they introduce their own problems of choices of entry, setting comparable tasks and determining comparable awards.

At the same time as greater curriculum and assessment diversity is being introduced into the system at Key Stage 4, the *ERA* introduces other mechanisms to control the activities of Examination Boards. Section 5 gives the Secretary of State powers to approve all qualifications and syllabuses for students of compulsory school age. Section 24 opens the way for that approval to be extended to post 16 qualifications and the Government has already signalled its intention to do this in the near future. In the context of enforcing the National Curriculum the powers are the means of ensuring that whatever is on offer to students at the age of 16 conforms to the curriculum and assessment targets which have been set, regardless of the Examination Board which makes the provision. However, for the Boards, Section 5 means that they can no longer decide what to provide for schools.

It is SEAC's responsibility to advise the Secretary of State on the qualifications to be approved and to approve on his behalf criteria for syllabuses or syllabuses themselves. As has been noted, the Programmes of Study allow little room for manœuvre and the new criteria which govern GCSE examinations in National Curriculum subjects provide a less flexible framework than did the original GCSE criteria. The inevitable question is, how many syllabuses are needed to provide schools with sufficient but not excessive choice? Should all syllabuses, however similar to each other they may be, which meet the requirements be approved, or only those which are distinctly different from each other? The greater the diversity, the greater the problems of ensuring consistent outcomes. SEAC's initial approach to this question was to adopt a Criterion of Need, whereby all syllabuses would be significantly different. The Criterion was dropped but, had it been enforced, it would have reinforced the trend to a central control of the operations of Examination Boards/Groups in such a way as to leave them with little control over their affairs. Nevertheless, the tensions between the setting of national standards and targets and the provision of a choice of syllabuses from a number of Examining Boards/Groups have to be recognised.

The debate about the number of syllabuses which might be

developed in relation to the Criterion of Need complicated the process of syllabus development for 1994. Other factors also made the task difficult, not least changes to the criteria governing syllabus development and uncertainties relating to the reporting requirements of the *ERA* as they applied to GCSE and the way in which these could be met. In July 1991 the Prime Minister in a speech to the Centre for Policy Studies expressed his preference for a largely externally assessed GCSE examination with the emphasis on terminal written examinations rather than course work. That speech led to a reconsideration of the place of course work in public examinations and to the need to rewrite the criteria which had been published 12 months previously for English, mathematics and science. It culminated in the Secretary of State ruling in November 1991 that new limitations on the weighting of course work in these subjects would apply from 1994 onwards. At the same time weightings were announced for other subjects to be incorporated in syllabuses as and when they came on stream.

The course work debate illustrates the degree to which control of their own affairs has passed from the Examination Boards to central government. Nothing that the Boards could say about the value of course work had an impact. The softening of the hard line of a 20 per cent limit across subjects resulted more from the emphasis on process in different National Curriculum subjects than from the Boards' assurances that their procedures for monitoring and moderating teachers' assessment of course work maintained a consistent standard. In one sense the course work debate is a microcosm of the tensions within National Curriculum assessment: the search for a balance between what meets curriculum needs with what is manageable and credible in assessment terms. The law comes down on the side of manageability with its emphasis on assessment 'at or near the end of the key stage', a requirement which has implications for modular schemes as well as the extent to which course work can contribute to the assessment process. In imposing limits on the weighting of course work, the Secretary of State interpreted the phrase less liberally than SEAC did originally when rewriting the criteria to match the National Curriculum. However, the Secretary of State's limits brought GCSE into line with what had happened already at Key Stage 1: the Assessment Orders make the SAT pre-eminent in the determination of the level, although there is some provision for an appeal process using evidence of work done during the Key Stage. At Key Stage 1 too the change from the course friendly SAT to the short sharp SAT demonstrated the emphasis on a more formal examination process. The post July 1991 GCSE was, therefore, consistent with developments at earlier key stages.

The limitations on course work apply as much to 'A' level as to GCSE. Principles which will govern future syllabus development in 'A' level lay down a 20 per cent limitation 'in most subjects'. No debate has taken place about what might be a weighting appropriate to the qualities and skills being tested. In some senses, therefore, the control being introduced at 'A' level is even more draconian than at GCSE. At this level too, the Government's view of what constitutes standards – 'A' level is referred to as 'the gold standard' and, like its monetary counterpart, shall not be devalued – takes precedence over what the Boards and many teachers believe to be the needs of post 16 students. The GCE Boards' freedom to meet those needs through new examination provision which does not meet the 'A' level standard will be curtailed by the extension of Section 5 powers to post 16 qualification. At post 16, as in the National Curriculum, therefore, central government is increasingly taking the lead in determining standards for schools, regardless of professional opinion.

There is also the question of the information about student attainment which the examination system must provide to meet National Curriculum reporting requirements. Section 22 of the act requires for each student at each key stage level to be reported for each Attainment Target and each Subject. Rules are needed to determine the basis on which levels should be awarded and the relationship between Attainment Target levels and Subject levels. It is SEAC's responsibility to lay down those rules and it is reasonable that the rules should be consistently applied across all key stages. The important question is, should the focus of the assessment be the Subject – the traditional approach of the GCSE and its predecessor examinations – or should it be the Attainment Target? The Key Stage 1 Assessment Orders for English, mathematics and science are clear: the focus is on the Attainment Target with fairly crude rules of aggregation to give a level for the subject as a whole, an approach which, if applied to Key Stage 4, would change the whole basis of the award of grades to candidates.

More than any other feature of the new assessment system which the *ERA* puts into place, an approach which denies control of awards at the subject level undermines the Board's responsibility to set, maintain and carry forward standards. For much of 1991 the Joint Council for the GCSE, speaking for the Examining Groups as a whole, attempted to impress on SEAC that the Secretary of State had a stark choice: to carry through to Key Stage 4 the principle of aggregation from the Attainment Target and thus give some semblance of consistency across the key stages; or to take a different approach at Key Stage 4, identifying Attainment Target levels within the context of the subject award, thus making possible consistency with existing standards of award. In the opinion of the Groups these two aspects of consistency were contradictory and irreconcilable.

SEAC's July 1991 advice to the Secretary of State described the dilemma:

> The Council considered three options. The first option follows on from our work on national curriculum tests and examinations, across the various key stages, which has been intended to yield outcomes for individual attainment targets.... The expectation has been that attainment target scores would be aggregated to yield whole subject outcomes, using appropriate aggregation rules taking account of any agreed weighting for attainment targets.... If we proceed this way ... there can be no guarantee that the proportions of candidates obtaining the various grades or levels in 1994, subject by subject, will closely match the corresponding proportions for earlier years....
>
> Despite this problem, there are merits in this approach. It would be seen to reflect the structure of the national curriculum and the intention to set performance targets. There would be continuity with the approach to aggregation envisaged for key stage 3 .... It is only because it is intended to merge national curriculum assessment at key stage 4 with GCSE that a problem has arisen.
>
> [An] alternative approach ... would be for GCSE awards in 1994 to continue to be made by examiners reviewing the whole of each candidate's performance across the range of tasks and questions set in that year .... This approach would deliver whole subject outcomes broadly consistent from 1993 to 1994, but would not yield individual attainment target outcomes. They would be assessed separately ... [using] teacher assessments made against the statements of attainment for individual targets. But ... a process of reconciliation would be required if they were to be reported in such a way that they matched the outcome for the whole subject ....
>
> This alternative could certainly ensure the maintenance of current examination standards .... It would however result in a discontinuity in approach between key stages 3 and key stage 4 .... This approach to continuity of standards might meet public expectations, and be seen to be fair to pupils at a critical stage of their educational development. Information at the whole subject level may be regarded as most important by a majority of the users of examination results.

SEAC went on to speculate about other possible resolutions of the problem but came to no firm conclusion, leaving the Secretary of State to decide where the priority should lie. In his reply of 25 July 1991, the Secretary of State indicated that it would not be acceptable for the Attainment Targets to be determined through a process of teacher assessment separate from the GCSE examination. He asked for further advice on how examiners might, within a system which yielded both Subject and Attainment Target scores, 'exercise an element of judgement, as now, in determining individual subject levels'. The reply also made clear that, if a choice had to be made, it would be in favour of consistency within National Curriculum assessment rather than consistency with current standards:

> I do not myself regard the need for precise continuity [of standards from 1993 to 1994] as overriding all other considerations. With the transition to a new grading scale, related to the National Curriculum Statements of Attainment which are themselves – at the top end certainly – more challenging than the existing GCSE criteria, we should expect no more than that GCSE standards should be broadly comparable between the two years.

The outcome of the exchange of correspondence, after further discussions between SEAC and the Joint Council, was a set of awarding rules for GCSE which reconcile Attainment Targets and Subject approaches. The focus of the assessment will be on the Attainment Targets and Statements of Attainment but the initial focus of the award will be on the Subject. Attainment Target scores consistent with the Subject award will then be identified. Whether this attempt to merge both sets of assessments will satisfy the competing demands of consistency across time and across Key stages remains to be seen.

Assessment is a central part of the *Education Reform Act*. The changes the Act has introduced are making their mark already on the system and affecting the work of the Boards and their relationships with other bodies. However, it will take some time for the full implications of the act for the Boards to be realised. Only when Key Stage 4 in the core subjects comes on stream in 1994 will the full nature of the conflict between the Boards' traditional role in the process of standard setting and the requirements of the act become apparent. All the indications are that the world of assessment is changing and the Boards could be pushed from its centre to the periphery. In curriculum matters the act has already marginalised the Boards and their exclusion from the creation of the National Curriculum reduces their influence on the standards required. Greater controls through Section 5 and the powers which the *ERA* gives to the Secretary of State limit the influence which the Boards have exerted on the system. The use of assessment throughout the key stages and the concept of assessment for all opens the process of assessment to all teachers and removes the secrecy which has often surrounded it. That greater openness offers great potential for the future, provided that mechanisms are put in place to ensure that the assessment of students across all key stages is carried out consistently. The levels awarded must be comparable, regardless of the context in which the judgements have been made. It is in the context of putting into place a consistent, reliable and coherent system that the Boards have most to offer in the setting of national standards. It is not too late to ensure that their considerable expertise and energies are used positively to achieve this end.

7 The changing perception of standards in the independent sector

The Impact of Era

Vivian Anthony

> There is little doubt that academic education is under threat. We have all seen it to some extent with GCSE – kitchen sink science, 'relevance', questions so easy that they make even pupils laugh. We are seeing it in the dilution of 'A' level and in the well-orchestrated efforts of those who wish to annihilate this examination. The content of science syllabuses has been reduced. Delighted as I am that so few of my pupils now fail 'A' level, I remain concerned that my colleagues tell me that the examinations are easier, that the scores are regularly higher than they expected, and that university dons now, almost universally, complain of the noticeable lack of knowledge among their current pupils as compared with those of three or so years ago.
>
> So said Geoffrey Parker, the High Master of Manchester Grammar School, in his Chairman's address to the Headmasters' Conference in Cambridge in September 1991 (Parker, 1991).

In primary schools

There is a growing body of support for the view that the expectations of teachers, examiners and others of what pupils can achieve must be raised, and further impetus was given in the report of 'the Three Wise Men' (Professor Robin Alexander, Chief Inspector Jim Rose and Chris Woodhead, Chief Executive of the NCC) on primary education (Alexander, Rose and Woodhead, 1992). That report accepted that standards had fallen in basic subjects partly because of the 'turbulence' caused by the introduction of the National Curriculum and partly because of 'highly questionable dogmas which had led to excessively complex classroom practice and devalued the place of subjects in the curriculum'.

What standards?

Whether we concentrate on 'expectations' or on 'achievements' it is important to be clear what is meant when these concepts are related to changing standards.

We are concerned with what this generation of pupils can do compared with those who have gone before. In some subjects comparison is a simple matter. If children of a given age are assigned the same mathematics problems as their forebears it is possible to compare the results. The same exercise can be applied to most straightforward tasks: spelling and vocabulary tests, factual recall of many kinds, performing activities which require basic skills, e.g. practical work in science or technology, and so on. Information from such sample testing makes possible not only comparisons over time but also between children in different countries or regions or in different parts of the educational system. It is on this simple philosophy that testing in the National Curriculum is based. In reality, comparisons are much more difficult to make. The body of knowledge and the complexity of questions in any subject is constantly increasing and syllabuses are regularly revised to take account of this. Items which were at one time at the heart of university courses are now the meat of 'A' level syllabuses and it is clear from National Curriculum Programmes of Study that a similar process has been going throughout secondary and primary education.

Content or skills?

The problem of overloading the syllabus which arises from this process has been particularly acute in science but the debate between the 'content' and 'skills' lobbies has spread over many parts of the curriculum. It is argued that if pupils are required to learn more and more information about a subject little time is left for them to develop the essential skills in that subject. To have learned all the facts about the French Wars of Religion is no substitute for being able to analyse the material, draw conclusions and be able to communicate them. Others argue that a reduction in syllabus content designed to enable the development of subject skills will leave the student with a partial and less effective grasp of the subject. You cannot be a true student of English Literature without reading a sufficient range of material on which to base further analytical criticism.

Breadth or depth?

These arguments are at the heart of the debate about the reform of the Advanced level. The critics say that to study only three subjects, to no matter what *depth*, is too narrow a programme around and even the then Secretary of State for Education, Kenneth Clarke, a staunch supporter of 'A' level, was prepared to accept that argument: 'The specialised study of two or three subjects, often closely related to each other, is for many students too narrow a preparation for the next stage of study or for work' (Clarke, 1991). He was, however, not disposed to accept the arguments advanced by the Opposition spokesman on education, Jack Straw, that if five subjects were studied there would be no reduction of standards. Those who want to see the standards associated with 'A' level maintained cannot see how this can be done if the amount of time spent on a subject and the syllabus for that subject are reduced by 40 per cent. They may not, however, be able to deny that studying five subjects, albeit to a lesser standard, may be just as demanding. Few commentators would claim that the International Baccalaureate, with three major and three subsidiary subjects, is not among the most challenging courses followed by students in this country (Barker, 1991). Moreover, the Committee sees this structure as the best way forward in reforming the Scottish system of 16–19 education: Highers and Sixth Year Studies being replaced by a Scottish Baccalaureate (Howie Committee, 1992).

Less subject content: same standard?

The Government has argued that the breadth missing from a straight 'A' level programme can be supplied by adding 'AS' level subjects. However, there is a certain inconsistency in the statement that 'AS' examinations 'offer what amounts to half-subjects *at the same standard* as 'A' level and make students spread their study across a broader range of subjects' (Clarke, 1991). If it is a half subject can it be *at the same standard* as the whole subject? There is a widespread ambition to allow 'A' and 'AS' syllabuses evolve 'without undermining the consistency of high standards' and a belief that 'establishing a framework of principles' will ensure the maintenance of quality.

'We remain convinced' said Kenneth Clarke 'that 'AS' is the best way of achieving breadth for 'A' level students. This is because it is of 'A' level standard – not at some intermediate standard which is unlikely to gain much credibility in higher education or elsewhere (Clarke, 1992). However, in their *General Scrutiny Report – 'A' and 'AS' Examinations 1990'*, SEAC ask for more 'attention to all aspects of parity between the two examinations'. 'In one subject the demands on the 'AS' candidates were considered greater than those of the 'A' level. In another subject, although some questions were considered to be of advanced level standard, others seemed easy and gave the impression of a paper aimed at candidates who had completed the first year of a two year course' (SEAC, 1992). There are many examples of schools using 'AS' as an examination course for 17 or even 16 year old candidates.

Grade inflation

One aspect of the complexity of comparing standards of pupils' exam performance over time arises from attempting to apply a sophisticated system of grades. It is much easier to make a general statement about the proportion of pupils passing an 'A' level than it is to compare performance at each grade. There are many teachers and examiners who believe that *grade inflation* has occurred in recent years but it is difficult to prove that there were, for instance, some candidates obtaining A grades in 'A' level Economics in 1991 who would have obtained B grades in 1966 when I first became an examiner.

Table 7.1 shows the percentages of candidates in each grade 1969–1990 (cumulative) for candidates in 'A' level Economics with the Oxford & Cambridge Board.

No doubt as teachers become more experienced at dealing with a particular syllabus they pass on to their pupils ideas for improving performance. 'A' level is often as much a test of the effectiveness of the teacher as the ability of the candidate. Whether improved grade performance is evidence of rising real standards depends partly on the student being able to perform to this standard after leaving school. Is it significant that those in Higher Education and in recruitment for employment have not held back from criticising the quality of those emerging from the 'A' level system in recent years? However, even those in Higher Education are not without their critics. 'Spurt in first class degrees renews fear for standards' was the headline in *The Times* on 17 February 1992 when 'University Statistics 1989–90' Vol 3 (Universities Statistics 1989–90) was issued. There was a rise of nine per cent in the proportion of undergraduates obtaining firsts in that year and a rise of 22 per cent in the previous four years. External examiners are employed to maintain the standard of degrees but critics have argued that it is surprising that in a period when more and more students are gaining places to read for degrees the proportion getting first class degrees should be rising so steeply. Nor is it easy to understand why in Bath and Aston the proportions are 13 per cent and 12 per cent respectively while in Leicester and Liverpool only five per cent obtained first class degrees. Moreover, the grades achieved by candidates have often surprised teachers and Heads. In surveys carried out in HMC schools in the last three years nearly 20 per cent of responses from

Table 7.1: 'A' level Economics results 1969–1990

Year	Number of Candidates	A	B	C	D	E	N
1969	1345	9.4	24.6	37.2	52.0	73.8	89.1
1970	1472	10.7	25.6	39.1	54.5	72.9	94.6
1971	1675	9.9	24.5	37.1	53.1	71.0	93.3
1972	1744	13.8	29.5	42.9	59.6	77.7	93.9
1973	1737	11.1	28.3	41.7	56.9	74.7	93.4
1974	1846	10.9	30.0	42.6	58.5	78.0	94.0
1975	2021	11.8	28.0	41.1	57.9	76.2	93.9
1976	2133	13.1	29.9	43.4	59.8	77.4	92.4
1977	2210	12.4	29.4	41.7	59.4	77.1	90.4
1978	2239	14.0	30.5	44.8	61.5	81.4	92.1
1979	2331	13.8	33.3	43.9	59.1	80.5	90.0
1980	2330	14.6	35.3	45.7	59.5	80.2	90.1
1981	2476	14.0	34.9	47.3	61.4	82.3	92.3
1982	2463	12.5	32.8	48.6	64.9	81.5	93.1
1983	2599	14.6	34.9	49.1	66.2	82.2	93.3
1984	2622	12.8	32.7	51.9	67.8	82.9	94.1
1985	2536	16.6	37.1	54.9	71.2	83.7	94.0
1986	2474	16.4	40.7	58.1	75.1	88.0	96.6
1987	2503	17.5	43.1	62.3	78.4	90.3	95.1
1988	2664	17.9	44.0	64.3	80.6	91.4	96.8
1989	3085	18.5	46.1	64.8	80.3	91.1	97.0
1990	3164	19.1	46.8	65.8	80.2	90.6	96.2
1991	2760	19.8	46.2	64.5	78.8	89.3	95.7

Heads of Departments indicated that exam results were better than expected (and this was true of both 'A' level and GCSE). This impression is reinforced by the experience of Chief Examiners when comparing school estimates with actual grades achieved which shows there are far more cases of the grades being higher than the estimates than the reverse. Moreover, in four reports to SEAC 'scrutineers were not confident that candidates had been awarded correct grades: some candidates received A and B grades whilst performing poorly on some sections of the examination and without showing the full level of skills expected at advanced level. However, in the majority of examinations ... appropriate grades had been awarded' (SEAC, 1992).

Grading differences between subjects

Even the JMB admitted 'the present 'A' level grading scheme has very serious defects' (JMB, 1983). 'The system of grades is based on ... "norms" (major departures from these norms has occurred in certain subjects ... reflecting the differences between subjects)'. 'The Secondary School Examinations Council (predecessor of SEAC) in 1960 established "norms" based on the expectations, founded on experience, of the quality of candidates entered ... and "to be regarded as no more than rough indications" (Ministry of Education).' In Table 7.2 the grades with cumulative percentages are compared with the actual grades awarded in 1990 in 'A' level Economics, English and Chemistry.

Table 7.2: Comparison of cumulative percentages with actual grades

Grade	Norm	Cumulative Percentages Economics	English	Chemistry
A	10	9.7	9.9	16.0
B	25	23.3	27.8	34.2
C	35	37.6	48.7	48.9
D	50	54.4	69.5	63.7
E	70	70.8	85.2	77.1
O/N	90	83.5	93.4	87.4
Number of Candidates in 1990		45,330	68,846	36,596

Source: SEAC 1991

It is interesting to see this difference in proportion in each grade between subjects and there are similar differences between boards. These are now published each year by the Schools Examination and Assessment Council (SEAC). Their report in March 1991 cautions the analyst that:

When considering the variation in results between boards it is most important to observe that candidates entering for the GCE examinations provided by different boards cannot, in any sense, be regarded as random samples drawn from the same candidate population. This situation is true even when the entry is large: large samples are not necessarily random samples. Each examining board has its own clientele and attracts candidates in different proportions from the various type of centre ... each board will show different percentages of candidates achieving a particular grade either in a specific subject or across all subjects .... It should also be noted that in particular subjects the syllabuses may represent alternative curricular and assessment approaches each of which may attract candidates from different achievement spans within the total population.

(SEAC, 1991)

Higher grades = rising standards?

How fair is it to associate the increase in the numbers and proportions obtaining higher grades with rising standards? The JMB paper states 'it may be reasonable to assume that, given a subject with a large entry (say 1,000 candidates), the skills and abilities measured by the examination will be distributed in a consistent way over the examination population from year to year. It is valid, therefore, to expect similar proportions of candidates to be awarded particular grades from year to year, provided that there are no major fluctuations in the quality of the entry and the effectiveness of the preparation for the examination' (JMB, 1983). It is, of course, the examiners who make the judgements on the quality of candidates' work but the process whereby the examiners' marks are turned into final grades is not simple. Exactly where grade boundaries are drawn is a matter for great discussion and heart searching rather than scientific calculation and yet the difference of a mark or two can result in hundreds more or less achieving a particular grade. Efforts have been made to tackle defects and ensure comparability but grading will never be a precise science. As we have seen in Table 7.1 in 1990 the 'A' level Economics examiners for the Oxford and Cambridge Board awarded A grades to 19.1 per cent of candidates compared with 9.4 per cent in 1969. Moreover, 90.6 per cent passed the subject in 1990 compared with 73.8 per cent in 1969. There is no doubt that a significant part of this improvement in grades achieved can be put down to rising standards. In 1969 Economics teaching in schools was still in its infancy whereas it is now well-established, well-taught by specialist trained teachers and is among the most popular of 'A' level subjects. All but a few of the candidates come from the major independent schools most of which have large

Sixth Forms and selective entries. In the multiple choice paper which is common to five boards, the Oxford and Cambridge candidates' mean score has always been the highest.

Nor was the high percentage of A grades achieved by O & C candidates only evident in Economics: it was achieved by 26.6 per cent in chemistry, 20.2 per cent in French, 37.5 per cent in German, 19.7 per cent in history and 38.3 per cent in mathematics. Yet when one looks at the A grade performance over all the Boards it is much closer to the 'norm' (see Table 7.2). It would seem that the rise in standards achieved by independent schools has not been matched in other institutions.

However, not all the increase in high grades should be ascribed to rising standards. Examiners have increasingly recognised the advantage of using the whole mark range and to be aware in their marking that candidates will not perform as well in an examination as they will in a prepared essay. This leads to higher marks than those awarded to course essays (see Table 7.3).

Table 7.3: Grades boundaries for an Examination Board's 'A' Level in one subject 1980–1988: maximum mark = 200

Year	Grades					
	A	B	C	D	E	N
1980	132	115	108	99	83	71
1981	135	118	109	100	84	70
1982	133	115	105	93	80	64
1987	144	125	111	97	83	69
1988	148	128	115	100	83	70

When grade boundaries are drawn awarders (chief examiners) will be aware of the boundaries drawn in earlier years and will want to see any improvement reflected in the percentage of higher grades awarded. Efforts have to be made to keep the standards in one subject in line with those in other subjects. SEAC and the Boards have stated the aim 'to maintain recognised standards of achievement through examinations based on approved syllabuses'. In order to ensure that standards are maintained from year to year SEAC and the boards have put in place a number of measures – notably SEAC scrutinies, inter-board comparability studies and various statistical comparisons carried out within the boards. HM Inspectorate also carries out its own monitoring activity (HMI, 1992).

Comparability

No subject expects to be left out of the general rise in grades awarded. If more history and geography candidates are obtaining A grades then the same candidates taking economics will be expecting similar grades in that subject. Nor is there much incentive for the Boards to hold back the upward movement. They are conscious that schools are likely to take their custom elsewhere if they consider their students are not being as well treated as they would be by another Board. It appears that similar processes are occurring in universities. John O'Leary, *The Times* Education Correspondent, has suggested that universities are attempting to achieve more balance between subjects: more firsts are being awarded in humanities and social science partly in response to the higher incidence of firsts in mathematics and science (O'Leary, 1992).

Appeals and scrutinies

The rising level of expectations on the part of teachers and students is one reason for the alarming increase in the number of appeals on results. In the past, few of these appeals were successful but now the number is growing and while it remains a tiny percentage of the total, appeals result in movements in only one direction – upwards. Fairness to all candidates requires parity between optional routes and optional questions within every examination. SEAC 'A' level scrutineers found that 'in some subjects optional topics were conceptually more difficult than others. Some topics were much broader than others .... Eight scrutiny reports commented on discrepancies in the demands and difficulties of the optional questions'.

More enter Higher Education

All parties concerned – pupils, teachers and even the Government – take pleasure from the steadily increasing proportion of young people passing at least two subjects at 'A' level. In 1990 that proportion reached 20 per cent when in 1969 it would have been little more than half that. It is the goal of both major political parties, by the year 2000, for 30 per cent of young people to achieve two 'A' level passes and for a similar proportion to go on to Higher Education. These are admirable goals: more young people staying in school post 16, more gaining success at 'A' level and more going on to Higher Education. However, if they are achieved by making 'A' level easier or by replacing 'A' level with less demanding examinations there will not necessarily have been an overall rise in standards and the universities will have to adapt their courses so that they start from a lower base. Students may well have to spend longer on their courses in order to achieve a first degree standard comparable to that which is currently achieved and is so highly respected throughout the world. Around 18 per cent of the age group at present reach this degree standard. A figure which compares well with other countries and is achieved with a much lower drop-out rate. Much of the credit for this goes to the quality of 'A' level as a preparation for higher education. It remains to be seen in the light of growing clamour for reform whether the Secretary of State can maintain the position declared at Oxford in 1992:

> We are not in the business of abolishing a successful examination which provides the basis for competitive entry into our excellent higher education system. 'A' level continues to be successful and ever more popular with pupils. More candidates are taking the examination each year and more of those candidates are successful than ever before. 'A' levels are doing their job.

Intermediate courses

However, not all students are suited to the 'A' level approach or capable of achieving its standards. There is no doubt that a wider range of approaches is needed if the goal of increased participation is to be achieved. The need for courses for those wishing to go beyond GCSE standard but not wishing to follow the vocational route and without the ability or maturity to reach *full* 'A' level standards, at least at that time in their development, remains unrecognised. The eloquent arguments of Dr Eric Anderson, Headmaster of Eton (Anderson, 1990), and the support of all associations responsible for teaching and examining 16–19 year olds were obviously not enough to persuade the Government that, unlike in most other industrialised countries, the needs of a significant group of students are not being met (SCUE, GSA, HMC, SHA and APVIC, 1992). The Government claims that in the 21st Century, schools and colleges will have the choice of a wider range of approaches, offering the possibility of links with vocational qualifications ... *without loss of standards or rigour* (Clarke, 1992). No doubt those who are persuaded to remain in full time education will achieve higher standards than had previously been achieved by those who dropped out but whether this can be 'secured effectively without the need for radical change to a highly regarded, tried and tested examination system' is much less obvious.

Vocational course

Sensibly, a range of general vocational qualifications is being introduced to cater for the needs of those who want to prepare for related occupations and do not want the 'A' level approach. There are dangers, however, in trying too obviously to link these approaches or to claiming that these courses are of the same standard. It may be that some vocational courses would offer 'an accepted route to higher level qualifications, including higher education' but the notion that they will be of equal *standing* with academic qualifications *at the same level* needs careful explanation. It would not be sensible to expect students on vocational courses to be able to tackle the same problems or demonstrate the same skills as those on 'A' level courses, and the reverse is also true.

A coherent system

Peter Pilkington has argued strongly the need for specialist tracks much as they operate in other countries like France and Germany (Pilkington, 1991). 'A principal weakness of our system', he says, 'is the lack of a single vocational/technical qualification which would command as much esteem, in its fashion, as the academic 'A' level. Indeed such a qualification, and the dedicated vocational institutions which helped to provide it, would be the greater safeguard against the dilution ... of academic standards.' Any attempt to make all courses operate at the same standard could only be achieved by bringing down the standard currently achieved at 'A' level and this would mean sacrificing the needs of the most able pupils to the needs of the majority. This principle has already been demonstrated in the move from 'O' level and CSE to GCSE and any attempt to impose a similarly all embracing 18+ examination would be even more effective in reducing the high standards currently achieved. There is much more support for a coherent and unified *system* of examinations with courses appropriate to the needs and abilities of different groups (SCUE, GSA, HMC, SHA and APVIC, 1992). In this way the standards of the majority could be raised while maintaining demanding courses for the most able.

GCSE experience

The restructuring of the 16+ examination system which gave rise to the GCSE has produced some significant effects on standards of performance and the introduction of the National Curriculum will be no less significant. Prior to 1988 there had been two examinations systems running side by side though with some overlap – the GCE Ordinary level and the CSE. When these were merged into the single system of GCSE some important changes were introduced not only in the system of examinations but also in the nature of the courses. Ordinary level had been appropriate for 25–30 per cent of the population and CSE catered, in most subjects, for pupils in all but the bottom third of the ability range.

The new GCSE was intended to be suitable for at least 70 per cent of the population and, in order to facilitate this, a new grading system A–G was introduced and, in some subjects, differentiated papers were introduced.

In place of the heavy content based 'O' level syllabuses new style GCSE syllabuses with greater emphasis on oral work, practicals, coursework and other skills and, in some subjects, a substantial reduction in the pure knowledge requirement. In order to cater for a wide ability range some of the questions on the GCSE exam papers became very simple. After four years of GCSE it is evident that it is easier to obtain A, B or C Grades than it was under the 'O' level system. One school has reported the results shown in Table 7.4 over the 20 years 1971–91, with no substantial change in the quality of its entry. A similar pattern has been evident in most of the returns from HMC schools.

Table 7.4: A school's results 'O'/GCSE 1971–91

	Subject Entries	*% A Grade*	*% A–C Grade*
1971–75	865	—	75
1976–80	969	—	78
1981–85	878	20	80
1986	857	23	78
1987	898	27	81
1988	841	28	84
	GCSE Introduced		
1989	884	40	90
1990	870	31	85
1991	949	36	88

GCSE = higher standards?

Various explanations can be offered for the improvement in the results of this and other HMC schools. Candidates produced improved performances because with the introduction of new courses and examinations they and their teachers worked a good deal harder than before. There is no doubt that whatever problems arose from the disappearance of 'O' levels with which teachers had been thoroughly familiar and even 'comfortable', a new energy and drive was evident as teachers and pupils strove to show that they could crack the new system.

Apart from the many in-service training courses, meetings of teachers in subject groups and meetings with chief examiners, each department studied the new courses with a freshness and enthusiasm that may have been missing in the final years of 'O' level. The pupils found the new approach in some subjects was more to their liking. Those who in earlier years would have left their work to a period of desperate final revision were now picking up some marks on coursework spread through the two years of the course. Those whose writing skills were limited picked up marks in orals and practicals. GCSE was testing different skills which enabled more pupils to show their talents. Overall the national pass rate (A–C) has risen from 42.5 per cent in 1988 to 45.0 per cent in 1991. A much higher proportion of young people leaving school at 16 with worthwhile qualifications but what of those going to Advanced or Further Education?

Some problems remain

Independent schools recognise improved standards among young people in the GCSE years at least in some skills. However, this improvement is not universal. The CBI, on behalf of employers, still campaigns for an improvement in core skills (CBI, 1990), drawing attention to communication, problem solving, information technology, numeracy, personal skills and a modern language competence as areas which need special attention. One of the subjects showing least improvement in performance has been mathematics. The national GCSE pass rate in 1989 (A–C) in mathematics (38 per cent) was lower than that of all major subjects. Only technology at 39 per cent had a similar pass rate. The problems with modern languages are different. A relatively small proportion of the school population continue with their study through to GCSE. In 1991 642,911 took English but only 292,497 took French. Concern has been expressed at the large number of these candidates in French obtaining high grades. In the past a pass in 'O' level French was a fair indicator of a pupil's ability to cope with Advanced level. Nowadays there are pupils obtaining A grades at GCSE who find themselves struggling when they face the more rigorous demands of 'A' level. This phenomenon, although less pronounced, has been recognised across a spectrum of subjects.

There may be strong arguments for emphasising the oral side of modern languages but if it is achieved at the expense of a good base of grammar and vocabulary then this is not a good preparation for 'A' level. Similar comments have been made about GCSE science and mathematics courses. One response to this problem has been to argue for the reform of the 'A' level. With more and more young people starting on 'A' level courses for which they are not sufficiently prepared to cope, the cry has been to make 'A' level more suitable or 'end-on' in the jargon. Does that mean 'easier' or at a lower standard? If it simply means adjusting 'A' level syllabuses to the new skills which GCSE pupils have acquired then there is support for this in the independent sector. If it means reducing the rigours of study then there will be even greater outcry for courses other than 'A' level which meet the needs of this intermediate group of students, who want neither the demands of 'A' level nor the commitment to vocational courses.

The more able
While recent developments at GCSE and at 'A' level may have benefited the group that was previously marginal in terms of required academic standards, there is a growing recognition that the group which has been disenfranchised is that which contains the very able; the group from which our top scholars, researchers and Nobel Prize winners will eventually emerge. It could be said that they will survive whatever schools throw at them but few will deny there should be courses available which challenge the most able. The Education Secretary has been influenced by these arguments in accepting the restructuring of the GCSE grading system so that the top grade level (10) will become a super 'A' level. It appears that in several National Curriculum subjects the demands at Key Stage 4 Level 10 will be substantially beyond anything which has been required in GCSE syllabuses. This attempt to push up standards will be welcomed by many in selective schools or with very able pupils.

Vertical flexibility
Schools that have made further attempts have been made to provide a challenge for able young people by allowing them to take 'AS' level examinations a year or two early but these courses were not designed for this purpose. The protagonists of 'vertical flexibility' – allowing students to take examinations when they are ready rather than at any particular chronological moment – are pleased by recent changes in regulations which allow students to take the National Curriculum Key Stage 4 tests (GCSE) in an earlier year. No doubt they would also approve of the American system which allows senior High School students to complete some of their college first degree courses while in their final year at school. Such schemes enable young people to be faced with challenges which make real demands on their ability. A similar flexibility is at the heart of the academic programme available at Winchester College. By such means higher standards are encouraged.

It is not only the most able who benefit from such flexibility. If young people of lower ability are persuaded to continue in full time study because they are not faced by the need to achieve what they consider to be impossible goals in too short a time, then their eventual achievements are likely to be higher. Too many pupils with modest GCSE results consider the jump to a full 'A' level course is too much for them. If the steps were more modest and pupils could take more time over them or even return after employment to part-time study then they would achieve qualifications currently considered to be beyond them.

The National Curriculum

This concern to raise general standards is at the heart of the developments embodied in the National Curriculum. The Great Education Debate inaugurated by James Callaghan and carried on by Shirley Williams, Sir Keith Joseph and others brought about a growing realisation that, in at least some substantial sections of society, educational standards had been falling. The *Education Reform Act* 1988 provided for the establishment of a National Curriculum consisting of foundation subjects to be taught to all pupils of compulsory school age in maintained schools. The intention is to bring the quality of provision in all schools up to that of the best. The days of inadequate curricula were over. In all foundation subjects appropriate Attainment Targets, Programmes of Study and assessment arrangements have been, or will soon be, identified. The Attainment Targets specify 'the knowledge, skills and understanding which pupils of different abilities and maturities are expected to have by the end of each Key Stage.' The programmes of study deal with 'the matters, skills and processes which are required to be taught . . .' (HM Government, 1988).

Assessment

When all the preparation is complete teachers in all maintained schools will have a clear idea of what they are expected to teach and how their pupils should be assessed. The results of this assessment will be available to all concerned – pupils, teachers, Heads, governors, parents, even future employees – and this information will give a clearer picture of changing standards than ever before. Comparisons will be made between the results achieved in different schools. Those who are interested in measuring the 'value added' during a child's school career will have better sources of information than ever before. As with the introduction of GCSE teachers will be stimulated into re-examining their approach and striving for even more effective methods. They will have a body of support in the curricular, assessment and training services which will be more thorough than anything available in the past. All of this should lead to rising standards at least in the areas covered by the National Curriculum.

Problems

It would, however, be wrong to suggest that these developments have been greeted with unequivocal enthusiasm or that progress towards higher standards is inevitable. The original proposals for 10 subjects – English, maths, science, technology, history, geography, modern language, art, music and PE – taught to all pupils through to 16 as full courses were considered certain to give rise to serious overcrowding of the curriculum at Key Stage 4. After much debate this was conceded and options were introduced to make this Stage curriculum more flexible. There are still those who consider the move away from 'entitlement' to 'flexible' choice retrograde but it has had several advantages including retaining a possible place for a second language or classics or economics in the curriculum.

Independent schools and the National Curriculum

The part played by the independent sector in campaigning for this and other changes was not without controversy for the 1989 act did not require independent schools to comply with its requirements. However, it is inconceivable that sooner or later all schools will not follow at least the essentials even if independence permits some variation from the basic model. This model is, in fact, very close to the curriculum which most HMC schools have been following for some time. There has been considerable determination to see that the good features of existing curricula are not abandoned. This conviction stimulated the build-up of a powerful pressure group in favour of retaining three separate sciences at Key Stage 4 (GCSE).

Separate sciences

Many schools with a record of success in preparing pupils for science 'A' levels were concerned that dual certificated science – i.e. three sciences taught in the time allowed for two subjects, with significant elements of integration between the sciences, and taught if necessary by a single science teacher – would be less good as a base for further study. They feared a further deterioration in the quality of science at Advanced level. While this view is by no means unanimously held in independent schools it was argued powerfully enough to persuade the Secretary of State to retain, as an option, the three separate science subjects at GCSE. The standards associated with Advanced level science and the preparation of young people for pure or applied science degrees are considered vital for the country's future prosperity. Some scientists consider students will be more attracted to 'A' level courses which build on combined or integrated sciences. However, the significant decline in the proportion of students willing to go down this route is a problem which must be addressed. Table 7.5 shows the results of a survey carried out in 27 city day schools in the HMC. Less than a third of sixth formers are currently studying 'A' level Sciences. The situation in 1981 and the results of a similar survey in girls schools (GPDST) are shown for comparison.

Table 7.5: Take-up of 'A' Level Sciences and Mathematics

HMC Day Schools	Total Numbers of VI Formers	Average Size of VI Form	Number and (Percentage) taking			
			Maths	Physics	Chemistry	Biology
1991 (27 schools)	5883	218	2636 (45)	1769 (30)	1766 (30)	1217 (21)
1981 (19 schools)	3966	209	1942 (49)	1600 (40)	1338 (34)	648 (16)
GPDST Schools						
1991 (24 schools)	2865	115	1018 (35)	488 (17)	822 (28)	911 (31)
1981 (24 schools)	2852	124	1100 (30)	689 (24)	862 (30)	863 (30)

Teacher supply and quality

The success of the National Curriculum in raising standards will depend heavily on the resources which the Government makes available and the most important resource is the quality of the teaching force. The 1992 report of HM Senior Chief Inspector Schools (HMI, 1992) supports this thesis in a number of ways. The report refers to 'shortages of particular types of teachers and a high turnover in parts of London and other inner-city areas'. The teacher shortages in modern languages, English, science, mathematics and technology, while lower than in previous years, were still worrying, especially because it left more specialists teaching these subjects. Moreover, 'supply teachers were (employed) often untrained for the National Curriculum and rarely used on the basis of their particular subject expertise'. HMI who observed 18,000 lessons saw some evidence of rising standards particularly at GCSE although over a quarter of the lessons were unsatisfactory and many teachers 'failed to challenge pupils sufficiently': their expectation of standards was far too low, particularly with the less able. There were significant differences in quality between schools not necessarily according to location but according to the nature of the intake: 'Meeting the requirements of the National Curriculum presented few problems in KS3 except in relation to assessment and to technology . . .'.

Initiative in curriculum development

Schools in the independent sector, in their search for higher standards of education, are not simply following along in the van of the National Curriculum. Teachers from this sector have played a full part in a wide range of curriculum developments. Nuffield Science, MEI Modular Mathematics, the International Baccalaureate, English with 100 per cent course work assessment, business studies, are but a few developments during my career which have depended heavily on teachers in independent schools. If they have been slow to fall in line with some recent government initiatives it is not because they lack initiative but because they doubt the wisdom. Key Stage 3 assessment is a case in point. There is a general worry that assessment will take up a disproportionate amount of the limited time available. There is, moreover, a strong feeling among those responsible for academic policy in the independent sector that, in planning revolution in the education system in England and Wales, much more careful study should be undertaken of the successful systems operating in other countries.

International comparisons

John Chubb of Brookings Institute and Terry Moe of Stanford University have published a study of the impact of the 1988 *Education Reform Act* in schools throughout Britain. Charles Hymas reports that this 'investigation coincides with an international survey which has found that English and American school children are trailing those in other industrial nations in mathematics and science' (Hymas, 1992). This survey of 175,000 children in 20 countries revealed significant gaps in the mathematical and scientific knowledge of our nine and 13 year olds: 'Pupils from Korea, Hungary, Taiwan, Switzerland, China, France, Israel, Italy and Canada score higher marks than English and American children.' Chubb and Moe argue that the position would be improved if schools could be freed from bureaucratic controls and allowed to run their own affairs: 'If enough schools were to follow the path (opting-out), the existing system would collapse and a very different one would take its place, a system whose hallmark is the most crucial foundation of effective education: school autonomy'. Improved classroom standards were seen by Chubb and Moe to follow from the greater independence of opted-out schools, benefits which have long been enjoyed by independent schools. It is possible that they will benefit further from the publication of exam results and school league tables, deplored by many, which will show that their results continue to get better partly because grades are being inflated and partly because standards are rising.

Conclusion

There is no cause for complacency: high standards must be safeguarded against ill-judged educational reforms. The *Education Reform Act* sets a real challenge to independent schools even if at present most of the clauses do not legally apply. ERA is bringing about a much demanded revolution not only in curriculum and assessment but in the actual nature of the educational system. The very existence of independent schools will depend upon their ability to respond to the changing circumstances with even higher standards in their overall educational performance.

References

Alexander, Robin, Jim Rose and Chris Woodhead (1992) *Curriculum Organisation and Classroom Practice in Primary Schools* (London: DES).
Anderson, Eric (1990) *HMC Working Party Report on Intermediate Level 16–19*.
Barker, R. (1990) 'The Need for Breadth' IPSET.
Barker, Richard (1991) 'Internationalism at Sevenoaks'.
CBI (1990) *Towards a Skills Revolution* (London: CBI).
Clarke, Kenneth (1991) *Education and Training for the 21st Century* (London: DES) p. 20.
Clarke, Kenneth (1992) Address to the Oxford Conference on Education.
HM Government (1988) *Education Reform Act* ch. 40, part 1, section 2 (2a).
HMC Working Party Report on Intermediate Level 16–19 (1990).
HMI (1992) *Education in England 1990–91: Annual Report of HM Chief Inspector of Schools* (London: DES).
Howie Committee (1992) *The Report on Upper Secondary Education in Scotland* (London: HMSO).

Hymas, Charles (1992) *Sunday Times* February 9, 1992.
JMB (1983) *Problems of the GCE Advanced Level Grading Scheme.*
O'Leary, John (1992) 'Boom in First Class Degrees Renews Fears for Standards' in *The Times* February 17.
Parker, Geoffrey (1991) Report of the Annual Meeting – Headmasters' Conference pp 10–11.
Pilkington, Peter (1991) *End of Egalitarian Delusion: Different Education for Different Talent.* (London: Centre for Policy Studies) No. 124.
SCUE, GSA, HMC, SHA and APVIC (1992) 'Joint Memorandum to the Secretary of State'.
SEAC (1991) *A and AS Examinations: Results by Board 1990.*
SEAC (1992) 'A and AS Examinations 1990 – General Scrutiny Report'.

8 To lever up educational standards?

John Horn

The *Education Reform Act* of 1988 according to the Secretary of State at the time, Kenneth Baker, had the 'fundamental unifying purpose to lever up educational standards'. Sceptics were quick to question whether such a comprehensive assortment ('ragbag' might be a more appropriate term) of separate measures, could ever be regarded as having a unified purpose, or if it had, that the Secretary of State had correctly described it so. Consider the range, the introduction of the National Curriculum with its whole gamut of content and assessment; the proposals for increased financial delegation to schools, and, in its more extreme form, the creation of Grant Maintained Schools and City Technology Colleges; the attempt to rationalise charging policies; the abolition of the Inner London Education Authority, to say nothing of the proposals for Higher and Further Education, which are not the concern of this chapter. Was there not here the impression of a confused attempt to tackle a number of political and educational issues perceived by some in the Government as problems (a perception not necessarily justified by the facts), on what might be described as the shotgun principle – spray around a large number of bullets in the hope that at least one or two will hit the target? The fact that the effects of some clauses of the Bill were likely to work against the effects of others thus securing the worst of both worlds was ignored. A simple example – unless the National Curriculum was intended (though some imagined it was) to confine education to chalk and talk in the classroom box, the charging regulations were hardly likely to improve educational opportunities.

From such a flawed base it is hardly surprising that considerable reassessment has taken place in the intervening three and a half years. As is acknowledged elsewhere, to disentangle developments that have occurred as a direct consequence of the *Education*

Reform Act, from changes brought about by shifts in government policy making, not dissociated, as one would expect, from the characteristics of later Secretaries of State, is difficult. Certainly modifications of the original Act were inevitable. The Government might not have been persuaded during the passage of Bill into Act in 1987/8 that they were introducing an unworkable curriculum, but few doubted that they were. One could almost see an inverse correlation between the vehemence and intransigence of government supporters of the Act and the certainty of the need for future change. Whether the changes that have necessarily occurred suit all tastes or indeed whether they in turn are any more likely than the original Act to meet the stated purpose of raising educational standards, it is too early to say.

Disentanglement therefore is one problem for any current assessment of the success of *ERA*. Timescale is another. It cannot yet be realistic to assess with certainty success or otherwise – trends there may be but it would hardly be fair to come to any definitive conclusion. It is not for me to comment on primary school performance but to the outside observer it could appear that recently expressed concerns about reading and mathematical standards at Key Stage 1 have their roots in two other requirements of the *Education Reform Act*. First the broader curriculum compulsory at all ages presumably allows less time for concentration on basic skills, and second the consequences of the amount of time devoted to assessment as opposed to teaching. Moreover judgement on whether that broader curriculum will produce better scientists at age 16 and beyond will have to wait until the summer of 1999. That in turn will depend upon intervening developments in assessment procedures at 16+ – should current concentration on final tests and the demotivating reduction of coursework be maintained, even then it might not be possible to make a realistic assessment of the scientific abilities of the 16+ age group. That particular problem already looms nearer for current secondary school pupils whose performance in English, maths and science based on teaching programmes in Key Stages 3 and 4 will be assessed in 1994. Again one suspects that trends, not certainties will be discerned for two reasons. A true assessment will only be possible when the whole range of National Curriculum subjects are in place – changes in time allocation may yet prove necessary, and as mentioned already other aspects of *ERA* are already having contradictory effects which make assessment of the precise success of changes in raising standards difficult to evaluate. One thinks of staffing difficulties caused by the introduction of local management of schools, of which more later.

However let us accept that the intention of *ERA* was to raise standards and consider in practice what chance it had of achieving its stated aim. Have standards been raised and, if so, has it been because of or in spite of *ERA*? For me the latter must be true, certainly for the Act in its original form. Not surprisingly it was the National Curriculum that took pride of place in the Act and the curriculum to be imposed to raise standards was identified in Clause 2:

> The curriculum must be balanced and broad and must promote the spiritual, moral, cultural, mental, physical development of pupils at the school and of society, and prepare pupils for the opportunities, responsibilities and experiences of adult life.

Schools with this curriculum would improve the educational standards of their pupils. Strangely Independent schools and City Technology Colleges were not to be included. Was this to be interpreted as uncertainty on whether the precise detailed proposals would actually achieve the stated aim, or must paying customers in Independent schools be allowed to choose an inferior, albeit costly, curriculum? Certainly there quickly appeared a manifest advantage for such schools – quite simply more time to teach, as they would be spared the hours that maintained schools would have to devote to assessment. Nonetheless such a commitment to establish an entitlement curriculum, offering progression, continuity and coherence for all pupils, and raising expectations for pupil achievement, had little difficulty in achieving universal support.

Hindsight has now confirmed what many commentators said at the time. On curriculum the Act should have stopped there. The Government should immediately have established appropriate bodies, call them NCC and SEAC if you like, though commonsense would suggest that one unified body would obviously have had a better change of success, to consult widely *before* producing more detailed recommendations for an entitlement curriculum suitable for all pupils, whatever their abilities and aptitudes, calculated to deliver the overall aims of the National Curriculum. From this single error, the failure to ensure that there was sufficient curricular thought before overprescription by legislation, have stemmed most of the difficulties for schools in these intervening years. We have lived hand to mouth. The wiser secondary schools did not immediately set out to implement Key Stage 4 on the grounds that legislation had been passed. The original concept was not only incapable of implementation but also totally inadequate to meet the National Curriculum's own stated purposes. Developments since 1988 have given more potential for choice for students at 14+. We have acknowledged that many topics essential for preparing all pupils for adult life are best developed through non-examined General Education programmes comprising Personal and Social Education, Careers Education, Education for Economic Awareness, and Health Education. We have sought and gained more flexibility – some would say too much, certainly those who believe that the arts are too important to merit their present possible exclusion from the curriculum for some pupils Post 14. It was this year's President of SHA, Mike Pugh, who, when welcoming new found freedom, feared that licence had been given for curricular weeds to grow.

Whether the content of the proposed National Curriculum, either in its original or adapted form, could by itself raise standards, must be a matter of individual judgement. Schools, it seems to me, must continue to plan their own curriculum interpreting the National Curriculum to take into account the individual needs of their own students. But more critical than content, it would appear, for the Government, in its determination to raise standards, was assessment. There was already sufficient evidence, even before Key Stage 3 testing for mathematics and science reached secondary schools in the summer of 1992, that immediate concerns both in principle and practice regarding the whole paraphernalia of tests at seven, 11, 14 and 16 were fully justified. In practice there would be serious interference with the time available for teaching, with too much concentration, because of the stated intent to use published results as the prime aid for parental choice, on rehearsals and practice, certainly curtailing the flair and initiative of teachers. The administration and marking of the tests are giving an arduous additional workload for teachers until improved pupil/teacher ratios allow significantly more non-contact time.

Concerns on principle were more deeply rooted. Is competition pupil versus pupil, teacher versus teacher, school versus school the best way to raise standards? Has not the development of Records of Achievement emphasising success not failure shown a better way? Did we want to return to an 11+ scenario, brought forward to seven+ where pupils at an early stage meet a sense of failure? Did we want to return to a 'positions in the class' mentality, a sure way consistently to identify and emphasise failure, thus depressing motivation and achievement and leading to lower standards rather than stressing individual positive achievement in relation to potential?

Despite the reservations above, let us nonetheless assume that National Curriculum arrangements for both content and assessment had some prospects of raising standards. For whom did the Government have that intention? One presumes for all pupils and indeed even for Independent schools, when deciding whether efficient and suitable instruction was being given, consideration was to be given on how far the curriculum offered matched the National Curriculum. It has long been my contention that the only worthwhile purpose of Government is to provide 'the best for all'. For pupils this means an educational system with equality of concern and access for all, the best possible opportunities for all pupils to develop whatever talents and abilities they have, taught by the best possible staff, with the best possible resources and facilities. Could the *Education Reform Act* 1988 lead to the creation of such a system. Not so, I believe, in the context of other parts of the Act.

The issue is simply whether measures to raise the standards for some positively diminish the chance of better standards for others. In *ERA* I believe the proposals both for City Technology Colleges and Grant Maintained schools were likely to have that effect and in fact have done so. Consider first City Technology Colleges – the Government's intention was that pump priming by themselves would generate greater income from Business and Industry and that such resources could only be guaranteed by offering Business and Industry a curriculum with a particular slant they could support. It is common knowledge that the scenario has been exactly the reverse of what was intended. Finance has been provided approximately in the ratio four to one by government rather than Business and Industry providing 80 per cent as had been planned. Too little is yet known on whether CTCs internally have actually improved standards though there was a certain irony in the fact that the first published evidence from HMI was critical of some of the technology curriculum being offered. There does remain the inconsistency in maintaining that the National Curriculum is the appropriate curriculum for most though not for CTCs. But in resource terms the CTC programme has adversely affected the standards of others, and has distorted the balance of neighbouring schools. Nor is it that other proposals were not available. One could easily concede that a more technological bent in the curriculum was best for all, but the proposals to introduce it were too partial.

An alternative strategy to raise the standards for all students in a community was put forward by a group of SHA Heads in the Doncaster and Rotherham areas led by Tony Storey of Hayfield School, Doncaster. The concept was to create a Staff College as an alternative to a CTC in the belief that it would unite industry, local government and the teaching profession, and would not create demotivating and divisive tensions in a local area. It would propagate the ethos and approach to teaching technology. It would provide a lively, forward thinking educational environment as a basis for industrial and commercial development. It would assist in raising standards for all, in recruiting for all students a well motivated, skilled teaching force, by offering high quality inservice training and access for students and staff from all schools in the area.

In the approach to raising standards for all I have no doubt that this approach would have been markedly superior to the CTC programme and even more importantly would have undoubtedly secured much wider support from Business and Industry who would have supported such an initiative with more vigour than the faltering CTC programme. Sadly the Government could not even be persuaded to support one major company in such an initiative when at the very least it would have provided evidence as to whether a strategy alternative to City Technology Colleges would be a better way of raising technology standards for all.

Worse than the CTC programme as an antidote to any improvement in standards for all was the Government's proposal for schools to achieve Grant Maintained status – proposals calculated, intentionally or otherwise, to create division and chaos within local education authorities. It might have been better if two promises often made during the consultation period had been kept, first that a level playing field would be kept in that Grant Maintained schools would not receive any preferential funding over schools that remained in local authorities, and second that decisions on schemes for reorganisation (undertaken often at the behest of the Audit Commission in pursuit of cost-effective provision of resources to ensure a raise of standards for all) would be taken first. Both have been consistently broken. Schools that have opted out have not only usually received a disproportionate amount of local authority money, thus depriving other schools of their legitimate share. Perhaps even more significantly, many have received disproportionately large amounts of the Government's capital programme. As more schools opt out the gap is narrowing but in the first year when local education authority schools received an average of £18,000, the average for Grant Maintained schools was £227,000, a figure which in the second year was reduced to £40,000, – still a significant difference. The Government may have believed that Grant Maintained status would lead to higher standards for some but apparently was insufficiently certain that others would agree unless sweeteners were provided. My concern remains the impact on other schools, and the standards of their students.

Government thinking clearly was based on the premise that to involve parents more was a critical factor for the pursuit of higher standards and that Grant Maintained status was the surest way to do so. It is almost trite to stress that full parental involvement and co-operation with a school are a vital ingredient for good education. Pupils perform best where the parent, pupil, school triangle functions best. But equally it is clear that parents, rightly and properly, are most interested in the curriculum and progress of their own children. It would be a rare event where parents would put the interests of their own children, as they see them, second to a wider educational viewpoint for all children. Was it ever realistic to expect parents when making choices for their own school to consider the effect of that choice on other schools for other parents' children?

Such a fact has become even more relevant, now a third Government assurance, even promise, has been broken by the Secretary of State. There were to be no proposals to change the character of Grant Maintained schools for at least five years. Already it has happened. Suppose a comprehensive school tries to turn itself into a grammar school, thereby, by its decision, affecting the intake of neighbouring local authority schools and making them more akin to a secondary modern school. Convinced as I am that you can only raise standards for all within a comprehensive framework, the Government has facilitated the destruction of that system by the decision of one group of parents. Additionally the different admission arrangements, which incidentally will mean less parental choice and more school control over admissions, and the different disciplinary and exclusion procedures will inevitably ensure that over the years the majority of less motivated pupils, with the less supportive parents, will be concentrated in fewer and fewer schools – this can hardly be seen as a measure to raise the standards for all.

There will be other effects on schools remaining with the local education authority. Support for the Grant Maintained schools will obviously come from the more articulate parents, those most likely and able to generate additional financial support for their children's schools, those most able to keep LEA, governors, the Head and staff of any school on their toes. Such parents will be a serious loss to other schools and parental support will be concentrated on fewer schools to the detriment of others. The LEA will have diminished resources. The fewer the schools for which it is responsible the less resources it will have to generate all the necessary support services for all its schools. There will be no economies of scale. Thus, within an authority, there will develop a stark contrast between a few well funded, well staffed schools with good teacher morale and the remainder with falling rolls, poor resources and low morale. It cannot be right that a particular group of parents should so adversely affect the total future of LEA planning for an area in the narrow interests as they see them of their own children.

It might be thought by now that I see nothing in *ERA* to raise standards. Not true – not only have I suggested that a National Curriculum introduced in a less peremptory manner and on a basis of national consultation, would have raised standards, but the proposals for Local Management of Schools in theory offered great opportunities to raise standards in individual schools. Sadly successful implementation has been impeded by other factors, one internal, others external. There can be no doubt that the flexibility and responsibility given to schools in managing their own finances has released considerable potential for raising standards in a cost effective manner. It is a matter of regret that too many LEAs have not yet accepted the challenge of developing a more positive supportive relationship with their schools on the voluntary basis that local management requires, but rather have been singularly reluctant to accept reality, still have wished to interfere unnecessarily on points of detail. Thus some schools, for no other reason than a sense of frustration, have turned to a Grant Maintained status, a move which even so resolute an opponent of Grant Maintained as myself can understand. Without doubt in this new climate LEAs should set out to have such good relationships with their schools that none would wish to leave their fold. Too often that has not yet proved the case.

On one issue I have sympathy with local authorities – that of resources. I referred earlier to one inherent weakness within Local Management of Schools, that is the requirement of schools to be funded on average salaries, taking too little account of the actual salary bill. This has caused significant staffing difficulties for schools either in terms of total staffing or the correlation between the teaching expertise and experience of staff and the curriculum to be offered. This I do regard as one of the major contradictions in government policy. They passed *ERA* to raise standards by the National Curriculum but implicit in other aspects of the bill they made it more difficult for schools to appoint and employ the relevant staff. Either staff could not be recruited or the curriculum meant that those employed had to be deployed in teaching a second, third or even fourth subject.

Even worse than that, though not the responsibility of the Education Act, is the way that funds are distributed to local authorities through other government policies. Bluntly the iniquitous system of standard spending assessments funding education, assessments based on inadequate and out of date information, taking little note of what actually needs to be spent, seriously damages the prospect of raising standards in schools. Inequality in and shortage of resources pose great problems across the country. There is at the moment no attempt to establish objective criteria for the resources necessary to deliver the National Curriculum for pupils of any age wherever they live. There will be elements in any such context which vary across the country – for example students in London will always cost more per capita in that their teachers are paid their London allowance. There may be other local factors which could be decided at the local level. But resources from government should recognise much more the similarity of resources required.

Capping adds to the difficulties. I have never yet understood what appears to be such a basic contradiction in Government policy. The Poll Tax was introduced so that local people would know precisely who was responsible for the level (high or low) of local taxation and could then take the appropriate action at the next election. Councils with unnecessarily high poll taxes would be thrown out. But Government then decided it could not trust that that would happen. They would determine centrally the level of local taxation not even allowing councils the opportunity to set budgets that would cause their own demise. Consequently capping has meant severe cuts in education, cuts that have had a serious effect on the availability of resources for schools, so that schools, given by *ERA* the opportunity to manage their resources better, thus raising standards, have then been denied sufficient resources to manage. One might believe the Government has acted thus to give a twin pronged impetus to the Grant Maintained movement in that schools denied sufficient resources from their local authorities (themselves scared of capping) have sought the richer pastures of Grant Maintained status. Recent events in Gloucester and Kent would support this argument. It is relevant that a similar incoherence between policy and resources has recently surfaced with regard to Social Services and the Community Care programme. What is clear is that the Government has never had a coherent policy for raising standards for all.

Amidst such a maelstrom of change in the past few years, one would be forgiven for assuming that standards had not risen. I comment not on the evidence provided by early SATS for primary school students, because I regard that as yet inconclusive. Moreover if standards have not risen the fault may lie in the *Education Act* itself. But at GCSE and 'A' level the evidence is clear – standards have slowly but surely risen at both levels. At

GCSE the reformed examination has allowed students of all abilities more opportunities to show determination and effort, the thorough research required by course and project work, and most importantly to show the skill, knowledge and ability they have, not tested by the single attribute of memory. Prophets of gloom who forecast that such changes to 'O' level would spell disaster for 'A' level results, have been thoroughly confounded. Improved methodology and study skills at GCSE were followed by the same at 'A' level with a consequential impact on student numbers for higher education. This is cause for rejoicing, one would imagine, for a Government determined to see standards rise, but not a bit of it. Rather the rise in standards has been questioned, coursework denigrated and reduced. Sadly such views have been supported by some in the traditional bastions of so called academic excellence; bastions not noted for their receptiveness to change and perhaps over-concerned that their traditional primacy in academic matters has been challenged by the widespread rise in standards.

That standards have risen is not least the responsibility of the teaching profession, who, despite late and inadequate notice of change, despite an alarming lack of resources, despite too little in-service training, have nonetheless made GCSE work. No tribute can be too high for those thousands of teachers across the country who have triumphed over difficult circumstances, at considerable expense to their time, energy and, in many cases, home life. Such has been their commitment to the individual students they have taught, commitment not yet itself matched by the Government's financial commitment to its oft-stated purpose of recruiting, motivating and retaining a high quality teaching force.

And therein perhaps lies the final answer as to whether *ERA* will have any chance of achieving Mr Baker's original purpose. Good teachers will make the curriculum work, against the odds. Courageous curriculum planning will be needed, and perhaps the confidence to ignore at times the imminence of SATS, prepared to teach beyond such limiting factors. Teachers and schools will need confidence in their abilities, their own standards, their own curricula, the confidence to maintain a sensible balance between the needs of teaching, and the requirements of assessment, the confidence not to be constantly looking over their shoulders, anxious that at some intermediate level, neighbouring schools might appear (I use the word 'appear' advisedly) more successful in the eyes of parents. It might be pertinent to comment that the 1944 *Education Act* was never implemented fully – perhaps the 1988 version never should be either.

And there we have it. *ERA* 1988 was too full of internal contradictions to meet its purpose. The curriculum planning was flawed, the creation of CTCs and GMS threatened the standards of many whatever it may have done for the few, and Government systems of finance cannot deliver to schools what is required. Inevitably one is led to the conclusion that the Bill was drafted and the Act passed by those who do not fully understand the maintained system of education, probably because they have had no personal acquaintance with it. Persistently the Government has shown a lack of empathy with the real situation in schools and without such empathy there must be actual experience. The Government stands charged with having acted to raise standards by imperfect legislation for 'other people's children'. This cannot be the purpose of Government which should strive to provide the best for all.

9 Choice or chaos?
Peter Smith

The history of consumer choice in education is relatively short. We need to place the *Education Reform Act* firmly within the context of the history of post-war compulsory schooling. We need to ask to what degree the legislation is really revolutionary. I believe we should pause to ask to what extent it is rather an evolutionary, almost inevitable development. Most important of all, we need to ask if it will work.

It is only recently that most parents have been able to exercise real choice over the schools their offspring attended. The 1944 *Education Act* admittedly gave parents the opportunity to send their children, without payment, to denominational voluntary schools. But in practice the freedom was limited, partly, though not solely, by the limited availability of places.

The 1944 act is, in any case, not now remembered mainly as a piece of consumerist legislation. It is more associated with the provision of free grammar school education. But though the grammar schools did not charge for admission, competition for places was almost always so intense that demand well outstripped supply. The fact that they were called 'selective schools' was in itself significant. The educational suppliers chose their customers, not the other way round.

The direct grant schools were able to be more selective still. Although there were concentrations of these schools in some areas, over the whole country they were very unevenly spread. Drawing pupils from a wide, but by no means panoramic, social and economic spectrum, their fees – in contrast to the fully independent sector – were low. To parents whose LEAs funded places at them, they often cost nothing at all. Even so, direct grant schools maintained their high academic reputation by picking and choosing their pupils from amongst the ablest. Even more than the grammar schools, they could hand select their clientele, and they did.

In the independent sector itself, boys' schools, whether

charitable in origin or not, increasingly came to cater for the able sons of the better off. There was, none the less, a marked shift in their intake: as the traditionally middle class professions waned in prosperity and influence, and, as a prosperous new business class emerged, so the independent school market changed. They now rely little on old money and the social structure which provided it, and much more on an aspiring, commercially minded *nouveau riche*, prepared to buy high quality education if the price is right, but wanting to see a visible return for their money.

The girls' independent schools, usually far less well endowed, were, at one end of the scale, vaguely academic establishments, which concentrated on turning out onto the marriage market the well brought up rather than the well educated. At the other end, they were rigorous, scholarly institutions which aimed to send young women out into employment, usually into the respectable, caring professions.

Those traditions linger on, but only just. It is now accepted that a girl's education is not just a social accomplishment within marriage or an insurance against unemployment in spinsterhood. It is increasingly seen as the essential qualification for an income generating career, during which marriage and child rearing (if they occur at all) will be one feature of a woman's career rather than its major objective.

Despite these changes, however, independent schools, continuing to enjoy high academic and social esteem, have largely continued to choose their intake on the basis of parental capacity to pay or pupil ability, or a combination of the two. Ever since the 1944 *Butler Act*, policy makers have been troubled by one of its central effects: that schools, whether maintained or independent, chose their pupils, not pupils their schools.

Successive post-war Labour administrations took one view of the issue. Their analysis was part ethical and part economic. They considered that the academic achievements of selective schools, whether grammar, direct grant or independent, were outweighed by two major disadvantages. The status which attached to them was, they argued, divisive. Their continued existence was a major obstacle to the emergence of an egalitarian, class free society, in which success would be the result of individual merit and effort rather than parental advantage.

They judged that the most important legacy of the 1944 act was not the educational advantages extended to grammar school children. It was rather the opportunities denied to those unable to attend them – and not merely while they were at school, but later because of their limited access to further and higher education. Those who went to the poorly esteemed (and often undervalued) secondary modern schools were alienated by their sense of failure. The result was the wholesale waste of their talent at school and in later life, both in terms of their personal fulfillment and in terms of their potential contribution to the economy.

Their judgement was that the country's education system was both unfair and inefficient. And in power, successive Labour administrations introduced a series of changes, changes quite as fundamental, and every bit as controversial, as the *Education Reform Act*.

As the grammar school system was almost completely dismantled and replaced by all ability comprehensives, selection at 11+ was abandoned. The period of statutory education was lengthened by raising the school leaving age to 16. The direct grant category of school was abolished. The few local authorities which financed places at independent schools were effectively prevented from doing so, and the independent sector itself placed on the Labour Party's longer term agenda for abolition.

That attitude to choice in education was, if nothing else, consistent. The post-1944 system was certainly not producing (as had been intended) a system in which different kinds of school enjoyed parity of esteem. Nor were the different categories of school equivalently resourced. The Labour answer was to remove the capacity of those which selected their pupils, either on academic ability or parental income, to do so. All schools, publicly funded according to their needs, would then provide equality of opportunity for the pupils who attended them. On such an analysis, parental choice of schools was an irrelevance. There would be nothing to choose between a system in which unfair competitive advantages between schools and parents had been removed or neutralised.

The long term impact of implementing those policies has been interesting. It has become generally accepted that a non-selective system of maintained schools at primary, secondary and, more recently, tertiary level is inherently fairer, and potentially more efficient, than a system which restricts access. Where local politicians have proposed reintroducing grammar school education in recent years, for instance, they have stimulated considerable controversy, but commanded little sustained support amongst voters. No political party at national level appears to advocate their wholesale return.

But for all that, the large scale introduction of comprehensive education did little to satisfy the general public that maintained education had been improved. If anything, it came to stimulate intense and widespread anxiety about educational standards. The disappearance of the 11+, however arbitrary that selection process may have been, deprived parents of any mid-course bearing on their children's educational progress.

Those who had experienced a grammar school education themselves, and whose children might have passed the 11+ if it had been there to sit, suspected a relaxation of academic standards. The fact that primary education methods were changing so that their children were being taught in a way they could not understand, with results they could not judge, increased the fear. Neither did the removal of the 11+ and the use of new teaching techniques satisfy the parents of children who would previously have almost certainly attended secondary modern schools. They had been encouraged to entertain academic aspirations for their children which the comprehensives did not, often because they could not, satisfy.

The fact that there was, throughout this period, a considerable rise in the number of children achieving success in public examinations and gaining access to a greatly expanded higher education sector, ironically did little to allay public concern. If anything, it aggravated it. The higher success rates were accompanied by changes in the way that children were examined too. That led to accusations that schools were deliberately lowering standards to achieve a spuriously high pass rate. Parents whose children did not achieve success, despite the examination reforms, blamed the schools. Had they not been told that a CSE Grade 1 was equivalent to a GCE pass? Why were their children failing to achieve what had been held out, even promised, as an attainable standard for all? As is so often the case, teachers found themselves in the firing line because they could not deliver the politicians' propaganda commitments.

As for the abolition of the direct grant, that had the effect, presumably unexpected, of tipping most of the recipient schools straight into the independent sector instead of injecting their academic adrenalin into the comprehensive system. For many parents that created a two-fold impression: one was that the Labour Government's assurance of concern for academic standards was bogus; the other was that it was determined to limit yet further what little apparent choice there was.

Although Conservative administrations approached the issues in a different way, it would be wrong to think that there was not a good deal of common ground between them and their political opponents. They did not, for instance, seek to reverse the tidal introduction of comprehensive education in any serious way. If anything they facilitated it. Nor did they oppose the raising of the school leaving age. It was common ground between the parties too that education should be extended at the very start with widely available, free nursery education, a cause championed by Mrs Thatcher herself. Both parties agreed that one of the ways in which school standards might be improved was if parents were to become more involved, and so Labour and Conservative governments both promoted the introduction of elected parent representatives on to school governing bodies. Both saw public examination reform as a route to providing less academic pupils with tangible evidence of their achievement when they left school.

Conservatives naturally deplored the abolition of the grammar and, later on, the direct grant schools on the grounds that able pupils were deprived of demanding academic challenge, and their parents of choice. For the same reason they opposed root and branch the Labour Party's oft repeated intention to abolish the independent sector, a threat never actually embarked upon.

And that emphasis upon choice proved to be the most important difference between the two parties. Initially the Conservative commitment to parental choice was on grounds just as ethical as Labour opposition to what they saw as privilege.

It was, Conservatives argued, a civil liberties issue that, in a free democratic society, citizens should be able to spend their money as they chose. If parents decided to spend it on education, it was wrong, and oppressively so, to prevent them.

Sensitive to the charge that only a limited number of parents could actually afford to meet the mounting costs of private education, they attempted to increase access by the Assisted Places Scheme. These government subsidised places were promoted as the academic escape route for the clever children of poor, working class, inner-city families, but few of their originally intended clientele took up the offer. For them, its effect was marginal, and there seem to be no plans now to extend the scheme.

Quite apart from anything else, the Assisted Places Scheme did not get to the heart of the most important concern – the worry that the maintained education system, notwithstanding a wholesale shift towards comprehensive schooling, appeared to be failing large numbers of young people who left school at 16 with little certificated evidence of achievement, and no appetite for further education or training. That anxiety was shared by all the main political parties. Concern about these youngsters united such unlikely parliamentary bedfellows as James Callaghan and Keith Joseph.

It is the Conservative response to that long term anxiety that finally led to the *Education Reform Act*. Previously, the Conservative government had proceeded gingerly – or so it seems, with hindsight. They appear to have thought that the fall in the child population and the accompanying increase in the number of places available in schools would, of themselves, give parents the consumer advantage. If they were to use it, they needed to be better informed.

They were given the right to appeal against local authority school placements. HMI inspection reports were, for the first time, published. Schools had to provide brochures describing their curriculum provision and public examination results. Governors were required to report to parents annually. Schools would have to take out their skeletons and display them in the shop window alongside the trophies. Anxious head teachers suddenly started to talk obsessively about accountability.

Those changes, controversial at the time, had some impact. As the child population fell, schools vulnerable to reorganisation or closure, and therefore anxious to court popularity, became far more forthcoming. There was an upsurge in admissions appeals. But for the Government, the change was too slow. Parents did not, in practice, rush to become as involved as Conservative policy makers had thought likely. Closing schools was a lengthy, bureaucratic and often unpopular business. Meanwhile, visible and measurable improvements in the knowledge, skills and understanding of 16 year old school leavers were slow in coming.

It became increasingly clear too that the country was facing an acute skills shortage in the 1990s and beyond, at the very time that international trading competition was growing ever fiercer. The long and acrimonious teachers' pay and conditions dispute reinforced, or even focused, the widespread perception that education was in a mess and needed sorting out. The drawn out dispute was not in itself the major cause of legislation, but it helped to create the political climate which made it possible.

The culminating legislation was, of course, the *Education Reform Act*. It stood the classic Labour analysis on its head. Labour governments had sought to establish an administratively coherent, LEA managed system of comprehensive schools, and had permitted, if not consciously encouraged, curriculum diversity within it.

The Conservative legislation moved neatly in the opposite direction. It promoted a wide variety of schools and virtually unrestricted choice between them, but required a standard national curriculum, and centrally established measures of assessment for each stage of a child's education.

The consumerist philosophy which underlay *ERA* is now familiar enough. The educational menu which publicly funded schools offer will need the National Curriculum's Good Housekeeping seal of approval. Forced into competition with one another, schools will have to maintain and improve their reputation with parents if they are to attract the pupils who provide most of their income. Running their own budgets, determining their own priorities in the competition for pupils, they will become more efficient. Those which do not will go to the wall.

Will it all, in the long term, work? It might just, but the obstacles are formidable and the risks are high – possibly too high. There is too much evidence that what some members of the Government saw principally as a sensible redistribution of managerial responsibility within the education service, others wanted mainly as a mechanism to reduce the power and financial autonomy of local authorities, no matter what their political colour or local circumstances.

The two objectives – one political, the other educational – are not the same. The attempt to achieve them simultaneously meant that many schools were in the tight grip of budgetary nutcrackers, which left them no more room for manœuvre than a helpless wriggle. They stood to lose able teachers they badly needed, with the risk that the quality of education would be lowered at the very moment that the educational reform programme had scheduled it to rise.

Unless there is a national strategic plan for the sustained development of an adequately funded education service, with a set of sensibly determined and manageable priorities, then we will be in deep, deep trouble. Even if market forces alone will promote the good and drive out the unsatisfactory in education – a proposition which begs a range of questions – the Government must acknowledge that the education market moves much more slowly than the business world with which they are more familiar.

While it is moving, it is essential that it receives careful, sensitive steering, for we cannot afford to take any risks that it will flounder. We need a well managed, nationwide education service capable of secure forward planning, rather than a highly fragmented, unstable, chaotic and uncontrollable mix of semi-autonomous schools, vulnerable to every inflationary blip. Otherwise we risk moving towards a Britain of educational penny bazaars, competing with each other to provide the cheap rather than the good.

Nothing short of such a nationwide strategic plan will secure the long term answer to the underlying challenge of educating our young people responsibly. For we are in the last decade of the 1900s. The young men and women of the early 21st Century are already in our classrooms. They are embarking not just upon Key Stage 1 of their education, but upon key stage 1 of the rest of their lives.

Certainly, one major question that we have to ask is whether the *Education Reform Act*, any more than the 1944 *Education Act*, gets to grips with a fundamental cultural and economic problem we have suffered since the war, and almost certainly earlier.

It is the low status that we in Britain continue to accord to applicable knowledge and practical skills and technologies. We prefer the pure to the applied, the abstract to the real, the professions to manufacturing industry, thinking about it rather than doing it or making it, designing it rather than selling it. It has been the cause of our gradual but serious national decline.

The 1944 act tinkered with the problem by establishing central schools. Some local authorities later set up technical high schools. Neither achieved real status. If anything, they reinforced existing national prejudices. Like special educational needs, technological learning received no real emphasis or importance.

What *ERA* did was to create a few highly resourced City Technology Colleges. They were not in the areas originally planned. The level of funding that the Government expected from industry was not forthcoming. Only a small number of pupils could attend them. On the most optimistic analysis, they were only ever likely to constitute a small-scale, marginal solution to a large central problem. Despite the inclusion of technology in the National Curriculum, a major opportunity was missed.

History will show that what was really needed was a substantially increased long term investment in the Technical and Vocational Education Initiative, and – perhaps even more important – immediate and substantially greater spending on primary school science and technology. What was wrong with TVEI from the beginning was that 14 was far too late an age for pupils to start it.

We should, as an urgent national priority, be providing properly funded, high quality in-service training for primary teachers to deal with these subject areas, rather than relying on poorly financed, unco-ordinated local initiatives. We should be mounting a real drive to attract suitably qualified graduates into the primary classroom. We should be providing first class physical resources. And we should above all be providing the time for the teachers to make the real impact on the curriculum which is so obviously necessary.

My concern on this issue is closely related to my anxiety over another challenge which *ERA* may not meet. I greatly wonder about the extent to which it will help us to raise standards and opportunities for those children who live and grow up in the increasingly deprived areas of our turbulent inner cities – not that deprivation is confined to towns and cities. None the less, concern about inner-city education had been widespread for years: it was a mainspring of reform.

What will *ERA* do for the socially disadvantaged, those with special educational needs, those from the ethnic minorities which continue to experience prejudice and whose members live at the margin of an affluent, self-interested society from which they feel increasingly isolated? Our responsibility for educating those children goes far beyond preparing them for employment. It is to help them to develop into responsible adults, ready to take their place in a society which is not just an economic machine but a civilised, democratic, questioning but responsible, law-abiding community.

Will they wish to do so if the only work which is available to them carries such little esteem or worth in our society that it is almost less shameful to be on the dole? Unless our education service substantially improves their lot in life, then future generations will see *ERA* as so much well-meaning but irrelevant waste paper.

No legislation can, of itself, cure these problems or meet these challenges. But the bold claims made for *ERA* set the standard by which history judges it. Responsible teachers do not want the reforms to fail, for if they do, it is children and young people who are the victims of that failure.

Let us hope that the political architects have got it right. We cannot judge that now: we are too close to it. All that we, who have to educate these children, can do is warn the political architects that, on their present investment of resources, they do not impress us as quantity or quality surveyors.

Part IV: PARTNERSHIPS

10 Captive audience

Joan Sallis

Many people inside education respond to the current pressures to test-and-publish, the pursuit of teacher appraisal and the search for acceptable performance indicators, by saying that you don't make anything longer by measuring it or heavier by weighing it. Most people outside the service on the other hand believe that every human activity is capable of improvement and that you must have the means to guide you in that process. Some would say that the absence for so long of published information about the performance of schools was intolerable in a public service spending public funds, especially, they might add, considering the unique importance of that service and the unavailability of redress for victims of its failures: its consumers are after all captives within it, with no chance to opt out of education altogether. Teachers believe that in resisting the publication of information they are protecting children. Politicians say they are only protecting themselves. That is the basic conflict.

All these arguments are crude and simplistic in some ways and the process of picking them apart is tedious and fraught with unreason on both sides. The radicals of the system see all too much cohesion in the *Education Reform Act* – you need a more standard product so that you can test; you need to test so that people can compare schools; you need open enrolment so that they can act on the comparison; you need LMS to relate school income more or less directly to numbers; and you need the last exit of opting out to enable those who have played the system well thus far to make their gains secure.

The critics of this package would say that it's nothing to do with raising standards for all but merely a device to give the strong the means to segregate themselves, pull up the ladders and allow the weak to drown. Far from creating a more standard product, they will say, the combination of open enrolment, market driven finance, heavy reliance on parents' voluntary contributions, and the establishment of grant maintained schools and City Technology Colleges will in time produce a highly differentiated product, with several grades of publicly provided education and greater inequalities than ever.

There is no lack of evidence for this point of view. One needs to say, however, that while the 1988 Act resulted from the leap to the top of the agenda of certain ideas previously regarded as the preserve of the extreme or even crackpot Right, the themes of measured performance, more information for parents, greater accountability of schools, which are now woven tightly together with the market orientated philosophy, can be traced back a very long way. These themes have all-party support and entered into public debate as long ago as 1976 when Callaghan spoke about them at Ruskin College and when the Taylor Committee appointed by his Government in 1975 was already halfway through its work. The sad part is that the wounds inflicted on educators by the thrust of competition bleed uncontrollably onto their feelings about the accountability and participation now associated in law with that newer and less acceptable theme.

What of the poor bewildered parents, the captive audience watching this drama unfold? What do they make of their new rights to information, their new freedom of choice, and their new entitlement to representation? How do they judge schools? On what criteria do they choose schools? What use do they make of their representation in the running of schools? Do they feel that their children will actually be better educated as a result of testing, publication of results, teacher appraisal, the development of performance indicators, and the right to demand inspection? Do they feel that they are able to use choice to enhance their children's life chances? Do they consider that their own right to a place around the table actually affects the quality of the meal?

Difficult questions. What *is* certain is that parents as well as politicians became worried about the degree of freedom schools appeared to enjoy in the 1950s and 1960s, the amount of experimentation to which they thought their children were subjected, and the lack of familiar landmarks in the curriculum and methodology of schools as they perceived them. We are suffering grievously for that now. Schools have since then made enormous advances in welcoming parents, informing them about their children's progress and explaining their methods, but only modest inroads have been made into the prevailing confusion and unease, especially with those parents who still find schools and teachers intimidating and may see closed doors where there are none. This is now worrying, since inevitably and legitimately as testing is established, parents will become more anxious about whether the way the school operates is going to deliver the goods, and will also want to know more about the schools on offer, how to make an informed choice, how the chosen school monitors its own performance and what it does about the results. Some still haven't found out why children in primary schools draw around their feet, weigh rice, sail corks and pour water; why those in secondary schools record the contents of trolleys in supermarkets, look at their local census records for a hundred years ago, make up plays, invent gadgets; these may reach near frenzy. What has a walk to the churchyard to do with the National Curriculum? Is it RE, science, history – or just subtraction?

Schools will have to take this seriously because the broad curriculum, already perhaps in danger from the fears of teachers, will be further threatened by the anxieties and pressures of parents. Teachers' fears may make them reluctant to stray from the paths, forgetting that flowers grow beyond the paths, forgetting too that many children never go on any voyage of discovery unless they go with the school. This would be a tragic outcome, since a narrow curriculum will rob those who don't have many windows opened at home – the lucky homes will make up any shortfall. But if schools are to protect the best they will more than ever need the support and encouragement of parents, and this must be worked for. Parent activists – PTAs and parent governors – can be good ambassadors if they are well-informed. What I am saying is that the first route to be signposted for parents in the quest for connections is the route from classroom practice to learning targets. Without that they can't judge anything. How can you measure the distance if you don't know the route?

Schools fear that the public will judge schools by raw examination and test scores and will make their choice on the basis of ill-informed comparisons which don't allow for the economic and social factors in a school's catchment area affecting its performance. I don't actually think many people are that stupid, and even if they show signs of such folly, schools and LEAs must give them a little guidance not just on how to look at examination results (even question whether a school which puts its all into exam performance is actually going to get the best from *every* child – yours for instance) but also on what other criteria to use and how to get at them. In my own LEA area the publication of exam results (two years before the law required it) caused no drama and there is still little evidence of crude comparisons being made. In the school I am involved in the first issue of Records of Achievement 10 years later probably evoked more warmth and appreciation from parents than anything else the school had done.

The most important thing to say about test and examination

results is that if schools and LEAs do not use them to help them make decisions, they are worthless as a means of raising standards for all. I have seen many good governing bodies and parent organisations encouraged to look at their own school's results with positive motives, not comparing their school with others but just looking for progress year on year, comparisons between subject areas or year groups, clues as to where to look a bit closer, where to put in resources, what changes to make in organisation, where staff development may be deficient. Similarly with the LEA. If it doesn't use results (and parental choice patterns for that matter) to guide it in the exercise of its responsibilities, do something about the schools which on that evidence and in all the known circumstances need support, resources or a kick up the pants, its existence is not justified. That sounds obvious, but I often observe LEAs behaving like spectators in a play called 'The Market Place'. These deserve whatever fate awaits them.

The various surveys of parental motivation in choosing schools suggest that they do in fact consider a lot of things besides exam results, press scandals and gossip. Contrary to the impressions given by some politicians, they seem to be very concerned about whether their children will be happy, sympathetically helped with problems, valued, cared for, protected from bullying, in a pleasant environment, given opportunities to take part in worthwhile activity outside the classroom. They rely on the reports of other parents and children for this evidence. It would be good if all schools produced more information about how they set about making the school a safe and happy place, what they do about bullying or loneliness, what clubs are available, and above all perhaps how pupils are themselves informed and consulted about school rules and policies and given a chance to say how they feel about school. I suspect that a number of 'bad' indices, bullying, truancy, vandalism, might respond to a greater sense of ownership by pupils of their school and its reputation.

The behaviour of pupils outside school is obviously a strongly observed measure. Schools sometimes dismiss it, either taking the legalistic line that they are not responsible, or the line that a small minority cause all the trouble. This is a pity, since the community image must be watched. Sometimes a very small reform like negotiating for an extra service bus at exactly the right time, a member of staff on duty at the gate, the sweet shop or the bus queue, works wonders. Neighbours troubled by noise and street parking on school play night might be charmed by a leafleted invitation to the dress rehearsal and a plea for tolerance for one evening. You tell your neighbours when you have a party, after all.

What of the judgements parents make about the quality and dedication of teachers? I would think these were often fairly accurate. Children and parents know which teachers are poor time-keepers, slow or sloppy markers, boring in their presentation or hasty or unfair in their discipline. One very frustrating thing is that schools build such a high wall around staff problems that parents go mad with frustration thinking that they are the only ones who know there is a problem. I am not of course suggesting that Heads should be disloyal to individuals or that they should discuss their staff problems with members of the public. Nor am I suggesting that the process of teacher appraisal and its outcomes should be public property. All I would urge is that schools say frankly and often what they do in general to ensure good teaching, and admit that vigilance is needed and applied. Parents only need to know that there's a *system*, that new teachers do get watched and helped; that weaknesses are identified and dealt with at least by guidance, in-service training or a good talking to; that there is a reason for having students and that they are not left to cope alone; that comments made by parents are heeded. Then when teacher appraisal is well established, the process should at least be described to parents. It would be so reassuring.

So far I feel that I have only skimmed the surface of public criteria for judging schools. I want now to try to explore a little more deeply the complex of issues centring on choice, information and representation, since I think one has to pick these apart to get anywhere near the truth about what access means and how the availability to parents of information, choice and influence might actually improve the quality of what is available to children, their children and all children.

When my children started school I knew that it was my duty to send them there, indeed that it was my duty to see that they had full time and suitable (suitable?) education. This duty was not then matched by any rights, and was deemed to be fulfilled if you presented your child at a school catering for the age range and left him or her there all day. What did it mean? If you had no choice, no information, and no access, how could you possibly perform that duty in any meaningful way? If you didn't have information how could you choose? No matter, you didn't have choice as a right anyway. How therefore could you say it was suitable? Well it may have turned out to be suitable in the end, though you could hardly have been said to be very active in your duty. How could you judge its success? You didn't know anything about what it was aiming at, and even if you did you had no access to satisfy yourself that it was being achieved. And if you had access, and weren't satisfied, what could you have done about it? Back to choice again. It was ludicrous. I hope those keen and for the most part well-judged critics of the increased consumer voice in education will look back sometimes at how it was, and will see that it was intolerable.

The legislation of 1980, 1981, 1986, 1988 and 1992 has certainly changed the landscape. So how has it changed? Choice is not absolute, never can be, but it may not now unreasonably be denied even across LEA boundaries; it may not be denied at all if the school has room. Whether choice has genuinely increased is more debatable. What about information? Big advances here. Schools have to give parents a great deal of information about their curriculum, their rules, their results, their policies on RE and sex education. Parents have a right to see the governors' papers, the school budget, their own children's academic records, syllabuses and schemes of work. Very welcome, these. In all these categories of information, parents can get some clues about how well the school is doing. Access? Well, no right of access by law, though of course schools are much opener than they were, and it would be a rare school where parents were not able at least to talk to a teacher by appointment.

Yet when you look at the legal rights parents still *don't* have, it is quite surprising. No right to form an association which meets in the school. A right to reports on their children, but no chance to contribute to the assessment except in special needs cases. No right to an explanation of school policies, much less to consultation, no absolute right to an appointment with a teacher or an assurance that the school would contact you if it were concerned about any aspect of your child's work, behaviour or welfare. Of course a good school offers all these things. But as seven members of the Taylor Committee, in their note of extension, said, if that's a good school why doesn't everybody have the right to a good school, why is it not a legal requirement to do those things? Fifteen years later that question has not been answered.

I am trying to expose something very unsatisfactory, which is that in the main the rights parents have to information are all related to choice. We are thought to need information only so that we can make an informed choice. That is the basic consumerism of government policy. Once you have made your choice, there is little more you can do. But does more choice improve the quality of education? Politicians on the right obviously think it does, while those on the left would sooner do violent good to you.

Choice would be real if all schools were equally good and if all parents were equally mobile, confident and well-informed. If these conditions applied choice would also be a very boring subject and nobody would ever discuss it again. It is only because there is inequality, both between schools and in the skills and social advantages parents bring to the task, that choice is a subject of debate. That and the suspicion that once the school gates close, there isn't a lot of influence you can have, so you'd better choose the right school gates. What I am saying is that influence and choice are in the balance – more of one makes the other weigh less with parents. Parents are obsessive about choice because they feel they have little influence. If they had influence they would not be so bothered about where they exercised it, would settle perhaps for the nearest school where they had so many natural advantages.

So those missing rights to good habits of communication, to a legally protected partnership *as an individual* are still very important, even when parents have rights of representation on governing bodies, which is undoubtedly an enormous advance. If governors are supported and encouraged in that role, if schools debate openly and share genuinely the policies they adopt, if they offer governors high expectations, good structures of involvement in the school day by day which improve their decisions, I am hopeful that the position of the individual parent in the process will be strengthened and that children will benefit from the joint effort on their behalf, but I would still not consider that the right, as an individual, to be treated as a partner became less important, even with wise and well-supported advocates in the counsels of the school.

I believe I am saying that parents, individually and collectively, will only be able to make use of the proliferation of tests and indices of the quality of schools if they understand their meaning in relation to the daily life and purposes of the school. That means access. It means the chance to observe for themselves, and therefore make better judgements of what is important. It means being able to comment and contribute. In the last resort it means a sense of part-ownership of the school's values, so the means to judge it by reference to what it sets out to do. *I am convinced that consumerism in the market place sense will reign supreme, with all its cruel consequences in terms of inequalities between schools and among families, waste of talent, self-fulfilling prophecies, stagnant social structures, until we can put something in its place.*

That something is of course partnership, or, better expressed, mutual accountability for a shared process. Parents know that without agreement about the objectives and debate about the methods there is no accountability, and therefore no basis on which to evaluate. This is uniquely the case in education because it is not a transaction and not a professional service, but legally and practically an active joint enterprise. Parents do not want to make schools accountable for failure – that is too late. They want to co-operate to prevent avoidable failure. They don't want to judge schools. They want to help make them better.

Further Reading

HM Government (1980) *Education Act.*
HM Government (1981) *Education Act and related regulations.*
HM Government (1986) *Education Act and related regulations.*
HM Government (1988) *Education Reform Act 1988 and related regulations.*
HM Government (1992) *Schools Act.*
Taylor, Lord *The Taylor Report: A New Partnership for Our Schools* (London: HMSO).
Sallis, J. (1977) *School Managers and Governors: Taylor and After* (London: Ward Lock Educational).
Sallis, J. (1988) *Schools, Parents & Governors: A New Approach to Accountability* (London: Routledge).

11 Developing school governor effectiveness in the 1990s

Mike Kelly

In an on-line literature search of the articles and papers listed in the *British Educational Index*, conducted in the Summer of 1991 for the previous 12 months, a total of 1,156 contributions were found on the subject of the management of schools; only 65 of these considered the role and activity of Governing Bodies in that management task, and in around a third to a half of them, the consideration of Governor activity was peripheral to the main purposes and scope of the articles.

Other documented and anecdotal evidence from a variety of sources, including small scale research, press and journal articles, and from my contacts with some 400–500 governors in the course of a variety of training sessions conducted by and for LEA and cross-LEA groupings in the North West, appears to indicate that governors' awareness and knowledge of the changes arising from *ERA* 1988, and the education acts from the earlier 1980s, and the implications of this legislation for the governance and management of schools is:

(1) *Patchy and uneven* – without doubt, there are individual Governing Bodies, and more occasionally, school clusters and even LEAs, where the levels of awareness and knowledge of the powers and responsibilities of governors are reasonable, and effective, with a sound grasp of their implications for the changed scenario in which educational organisations are working. However, it does not appear that this situation is widespread – indeed, it seems to be the case in the minority of schools. In too many institutions, the understanding of the governors' roles and powers in the key areas in which they need to be effective,

such as the *focusing*, *marketing*, *employment*, and *reviewing* aspects of running their educational enterprises, is patchy and uneven, and in some cases, incoherent and misled

(2) *discontinuous with management training and development in general* – the training and development investment for Governing Bodies needs to encompass and be articulated with that for the managers of schools, the senior management teams, and, pre-eminently, the Heads of institutions.

The reasons for these uneven levels of knowledge and awareness, and the unsatisfactory state of training and development, are complex. They lie in such things as:

— the pace of the introduction of changes in the structure and objectives of educational institutions;
— the often politically motivated 'collusion' between professionals and providers in keeping levels of understanding and action in the 'soft' areas of the organisational activity of schools;
— the gradualism with which LEAs are introducing full delegated status into schools;
— and, sometimes, simply in the poor quality of the trainers who have been given the job of raising and developing governing body awareness and capability levels.

But, in a way, these are symptoms, not the problem. What has happened as a result of the education legislation from the 1980s is that an additional set of *active* players have been introduced into the already complicated and difficult activity of managing *change* in schools – Governing Bodies have been added to what David Hargreaves and the Cambridge Institute group have called the 'management arrangements' of schools, without too much of an attempt to integrate them into these 'arrangements'. In situations of change, and where there is such a rapid rate of change, the simple lack of knowledge about one's scope of control is only a symptom of wider and deeper problems. The changes brought about by the legislation, and, more importantly, their implications for school managers, are marking a 'step change', what has been called a 'second order change', in the way the state school system in the UK is to be managed. It is the focus of this chapter that such a second order change needs to be internalised and institutionalised by the managers and by their organisations extremely rapidly, if the institutions are to survive and grow – and that the partners in the enterprise, primarily the parents, pupils, staff, and governors of schools, have an essential need to contribute to each others' understanding of the change, and of their roles in their school's management and development.

The contribution of governors to the management of the changes in schools arising from 1980s legislation

Baginsky, Baker, and Cleave (1991) suggest that the major responsibilities of Governing Bodies consist in the overview of curriculum, the employment (or not) of staff (including the arrangements for their contracts, pay and conditions), financial management, and the interactions and structural relations with outside agencies, including parents, the LEA, the community, and contractors.

Ormston, Holmes, and Shaw (1991) identify a change from the traditional LEA/schools 'command culture' towards a 'partnership culture', with, in some cases at least, a further move towards a 'service culture'. This last move is confirmed by research in progress for the then DES (Bowles 1991) on the service role of LEAs. In schools, this movement is seen as leading to the governing body seeing its role as target setter, and target checker, for the professional and other staff of the school.

Ormston *et al* argue that the primary objective for governors will be to develop their pivotal role in the management of change – in order to do this effectively, they suggest that they must select a very few tasks, central to their mission, and concentrate on doing them well. Four tasks are proposed:

(1) Knowledge of, and commitment to the School Development Plan, the targets therein, and the evidence of success;
(2) Developed confidence in the management structure of the school, as 'fit for purpose', so as to be able to leave the management to the professionals;
(3) Care for the staff as the key resource;
(4) Approval of a budget which supports the learning opportunities for pupils and students.

In *The Empowered School*, Hargreaves and Hopkins (1991) propose the involvement of governors in the partnership which creates the Development Planning process as the key way in which the partners may be able to manage the changes in dynamic and effective ways:

> Development Planning creates a partnership in which there is a

shared commitment to the school's improvement, and a shared responsibility for the school's progress and success in achieving such improvement ... a partnership of mutual support and accountability.

In this way, they see the Governors as part of the management arrangements of the school, involved in the establishment of agreed frameworks for action, clarified roles and responsibilities, (including, for governors, new relationships with staff), and rewarding ways of working together. They also include the role of reporting on action, primarily through the provision by the Head of information to the Governing Body, and the parallel provision by the Governing Body of information to the parents and the wider community through the Annual Report.

Getting results and developing effectiveness through governors

It is with the caveats and suggestions discussed above in mind that this chapter goes on to propose a series of key areas in which governors in particular must get results which support and enable the organisational goals and outcomes of their schools. It is essential to acknowledge that, although they will, and should, aim to act in partnership with the others in the enterprise, in the last analysis the legislation places the responsibility, and the accountability, on their shoulders, within the constraints of the legal and resource framework currently in place.

The overall key results areas

In general, governors will need to get results in three overall Key Results Areas (KRAs), which this chapter describes as:

— organisational focus and direction;
— organisational productivity;
— review of progress.

Each of these overarching KRAs will be subdivided into a number of working areas. The three are identified so as to give Governors, (and the other partners), a shorthand formula for checking that what they find themselves engaged in during their meetings, visits, discussions, etc. is legitimate and appropriate to the needs of the organisation and their role in it. Tables 11.1, 11.2 and 11.3 summarise the three KRAs, and their sub-areas.

KRA 1 – Organisational focus and direction

Table 11.1: KRA 1

Element A	–	Policy initiation
Element B	–	Policy maintenance
Element C	–	Policy development
Element D	–	Legal and quasi-legal arrangements
Element E	–	Constituency representation
Element F	–	Partnership development

This is a pre-eminent need for those running organisations, particularly in times of rapid change. Governors, in partnership with the staff, customers, and consumers of the service, can play an essential part in helping the professionals to identify legitimate and appropriate activities for the school to engage in, and, perhaps more importantly, what *not* to engage in. A major difficulty for schools at this time is to prioritise its activity, to focus on certain aspects, and to hold back from others. Identifying and agreeing 'what we do here', taking into account the philosophies and needs of the various stakeholders, is a complex activity, which needs considerable and careful deliberation – the problems of the school development planning process currently occurring in UK schools are substantial examples of this complexity, pre-occupying practitioners in the schools, and researchers such as the Cambridge Institute group. Too many organisations are unfocused and weakly directed, tending towards a backward perspective, rather than one which takes up the needs of the next 10 years. Governors have a prime role in ensuring that schools have an agreed, and if possible shared, sense of direction and focus, preferably by establishing its business plans and priorities in open, formal, and accountable ways.

KRA 1 – Element A: Policy initiation
How do Governors *initiate* policy? I suppose 'play a part in its initiation' is a better description. Their tasks include setting parameters and areas – the curriculum, finance, staffing, and the marketing contribution to overall school strategy – and indicating their interrelationships, offering opinion and steer to the staff in the school, in such a way as to identify and help establish the desired culture and ethos of the institution. This activity needs to be preceded by an audit of current policy.

KRA 1 – Element B: Policy maintenance
The Governing Body's part in the maintenance of policy begins

with a check, through staff and inspection reports, on the implementation of the school's policies – what DES refers to as 'tracking', via the examination of activity at every level. For example, if the school has, with Governing Body help, initiated a particular curriculum policy on information technology, dipstick tests are made on its implementation at departmental levels, in classroom practice, in the school's written output, in attitudes and comments among all levels and types of staff in the organisation.

KRA 1 – Element C: Policy development
This is the key element where proactivity may be cultivated. In a period of constant and often discontinuous change, current policy needs continuous adaptation, and more importantly hard-nosed review, in order to monitor fitness to purpose, and purpose to context matching.

KRA 1 – Element D: Legal and quasi-legal arrangements
Tasks in this element involve ensuring the organisation operates on a legal basis, particularly in the areas of information and publicity, employment practice and policy, conduct in relation to pupils, health and safety, and the production and operation of the budget.

KRA 1 – Element E: Constituency representation
Governors all have to work from representative position, and will therefore have varying degrees of need to report to, and/or inform, their constituencies on their action, for which they must stand ready to be called to account in their collective action.

KRA 1 – Element F: Partnership development
A vital part of their key result area of setting overall focus and direction lies in the activity of developing the partners in the enterprise, not by accident, but by conscious pursuit. Inter-group rivalry and hostility feature strongly in group and inter-group research, particularly where power relationships are involved. A key to successful partnership development would appear to be accessible information, and clear communications, representing to each other action and implication.

KRA 2 – *Organisational productivity*
The governors have a shared role with the staff of the school to ensure that results are gained in the important area of productivity, i.e. that the school steadily becomes increasingly productive.

Partnerships

The governors' roles here are predominantly those of *pressure* and *support*. In the current arrangements for the management of schools, there is and will continue to be the need to ensure that

Table 11.2: KRA 2

Element A	–	Budget strategy and approval
Element B	–	Accountable school development planning
Element C	–	Market growth
Element D	–	The three Es
Element E	–	Communications intensity

they are doing what their stakeholders require, and doing it in the most efficient way possible. The stakeholders include the professionals, who will have an input into the goals, curriculum, and methodology of educational institutions, the community at large, who pay for the service, and the customers and consumers who are intimately involved with its ultimate quality – parents and children in the main.

KRA 2 – Element A: Budget strategy and approval

This I feel is the primary KRA element in ensuring productivity – the organisation's fundamental 'theory-in-use' (as opposed to the 'espoused theory' which may be seen in its nominal and written philosophy) is seen in what it spends its money on (and what it doesn't spend money on). Governors have to determine and approve the strategy for future expenditure, in line with its felt need and policy for the development of the school, and the focus it has consciously set in the light of the context within which it has to work.

KRA 2 – Element B: Accountable school development planning

Governing Bodies have to apply pressure, by setting deadlines, by structuring its budget, by making decisions on the allocation and capture of resources, and by receiving and approving the School Development Planning processes and products. It may give support by being involved in the initiation, production and review of the SDP, offering a concerned 'outsider' view on the effectiveness of the plans, and their implementation.

KRA 2 – Element C: Market growth

In times of major change, an organisation's ability to survive is dependent on its ability to develop to meet new challenges in new ways. I see no reason to suppose that schools in the 1990s and beyond will escape this 'market inevitability'. Tasks here involve identifying the organisation's systems for marketing, and customer care, needs identification, and appropriate service provision, plus the necessary staff training and development; analysing and developing the image, capabilities, and vision of the school; setting appropriate SMART targets; generating income for development activities, which are desired, but not currently funded; looking for new ways of providing services, particularly through the introduction and application of non-expert, non-professional, non-OK ideas; and identifying growth and retrenchment areas to raise the levels of challenge and achievement for the organisation.

KRA 2 – Element D: The three Es

All school activity should be demonstrably *efficient* (doing what it sets out to do without waste), and *effective* (doing what it sets out to do, and what is needed to be done). If possible, this should be done *equitably* as between the stakeholders, though it can be argued that the needs of the pupils are pre-eminent, and in the extreme, take overarching priority, at which point equity may become irrelevant.

KRA 2 – Element E: Communications intensity

In this element, Governing Bodies will aim to encourage and monitor powerful networks of communication, running horizontally and vertically throughout the school community, informing and elaborating a continuous and intensive debate on vision and pedagogy at all the organisational, group, team, and individual focal points – encompassing formal, informal, and inferential communication channels, with an emphasis on face to face activity as far as is possible.

KRA3 – Review of progress

Table 11.3: KRA 3

Element A	–	Monitoring systems
Element B	–	Review systems
Element C	–	Challenge levels
Element D	–	Achievement levels

The third overarching area in which governors need to ensure results is that of review of progress. This KRA includes the monitoring and evaluating functions of organisations, to establish, maintain, and develop the levels of quality being provided, the challenge of the curriculum and methodology, and the level of student achievement. Here the provision and implementation of systems loom large in the governors' brief, as well as the process of matching achievement to the focus and direction KRA 1 described earlier, to consider how far the school is meeting its goals in its eventual 'product', the seven year old, the 11 year old, the 16 year old, and/or the 18 year old.

The main sources of data upon which the Governing Body can base its review of progress are the reports it receives at its meetings, from the Head, from staff, from outside agencies such as the LEA or other inspection and advisory services, and from governors themselves; through class, pupil, and staff 'pursuit', visits, or shadowing; and through the development of the Governing Body as an interactive monitoring network.

KRA 3 – Element A: Monitoring systems

The governors need to be sure that the systems used in the school for gathering data on activity and impact are appropriate to the collection of meaningful and relevant data, are storing it effectively and efficiently, and lastly are being used to develop assessment and action decisions which can help to move the organisation into line with its goals and vision.

KRA 3 – Element B: Review systems

These are the systems whereby the Governing Body, and the other partners, change the activity of the school. They establish criteria for action, and evidence of that action, derived from what is going on in the school. They indicate, as unambiguously as possible, what is in need of re-orientation. They are embedded in the budget strategy, the School Development Plans, and their associated action plans, and in the inspection arrangements agreed by the governors.

KRA 3 – Element C: Challenge levels

Curricula can easily become self-fulfilling wishes, rather than challenging programmes – organisations have to ask continuously whether whether their levels of challenge fit their levels of capability. To help here, schools and the Governing Bodies need to indicate the 'challenge environment', preferably in SMART terms (specific, measurable, achievable, relevant, and time-governed), and regularly review them.

KRA 3 – Element D: Achievement levels

As well as indicating the levels of challenge to be offered to the participants in the enterprise, Governing Bodies need to consider the acceptable levels of achievement to be reached. Whether this be internally agreed standards, in addition to any national assessments, they need to cover in detail the academic and behavioural areas of activity of students, staff, and whole school achievement.

Areas for Attention and Development

All three Key Results Areas, goal setting, productivity, and review, pose problems for Governing Bodies, who are always part-time, often lay, and occasionally out of sympathy with the organisational milieu and culture they find themselves in. It is a challenge for such bodies, all 25,000 plus of them in the UK, to regulate effective, efficient, and equitable action in the organisations they are responsible for. The premise of this paper is that it is a challenge that can be met, and through which the education system can develop. The immediate area for attention is likely to be KRA 2 – I believe that this will be difficult in the short term, but that it is totally dependent on Governing Bodies being increasingly successful in their planning and review capabilities. Their abilities to anticipate change, to learn from their organisation's levels of skill in action, and to make their own changes and their own paths to the future, will be what contributes to the chances of survival and development of those fittest to achieve the standards their stakeholders want to be achieved.

Recommendations for action

The key trigger for effective Governor development is firstly experience. Governing Bodies can learn from their experience of the process of taking over their part of the reins of power in schools what works and does not work. Time is needed for them to experiment – and occasionally to fail. No training can substitute for this, or even prevent it – would that life were that straightforward.

As the Governing Body's store of experience develops under the gradual development of delegated status, the training needs can be met by the development of a national framework of management training with some possibility of it being reasonably effective. Examples abound across the country of headteacher management training failing to change much in the organisation and success of schools, and much INSET of the more general professional type for teachers at large has a pretty low rating from them on its effectiveness. It is therefore worth questioning what is the appropriate response to governor's needs. It is my view that what is the current order of need is something like:

— experience of the changes, and the challenges of LMS;
— development of a training framework for Governing Body needs;
— trainer training and development;
— Governing Body training courses articulated with management training arrangements for Heads, Deputies, and other school managers.

It is likely, however, that the second area above, that of the development of a training framework for Governing Body needs, could too easily become a rigid and bureaucratic nightmare. It is perhaps only possible to agree a national content and process for governor training, with guidelines on its structural characteristics and scheduling.

Research is needed into effective governor practice; effective governor training practice; and the development of a database on Governing Body activity in the fulfilment of their key results areas.

Of key importance for the development, even the continuance, of Governing Bodies in forms which will enable their effective contribution to the post-*ERA* schools system, is the radical re-appraisal over the next year or two of their size and structure, as well as of their actions. Though this is not the place or time to make definitive statements in these areas, it would appear that two essential principles are likely to be 'smaller rather than larger', and 'simpler rather than more complex'. Fine details should wait on the research mentioned earlier.

References

Baginsky, M., Baker, L., and Cleave, S., (1991) *Towards Effective Partnerships in School Governance*, NFER.

Bowles, G. N. (1991) *Support Services for School Management*, (London: DES).

Hargreaves, D. H. and Hopkins, D. (1991) *The Empowered School*, (London: Cassell).

Ormston, M., Holmes, G. and Shaw, M. (1991) *Governors and LMS*, Conference Paper, (Oxford: Oxford Polytechnic).

Part V: QUALITY AND STANDARDS

12 Total Quality Management and standards in further education

Edward Sallis

Challenges in the market for further education and training

Assuring the quality of service is a key issue for further education in the next decade. One of the most important challenges facing colleges is how to manage for quality. This paper will argue that the most effective means of assuring the quality and standards of service is through the introduction of Total Quality Management. While the paper focuses on further education the approach to quality outlined in it can apply equally to other parts of the education system.

The recent upsurge of interest in quality issues in FE coincided with the passing of the *Education Reform Act*. *ERA* placed considerable emphasise on the monitoring of the outputs from colleges. However, the performance indicators written into colleges' schemes of delegation provided only rudimentary measures of efficiency, and did not address questions about the quality of the student learning experience or the effectiveness of the delivery. They provided only proxies for the successful management and operation of colleges. They also did not address the issue of the customers' perception of the service. Many colleges consequently felt the need to look beyond performance indicators and started to develop systems for demonstrating and improving the quality of their provision.

Greater freedom has been matched by greater accountability. Colleges have to demonstrate that they can, on a reasonably consistent basis, offer particular levels and quality of service. Training and Enterprise Councils are specifying that colleges should install quality assurance systems as a means of demonstrating both their accountability and quality. The White Paper *Education and Training for the 21st Century* contains the expectation that colleges will have quality assurance mechanisms in place as part of their institutional framework when corporate status is achieved in April 1993. Additionally, there is an expectation that the financial allocations of the Further Education Funding Council will be informed by quality judgements.

Colleges face greater competition both from within and from outside the public sector of further education. Schools are moving into vocational education – the traditional market of colleges. National Vocational Qualifications (NVQs), which require workplace assessment of competencies, will increasingly be offered directly by employers. In areas where colleges catchments overlap there is increasing competition between them. The introduction of training credits is putting power into the hands of consumers. Colleges have to plan to become financially viable corporate bodies within an environment in which there is considerable uncertainty. In a period when colleges' traditional market is being deregulated competitive strategies are required which clearly differentiate them from their competitors. Quality may sometimes be the only differentiating factor in the market for education. Focusing on the needs of the customer, which is at the heart of quality, is the most effective means of facing the competition and surviving.

The importance of quality is reflected in the findings of the *National Quality Survey*, which the author carried out in the autumn of 1990. 66 per cent of the 260 colleges who responded said the development of a quality assurance system was a high priority for them. Only a handful replied that quality was not on their agenda. It is important for a college to be clear why it is developing a quality assurance system. The reasons can be summed up as follows:

(1) **The Professional Imperative** – the college itself wants to improve the quality of its service;
(2) **The Moral Imperative** – the college's customers deserve a quality service;
(3) **The Competitive Imperative** – other colleges have introduced a quality system;
(4) **The Survival Imperative** – the college has to because TECs and others are demanding it.

The Survey explored the motivation behind the development of quality assurance systems. The external pressures from Training and Enterprise Councils and other external bodies were found to be less of an influence than the desire of colleges themselves to improve the quality of their provision. Most colleges recognise the importance of offering a guaranteed level of service which meets the needs of customers and clients. The findings from the Survey suggests that there are a number of main benefits which colleges expect to flow from the introduction of a quality assurance system. These are:

— Improved service and client satisfaction;
— Change to the culture of the college;
— Improvements to teaching and learning;
— Improved staff motivation and morale;
— Improved managerial performance;
— Improved marketing opportunities;
— Improvements to the college's administrative systems and procedures.

There is no uniformity about the system of quality assurance being adopted. For colleges who see quality as an all-embracing holistic concept Total Quality Management has a greater appeal than the more mechanistic British Standard BS5750 'Quality Systems', which focuses on the quality of an organisation's systems and procedures. However, 27 colleges reported that they are combining TQM and BS5750. Other colleges are devising their own approaches and systems. The White Paper mentions three approaches to quality assurance which could be useful to colleges: British Standard 5750, Total Quality Management, and Strategic Quality Management (SQM is a system devised by Consultants at Work and which is entirely combatable with TQM). BS5750 and SQM are well documented elsewhere and this article concentrates on the issues and implications of introducing TQM. A TQM approach can easily accommodate BS5750 if external recognition is required for particular aspects of a college's quality assurance system. However, before TQM is explored the issues of what quality and quality assurance mean and how they relate to standards needs discussion.

What is quality and how does it link to standards?

The need for a definition of quality is a necessary starting point for introducing TQM. One of the fundamental problems is to ensure that there is not a confusion between quality, standards, and price. W. Edwards Deming has written 'Good quality does not mean high quality. It means a predictable degree of uniformity and dependability at low cost with a quality suited to the market'.

Quality is an interesting idea because it has a variety of contradictory meanings. It is both an absolute and a relative concept. As an absolute it is similar in nature to truth and beauty. It is an ideal with which there can be no compromise. This absolute definition implies that things which exhibit quality are of the highest possible standard and cannot be surpassed. Rolls Royce cars are 'quality products' in this definition, but not Ford Escorts. Such high and absolute standards are usually based on an aesthetic as well as a practical criteria. 'Quality products' are not only precision engineered, but are things of beauty. Hand in hand with such 'quality' goes a high price as they are usually costly to produce.

The relative or ascribed definition of quality is the one employed in quality assurance. Quality is not seen an intrinsic attribute of a product, but is something which is ascribed to it. Quality products, in this definition, need not be expensive or exclusive. They may be beautiful, but not necessarily so. They can be mundane, everyday, and throwaway – can openers, tins of soft drink and ballpoint pens. In this definition products exhibit quality because someone thinks that they are quality products. However, it is important to be clear who is ascribing an attribute of quality to a product. Is it the producer or the consumer?

The producer definition of quality can be summed up as conformance to requirements or 'fitness for purpose', as the British Standards Institution defines it. Quality is achieved because products meet their specification in a consistent fashion. Quality is demonstrated by a producer having a system, known as a quality assurance system, which enables a product to be consistently produced to a particular standard or specification. So long as a product consistently meets its makers claims for it then it is a quality product. In this definition both Ford Escorts and a Rolls Royces are quality products. They both conform to their manufacturer's specifications and standards. This producer view of quality is sometimes called 'quality in fact'. It requires consistency in meeting the standard which the producer has established. 'Quality in fact' is the basis of the quality assurance systems devised in accordance with the British Standards Institution in the BS5750 standard. The problem with 'quality in fact' is that consumers may have a different perception of the quality of the product from the producer. In the final analysis, it can be argued, it is the consumer who is the arbitrator of quality because without customers there is no business. This user-based approach sees quality lying in the eyes of the beholder. Quality in this definition is 'quality in perception'. Quality products are those which best meet the needs and wants of consumers. They exhibit 'fitness for use'. In this definition the consumers' views are sovereign. As an aside this definition does lead down some interesting avenues. For example, as the *Sun* and the *Daily Mirror* obviously please a great many consumers then they are, according to the quality in perception definition, quality newspapers!

When using the relative or quality assurance definitions a distinction has to be drawn between quality and standards. Quality and standards are not the same thing, although they are related. A standard is a predefined and measurable specification. Quality is consistent conformance to a standard. It is perfectly possible for a product to be of high standard but poor quality. This can occur when there is a high level of specification but a lack of consistency in meeting it. The obverse is also possible. If customers want a low level of specification at a low price then this represents a quality product to them. The important point is that quality products must always provide customers with value for money.

At first sight the issue appears to be who sets the standard? Is it the customer, the producer, or an outside agency such as government? Should standards be imposed, with the possibility of national uniformity, or negotiated between provider and customer and so open to considerable local bargaining? While these issues are important it assumes that standards can be easily expressed for a complex service industry, with a diverse range of customers, like further education. Standards in education have usually been expressed narrowly as examination pass rates and standards of behaviour. In reality, if the nature of what is being provided is carefully analysed then the standards for the service can be seen to be complex, multi-faceted and often conflicting. If further education is seen as a service industry then some of the standards which need addressing are outlined in the following table. There is more to the quality of service delivery than just pass rates.

Total Quality Management starts with a recognition of the complexity of the issues surrounding standards and offers a methodology for defining and negotiating standards, and ensuring that they are met wherever possible. It does, however, assume that sovereignty over standard setting lies with the customer. As the purpose of current legislation and policy is to deregulate further education and to empower the consumer then a TQM approach, whether or not the initials are used, will be essential to the future of colleges.

Table 12.1: Some Standards for Service Quality

Quality Characteristic	Standards
MISSION	Consistency of purpose
RELIABILITY	Keeping promises/consistency of performance
RESPONSIVENESS	Willingness to serve the client as the client wants and needs to be served
COMPETENCE	Staff with appropriate skills and competencies/systematic review of training needs and comprehensive development programme
ACCESS	Ease of contact with the service
COURTESY	Politeness/friendliness/client orientation of staff
COMMUNICATION	Keeping clients informed in an understandable way/informing and listening to staff
CREDIBILITY	Trustworthiness of staff/honesty/reputation of staff
SECURITY	Physical safety/confidentiality
UNDERSTANDING	Understanding clients needs and demonstrating needs in practice
PHYSICAL TANGIBLES	Physical appearance of staff, environment, etc
OUTCOMES	As specified in the mission statement/as specified in the contract with clients

What is Total Quality Management?

TQM is a philosophy of never ending improvement which is only achievable by the people who work in an organisation. It is a structured and integrated approach to management, which seeks to incorporate quality and the continuous improvement of quality into all functions and all levels of the organisation. Its origins lie with the resurgence of the Japanese economy in the early 1950s after the visits there of W. Edwards Deming and Joseph Juran. Japanese business conceived a long term strategy for producing goods of outstanding reliability and competitiveness which would deliver long term world economic dominance. In the UK, until about 10 years ago, terms such as quality and quality assurance were obscure and seen as technical concerns in manufacturing and the defence industries. By contrast, in the 1990s ideas of total quality and the production of quality cultures are seen as a major aspect of strategy by organisations in all sectors. The influence of quality thinking has now spread to the public sector including education and the national health service. Total Quality Management not only transcends national boundaries it also translates from manufacturing into education. The ideas of client centredness, which are at the heart of the total quality approach, fits well with the underlying philosophy of the education service.

It is important to realise that TQM cannot be bought off the peg. Programmes need to be bespoked to fit the organisational culture of each individual institution. Industrial models can provide useful pointers and examples, but it is important to ensure that the approach used is realistic, workable and affordable in an educational setting. Neither is TQM something which can be introduced overnight. It is not a miracle cure. It is a slow process, and the benefits are seen long rather than short term. It builds on and highlights existing good management practice. Quality already exists in education. TQM is about enhancing existing quality and introducing systematic approaches to ensure that customers needs are met. No organisation has to adopt the message of total quality. However, the words of Edwards Deming sound a warning: 'Survival', he has written, 'is not compulsory'.

Whilst there is no one definition or approach to TQM the fundamentals of TQM are generally recognised to be:

— The definition of quality is continually meeting customer requirements.
— Leadership and commitment to quality must come from the top.
— A quality culture must be established which is people-led and management organised.
— The commitment to quality must be organisation wide.
— The ultimate standard is 'right first time' with zero defects.
— Prevention not detection assures quality.
— The organisation's focus is the customer.
— Customers are both internal to the organisation as well as external to it. Everyone in the organisation is both a customer as well as a supplier (the customer–supplier chain).
— Quality systems must be vehicles for the empowerment of staff not their control.

— All employees need considerable training in quality issues and quality improvement implementation.
— All staff are responsible for quality within their operational sphere.
— Teamwork is an essential ingredient of the process of assuring quality.
— Quality improvements should be rewarded and celebrated.
— Quality improvements must be measurable and measured.
— Customer needs and wants must continually be solicited.

TQM organisations put their customers and clients first. They recognise that their mission is to meet the needs and wants of their customers. They set out to match their products and services to the expectations and requirements of their customers and clients. Long term survival is only possible if the quality is that which the customer wants and not that which the organisation specifies. Without customers there is no organisation. A customer focus is, however, not by itself a sufficient condition for ensuring total quality. TQM organisations need fully worked out strategies for meeting their customers' requirements.

Education faces a considerable challenge in its relationships with its external customers. Its customers are often uninformed both about the product and what constitutes its quality. Furthermore, customers expectations of education are various and diverse. Often the quality of particular programmes is confused in the public mind with the reputation of the institution. A further difficulty is that the customer plays an important role in the quality of their own learning. Customers in education play a unique part in determining the quality of what they receive. There are difficulties with notions of consistency in the interactive process of learning. To overcome some of these problems it is necessary to ensure the motivation of both the learners and the staff. It is also important to making clear what is being offered and what is expected of learners. This could take the form of a statement of 'student entitlements', which lay down what the institution is offering and what learners can expect from it.

There is also the additional dimension of a professional workforce in colleges. Lecturers have traditionally seen themselves as the guardians of quality and standards. TQM's emphasis on the sovereignty of the customer may cause some conflict with traditional professional concepts. This is a difficult area and one that will need to be considered by any institution taking a total quality route. Total quality is about more than being 'nice to customers and smiling'. It is about listening to and responding to people's needs. The best aspects of the professional role are about care and academic integrity which are notions which fit well into a TQM culture. Blending the best aspects of professionalism with total quality is essential to success.

While at first sight the broad philosophy of TQM fits well first into an educational setting a number of the key concepts require translation. Perhaps the most pivotal is the concept of the 'customer–supplier chain', which embraces many of the main features and approaches of TQM. This simple idea is the basis of the culture of TQM. It revolves around the notion that everybody is the supplier and the customer of everyone else. The primary external customer of a college is the student. Nevertheless, equal attention has to be paid to the requirements of secondary customers such as employers, sponsors and parents, as well as to tertiary customers such as TECs, schools, the new FE Funding Council, and the college's wider community. Further education has a complex of overlapping sets of external customer relationships among whom there are often competing wants and needs. These can only be reconciled within a framework which involves not only close links but also the active seeking out of customer requirements. Customers must be nurtured and listened to.

Customers are also internal to the organisation as well as external to it. They are located at all levels in the college hierarchy. Everyone in the college supplies services to others and receives services in return. This is an important notion and has important implications for organisational status. Treating colleagues as customers requires every individual in the organisation to perform their tasks to the best of their ability whilst conforming to their customers' requirements in the knowledge that they can expect equal treatment in return. The customer/supplier chain is as strong as its weakest link. It has to be maintained by a management committed to making it work and an investment in people and their training. In a service industry where people deliver quality the resources required for delivering customer care are not all material or financial. Care, interest, listening, consideration, and service are of paramount importance.

Traditional notions of education have not seen the customer as sovereign. Supremacy has been given to professionals whose function has been to act as the gatekeepers of success and failure. It is still a very revolutionary concept to argue that all who pass through an educational system should of right leave it as a success. If consumer satisfaction is something new then the TQM notion of moving beyond satisfaction and 'delighting the customer' is a considerable challenge.

Teamwork has to be interwoven into the notion of customer/

supplier chains. It is not only course teams which need to be considered here, but teamwork across the institution. This is not just because course teams may be an outdated term in an age where the curriculum is being increasingly modularised and the idea of a 'course' is increasingly difficult to define. It is rather because TQM requires everyone in an organisation to be a team member. TQM is underpinned by a notion that everyone is responsible for quality. It, therefore, follows that teamwork must permeate the whole institution. Teams must be in place and be nurtured at all levels in the organisation – support staff, middle and senior managers, and teaching staff. Teamwork must cut across some of the 'caste' boundaries in a college. Teams consisting of academic and support staff meeting regularly to discuss areas of concern to students have not been usual features of college life. Teams can only function successfully if they are supported, nurtured, valued, and trained.

Another key concept is the idea of 'right first time every time', usually regarded as the quality standard of TQM. It underlies the striving for consistency which is a hallmark of the total quality approach. This is an easily understandable notion in a manufacturing environment. It sets the standard of producing 100 per cent of output to the required specification. Although even in a manufacturing environment the notion has its difficulties, because in a total quality culture 'right first time' applies equally to after sales service, enquiries and reception, and internal and external customers. In a college the translation will depend in part on the definition of the 'product' of a college. If students are seen as the college's 'product' the obvious translation of the standard is that all students will achieve their agreed aims from their college programme. This has a range of implications including the completion of an action plan for each student, having a system for monitoring progress, and taking corrective action if goals are not being met. It also involves having a system in place to ensure that the individuals' action plans will be implemented. 'Right first time' should mean that each and every student will make a success of their programme. This notion will cause enormous difficulties for colleges preparing students for external norm referenced examinations. Whether 100 per cent examination passes are aspirational targets or realistic goals will have to be a question of debate in the college.

TQM is accomplished by a series of small scale incremental projects. The philosophy of TQM is large scale, inspirational and all embracing, but its practical implementation is small scale, highly practical and incremental. Drastic intervention is not the means of change in TQM. Grandiose schemes are not the way forward because often they founder for lack of resources, and their demise can breed cynicism and discontent. Small projects seek to build success and confidence, and develop a further base for further improvements. The incremental approach means that implementation need not be a prohibitively expensive process. Spending money by itself does not produce quality, although carefully targeted it helps. What makes a difference is the people within the organisation and their motivation and commitment. Solid improvement is based on a long series of small and achievable projects. Over a period of time more is achieved this way than by trying to make large scale changes: 'The longest journey begins with a single step'.

TQM is management led and management driven. This is a key element, but one that often leads to misunderstanding for it does not imply that TQM is the responsibility only of the senior management. 'Management' in TQM reflects the idea that everyone in the organisation is the manager of their own areas of responsibility. However, staff will only work for quality if they are sufficiently empowered and have control over the essential aspects of their working lives. Quality circles and improvement teams only work if staff have both the power and authority to suggest and make changes. Senior management must give the lead and provide the vision and inspiration. The vision needs to be cascaded throughout the organisation. Many people, particularly in middle management, may find total quality difficult to accept and to implement. It involves a change in the management mind-set as well as a change of role. It is a change from the 'I'm in charge' mentality to one of management as both leader and supporter of the front-line staff. The key activity in colleges is clearly student learning, and the function of management is to enhance its quality and to support the staff who work with students. While this sounds obvious it is not always the way management functions are viewed. Traditional notions of status can lie uneasily with the total quality approach. TQM in effect turns the traditional college on its head and inverts the hierarchy of functions. It empowers the teacher and gives them a greater scope for initiative. A major function of management is to ensure the existence of effective teams and delegates to them the greatest level of responsibility combatable with the needs of accountability. Teams can only function effectively if they have the authority and resource to deliver quality.

TQM is about continuous improvement, it is not just another project. TQM is a journey and not a destination. For this reason TQM is not achieved, but is always something to be strived for. Organisations who are looking for the quick fix or a short term project for immediate impact will find little in TQM to attract them. TQM takes time to implement. People have to be convinced and taken along. Typical time spans are five years plus for programmes to make an impact. TQM is concerned with altering attitudes and working methods which are notoriously difficult to change.

Introducing TQM

A college seeking to introduce total quality needs to take a corporate overview of its planning process and it will initially need to tackle the following questions. Seeking answers to these questions provides clarity on the purposes of the institutions, its customers' requirements and the standards it needs to set.

— What is our mission?
— What business are we in?
— What do our customers expect of us?
— What do we need to be good at to meet customer expectations?
— What are our critical success factors?
— What are our critical processes?
— How are we going to achieve success?
— What means are we going to take to achieve success?
— Who should do what?
— How will we know if we have been successful?

The TQM planning process

There is no particular sequence when planning for quality. However, it is important to take a systematic approach to the planning of the corporate future. The following is a typical process for planning for TQM.

— What business are we in? *The Mission statement*
— What are our customers' expectations? *Market research*
— What do we need to be good at? *Critical Success Factors*
— What are our critical processes? *Process charting*
— What are we going to do? *Corporate and business planning*
— How are we going to deliver quality? *Quality planning*
— Who is going to do what? *Assign responsibilities*
— What will quality cost? *Quality costing*
— How do we know if we are successful? *Evaluation, monitoring and feedback*

Mission statements
These are nowadays well established in colleges. Some of the salient points of mission statements are:

(1) They need to be memorable and easy to communicate: 'We create Happiness' (Disneyland);
(2) The nature of the business should be clear;
(3) There should be a clear statement of the 'product range' being offered;
(4) It should include a commitment to quality improvement;
(5) It should state the long term aims of the organisation;
(6) It should *not* be a measure of performance;
(7) It should make reference to the customers.

Market research
TQM is based on responding to facts and data and not emotion. The planning process requires good market information and research. The purpose of market research is to establish the needs and wants of customers. Ideally, this should focus both on the current situation and on possible future scenarios.

Critical Success Factors
Critical Success Factors are indicators of what must be achieved if an organisation is to satisfy its customers and its mission statement. They are similar but not identical to the more familiar performance indicators. The difference between CSFs and PIs is that the latter are often generated by others and are not specifically related to the mission statement of the college or its customer requirements. CSFs are the key activities which the college identifies for itself.

A list of a college's Critical Success Factors should include external measures such as customer satisfaction as well as internal indicators such as the generation of income. The key to listing CSFs is to concentrate on the words *critical* and *success*. CSFs must highlight what has to be achieved and to what standard if a college is to achieve total quality.

Internal CSFs could include:

— Attainment of BS5750
— Greater customer satisfaction evidenced through surveys
— Improved examination pass rates
— Responsiveness to customer needs
— Improvements in teaching/learning strategies
— Improvements in teamwork
— Involvement of the majority of staff in improvement teams.

External CSFs could include:
— Increased market share
— Increased take up of provision by minority and disadvantaged groups
— Improved progression rates into employment and higher education
— Generation of additional income.

Process planning for quality

It is important to have a clear concept of the process by which the product of the college is produced and delivered. The quality of the final product depends upon the quality of the process which produces it. In turn the quality of the process depends upon an understanding of the factors which impact upon it. This exercise highlights the need to ensure that all the major components which impact on the quality of the process are identified. It is important to identify all the customers and suppliers, and to identify their requirements and your requirements of them. A typical organisation process diagram is shown in Figure 12.1.

Figure 12.1: Process planning diagram

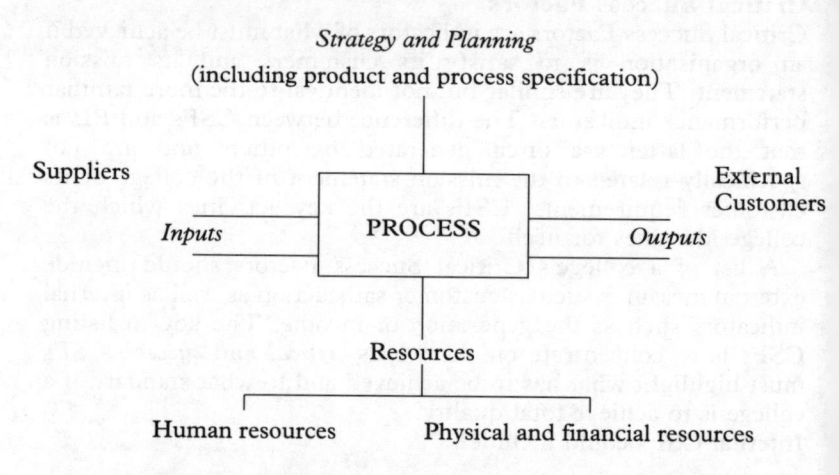

Strategy and Planning
(including product and process specification)

Suppliers → *Inputs* → PROCESS → *Outputs* → External Customers

Resources

Human resources — Physical and financial resources

Product and process analysis is required to ensure that all the components which are critical to the process of producing the product are correctly specified and delivered. Typical questions which need answers are listed below:

— What is the product?
— Is there a clear specification of the product?

- Is there a clear strategy to produce the product to specification?
- Have all the external customers been identified?
- Are we clear what external customers want and need from us?
- Are there gaps between the expectations of customers and the specification of the product?
- Can gaps between expectation and specifications be closed?
- Are the expectations of customers incorporated as fully as possible in the product specification?
- Have the suppliers been identified?
- Have the suppliers been as fully informed as possible about requirements?
- Are there gaps between supply and requirements?
- How are gaps between supply and requirements being closed?
- Have all the resource requirements been identified?
- Are the resources adequate to meet the specification?
- Are there gaps between the needs of the specification and the available resources?
- Can gaps in resource requirements be closed?
- Have the training needs of the staff been identified?
- Does the process to be used produce the product to the specification?
- Does the process meet the expectations of the customers?
- Have we defined what a successful outcome is?
- Have the critical success factors been identified for the process?
- Are there adequate monitoring mechanisms in place to measure success?
- Are there adequate feedback mechanisms in place to allow for self-checking and self-evaluation?

Corporate and business planning

The corporate plan details the measures which the college intends to take to achieve its mission. It sets a medium term time scale usually over a three year period. Its aim is to give the college guidance and direction. However, a plan is not a rigid instrument and should be modified if significant internal or external events require it. The business plan is the short term, usually one year, detailed plan for achieving particular aspects of the college's longer term corporate strategy. It contains concrete measures and the financial implications of putting them into operation. As well as the direct financial benefits and costs it should include the non-financial benefits such as enhanced reputation, increased profile etc.

The quality plan

Quality cannot be left to chance. The quality plan shows how the process of quality improvement is to be made and maintained. Clearly, it must relate closely both to the corporate and business plans but its focus is different. It outlines the processes to be taken in the medium term to deliver quality improvements. As a result the quality plan must have clear aims and objectives in relation to quality and the methods through which management commitment is translated into action. Additionally, it must detail the mechanisms through which staff can participate in quality improvement teams. The quality plan should detail the improvement projects which the college intends to carry out. This is the document in which the grand design and the large scale aspirations are turned into practical and manageable projects. Achievement is important in quality implementation, and the projects should be small scale and focus initially on some of the main problem areas in the college. Such a focus will signal success as well as bringing about positive benefits.

It is important to communicate the vision of the quality plan to staff. Without it will not be possible to harness commitment. It is people who make the quality difference. They produce successful courses and satisfied clients. Internal marketing is a useful tool in communicating the organisation's goals. Simply, the idea of internal marketing is that new ideas, products and services have to be as effectively marketed to staff as to clients. Staff cannot convey the message of the college to potential customers without proper product knowledge and an enthusiasm for the college's aims. Internal marketing is a stage on from communicating ideas. It is a positive and proactive process which demands a commitment to keep people informed and to listen to their feedback.

Measuring the benefits of quality – quality costing

Quality costing is about measuring the benefits of quality assurance. TQM should be approached from the standpoint of measurable benefits for the organisation and not from emotion. A quality improvement project should not simply be a good idea. Good ideas have to be measured, costed and evaluated.

Any project should be approached with the expectation that it will bestow benefits. Another way of appreciating the gains from TQM is to measure the cost of things going wrong – the costs of failure or nonconformance. Frustrated customers, inefficient or ineffective ways of doing things, and simple mistakes cost the organisation. The costs are various – lost business, angry students, lost enrolments, extra work, lost income. The TQM approach is to try to make things right first time every time and to aim for zero defects. Complaints must be taken seriously and rectified. The feedback loop is important. There must be a system which takes up complaints and looks into serious mistakes and ensures that the loophole which created them does not occur a second time.

'Right first time' is a difficult concept to implement in a human activity like education, but we should always aim to get it right the second time around. Making honest mistakes, however, should not be seen as a matter for blame. Honest mistakes can be the result of innovation and initiative, and excessive caution can be a double edged sword. The important thing is to minimise mistakes with clear systems and procedures, and good teamwork. Careful and thoughtful planning is an important means of getting things right first time. The test of a TQM organisation is how well it responds to mistakes, ensures that they do not reoccur, and learns the lessons for its future operation. Reoccurring errors and mistakes demonstrate a lack of system and ineffective or inoperative methods of feedback.

There are various ways of measuring quality costs, but an essential distinction can be drawn between the costs of prevention and the costs of failure. The costs of prevention are essentially those costs required to stop things going wrong and to ensure that things are done properly. Under this heading are the costs of quality assurance, the setting up of quality systems, the salaries of co-ordinators and quality managers, training, and supporting teamwork. These costs are direct costs and can be readily quantified. The costs of failure or non-conformance are often more difficult to measure and are usually opportunity costs, which are measured via lost opportunities and business. Included in these costs are student dissatisfaction, lost business, student failure, reworking and redoing things which should have been done correctly first time, time wasting and frustration. In fact, the things that take the pleasure out of managing and working in colleges.

The real costs of quality are those involved in eliminating non-quality. The aim with quality costing is zero quality costs. Quality costs are after all the cost of failure and non-conformance. Quality assurance is about preventing things from going wrong and ensuring that they are improved next time.

What are the barriers to implementing TQM?

Many of the barriers to implementing a total quality approach involve an element of fear and uncertainty. Fear of the unknown, of doing things differently, of having to trust others, of making mistakes are powerful defence and resistance mechanisms. W. Edwards Deming recognised this and the last of his famous 14 points is 'Drive out fear so that everyone may work effectively for the company'. Staff cannot give of their best unless they feel secure and are trusted. Being secure and trusted involves being able to express ideas, ask questions, and question decisions and established routines. It also can only exist if people are allowed the freedom to make honest mistakes. Total quality can only exist in an experimenting and self-critical institution.

Fear does not only affect the workforce. There is also the fear by management of adopting new methods and approaches. Too often there is lack of trust in the staff by management, and a belief that staff are responsible for the organisation's quality problems. The 85/15 rule of another 'quality guru' Joseph Juran is instructive here. Juran argues that as management controls 85 per cent of the decision-making then it is management which is responsible for 85 per cent of the quality problems. The professional autonomy of lecturers probably reduces the percentage in colleges, but the point of the argument remains. There can be a fear of disempowerment and loss of status by managers when confronted with many of the ideas of TQM. This combined with the comfort of the status quo is usually the reason why a start is not made.

Barriers can be overcome by sharing with staff the college's vision. They need to know where the organisation is going, how it will be different in the future, and the part they have to play in it. The leadership must come from the top. This does not imply that all the responsibility falls on the shoulders of senior management. Champions and leaders need to be recognised and celebrated. It is only by doing this that the inevitable scepticism and cynicism over new ideas can be overcome. The most powerful mechanism to move TQM along is training. This is expensive and time consuming and involves disruption, but there is no substitute for it.

Creating a quality college

> Obviously the obvious isn't so obvious or more people would be doing it
>
> (Peters, 1987)

The rewards for establishing a total quality college can be immense and should be quantified in the college's plan. Increase in enrolments, improved results, greater customer satisfaction, improved curriculum delivery are just some of the many potential benefits. In the industrial world fortunes have been turned around through taking the total quality route. The route is by now well trodden but just as hard. The driving force has to come from the top and the process has to be constantly nurtured and reinforced. Leadership is the key, but so is listening and learning. Managers must respond to suggestions from others as well as being a source of ideas. The task of management is to enhance staff commitment to quality improvement.

The management challenge is to carry all staff along the TQM route, but this should not be expected to happen overnight. Hundred per cent acceptance is an unrealistic goal. Cultural change is a long process. The industrial literature suggests that it is best carried forward by nurturing 'champions' and bringing people into the process by showing them the benefits. In industrial TQM organisations an often adopted performance indicator of success is the percentage of staff at all levels who voluntarily take part in improvement teams.

If a college aspires to be a total quality college it must act like one. It must innovate and drive ahead to achieve the vision contained in its mission statement. It should recognise that quality will always provide an edge in the market. Most importantly it must carry the message to its staff and ensure that they are partners in the process.

All organisations are different, and while external criteria and quality marks are important it is necessary for colleges to develop their own concepts and approaches. It should never be forgotten that people create quality. The task of management is to develop an improvement culture which will enthuse staff in order that they want to do a better job and to work towards total quality.

A reaction by many people to TQM is 'surely this is nothing new? It's just good management practice'. They are right. However, a caveat needs to be entered: 'It is good management practice *systematically applied and followed through*.' It is not just another good idea. Quality is long term commitment and has to be fought for and won. It requires both foresight and determination; breadth of vision and attention to detail, and it involves always paying attention and listening to the customer.

TQM is about partnership. It requires an internal partnership between the staff, the staff and the management, and the staff and the students. Equally necessary is a web of overlapping and interweaved partnerships of external customers – parents, schools, higher education, employers, validating bodies with the staff and management of the college. The standards of service required to meet the diverse and sometimes conflicting wants and needs of the partners will only be arrived at and met if the college has established the dialogue and has the mechanisms to plan the needs and to evaluate the results. Only by active partnership and responsive action will colleges survive incorporation and the needs of students be met.

Bibliography

General

Edwards Deming, W. (1986) *Out of the Crisis*, Cambridge: Cambridge University Press.

Juran, J. M. (1989) *Juran on Leadership for Quality*, New York: Macmillan.

Oakland, J. S. (1989) *Total Quality Management*, Oxford: Heinemann.

Peters, T. (1987) *Thriving On Chaos*, Pan Books.

Peters, T. and Waterman, R. (1982) *In Search of Excellence*, New York: Harper and Row.

Quality issues in colleges

Miller, J. and Dower, A. (1989) *Improving Quality in Further Education: A Guide for Teachers in Course Teams*, (Ware, Herts: Consultants at Work).

Miller, J. and Innis, S. (1990) *Managing Quality Improvement in Further education: A Guide for Middle Managers*, (Ware, Herts: Consultants at Work).

Miller, J. and Innis, S. (1990) *Strategic Quality Management*, Ware, Herts: Consultants at Work.

Sallis, E. (1990) 'Corporate Planning in an FE College', *Educational Management and Administration*, Vol. 18, No 2.

Sallis, E. (1990) 'The Evaluation of Quality in Further Education', *Education Today*, Vol. 40, No 2, Spring.

Sallis, E. (1990) *The National Quality Survey*, Mendip Paper MP 009, (Bristol: Staff College Blagdon).

Sallis, E. and Hingley, P. (1991) *College Quality Assurance Systems*, Mendip Paper MP 020, (Bristol: Staff College Blagdon).

Sallis, E. and Hingley, P. (1992) *Total Quality Management in Further Education*, Coombe Lodge Report, (Bristol: Staff College Blagdon).

Training Enterprise and Education Division of the Department of Employment (1990) *The Management of Quality BS5750 and Beyond*, (Sheffield: Employment Department).

13 In the pursuit of quality

Mike Ash

The pursuit of quality in state schools, particularly manifested in the inspection of the work of teachers, goes back to the end of the 19th Century when the state system was established. Many classic comments from school inspectors on the outcomes of their visits to schools have been documented and stand the test of time in terms of relevance to current issues. Education experiences and examples of practice, both good and bad, were identified and good practice disseminated. Many of the leading innovators and promoters of educational thinking between the world wars were HMI. Another key group of influencers were the teacher trainers. In Bradford the name of Macmillan is still remembered and cherished, as is Forster, who introduced a city wide system of schooling there before moving to London.

There is much current debate about HMI's role in promoting quality, or at least identifying situations where the quality level is unacceptable. Over recent years the inter-relationship between the centrally managed inspectorate and services run by local authorities has gradually but inexorably changed. As a young teacher I vividly recall being told that an HMI could dismiss a teacher summarily for not keeping a proper register. However, my main perception of the centrally managed inspectorate was in their role as 'monitors for the Secretary of State'. As a teacher, the idea of being 'inspected by HMI' seemed too remote to contemplate – like some sort of freak accident. The main thrust of HMI's work appeared to me to be the dissemination of exemplars and leading the development of educational thinking. At that time, local authority inspectorates (LAI) were mainly advisory and developmental. Often LAI teams consisted of advisers in those subject areas that had health and safety implications. The word 'Quality' might have been used about the work of students or, occasionally, an individual teacher, but it was not a regular part of the everyday language and culture of educational development. Similarly, the word 'Standards' – a much overused and underdefined word – was used in a very different context to the way it constantly appears today. If one was asked the question by a governor on one's views on 'standards' then it nearly always referred to 'standards of behaviour' or 'standards of dress'.

Ten to 15 years ago I had a number of interviews for deputy head and headships. I cannot recall the word quality, certainly in the sense that it is used today, being used at any time during those interviews. As an education inspector, and then officer, I have sat in on countless similar interviews over the last 10 years. I cannot recall any interviews over the last five years or so, where a candidate has *not* been asked his or her views on 'Quality' in education and how they would improve or promote it. Unfortunately, it has often been the case that the question is asked by one governor with an expectation totally contrary to the expectation of other governors. Such are the delights of obtaining senior management posts in schools in current times!

I moved from school management to become an education inspector. As well as purporting to be a specialist in mathematical education, promoting and developing this curriculum area in schools and colleges, I was expected to inspect all kinds of schools in the district and provide reports on those schools and colleges for their governing bodies. This process claimed to make those schools better. Not surprisingly Heads and teachers were very wary about both the process of inspecting and the reports produced. Governors were often torn between their natural inclination to defend the school and their understanding of their responsibilities as custodians of the interest of the pupils and parents. The process of formal inspection – be it 'structured visit', 'significant exercise' or 'full inspection' – is based on a philosophy of quality control. That is, identifying good and bad practice will enable those responsible for the schools to eliminate the bad and develop and disseminate the good. Simplistically, this has been described as the American industrial model, where quality control was exercised by supervisors checking on the work of operatives and faulty or inferior products being weeded out.

Looking back now it seems incredible that we actually believed that by reporting on what schools were doing wrong, whilst acknowledging that much of what they were doing was right, standards would actually improve or that schools would become more effective. It might have improved accountability, at least in the sense of giving information to members of governing bodies and education committees. The value of this activity was not perceived as commensurate with the resources required to support it and the intensive programme that was started in that medium sized London borough could not be sustained after two or three years. There is no doubt in my mind that this kind of exercise could continue to have a place in the system. HMI have been demonstrating for many years that the systematic and rigorous review of experiences in classrooms can lead to both a wider understanding of general issues and the ability to alert the system if a school or college is causing concern. It is interesting to reflect however that the system has not always been able to address this concern. It needs to be recognised that the ability to alert the system works most effectively when there is a general consensus amongst at least two of the three groups with responsibility for managing the education process (simplistically divided between teachers, governors and the LEA) that there is a real concern. I was not surprised to observe that, when HMI were recently critical of a Midlands grammar school, their analysis was rejected by the teachers and the governors because both groups were very satisfied with the examination results and behaviour of the pupils. With the coming of the *Education Reform Act (ERA)* and the new responsibilities of governing bodies, it is becoming increasingly clear that the quality control model is barely workable. The fact that much of the current debate is predicated on a belief that this model will enable schools to be more effective is a cause for considerable concern.

Many people working on the management and support of schools have already moved on to considering a concept often labelled as 'Quality Assurance' (QA). There are a great number of variations on the idea of quality cycles as part of the QA process. Essentially a policy framework provides a basis for advice and support for practice. This is reviewed and evaluated in order to inform policy development and identify the need for support. The cycle is regenerative and comfortable. The implication is that the values inherent within the process are shared by each of the constituent parties but different elements of the process are within the remit of different partners. For instance, formal review and evaluation might well be undertaken by advisers and inspectors, possibly building on self-evaluation within the school, whilst the responsibility for curriculum and school management policy frameworks rests with the teachers and governors, informed of course by the LEA Curriculum Statement and Management Development Policy, if such a thing exists!

The way that advice, support and development is delivered is becoming much more flexible as a result of the introduction of the local management of schools. The use of teacher trainers for traditional INSET activities is decreasing, whilst the establishment of 'clusters' of schools to support one another is rapidly expanding. Such clustering is a crucial part of the quality assurance process where it is working most effectively. It links the school based activities that are the fundamental building blocks of school development but have the risk of internalisation, with the external evaluation that can all too often be unrealistic in the specific context of the school. By using monies to release staff to work alongside one another and assist teachers with specialist expertise to disseminate their work in neighbouring schools much work on school effectiveness can be undertaken without the direct contact of an external facilitator.

The quality assurance model assumes that all the parties concerned recognise that the quality can be best assured by collaboration. It is also predicated on the belief that standards will not be raised without a process of development owned by all of the parties concerned.

The various models that fit the criteria of QA have had significant success but, I would argue, only in a context where the LEA is perceived as having the ability to control or at least influence the allocation of the resources necessary to enable developments to take place. Such a scenario is unlikely to be realistic in the future. Already it is being questioned in some LEAs and this will increase, particularly in the light of debate generated by schools considering Grant Maintained Status (GMS).

Recently many people working in the area of school improvement have looked at models that are inspired by the developments around 'Total Quality Management'. I prefer to call this 'Managing for Quality'. Such a model works on the basic assumption that all of the participants in the delivery of schooling understand what quality is and all are seeking to achieve higher standards. It is not necessary to tell teachers what is or is not effective learning. Rather, the process of management within the school must empower teachers to work together, discover for themselves how to articulate their aspirations and to support them in the review and development of practice. It would be easy to make the accusation that this approach is soft on accountability but it is fundamental that formal and rigorous accountability checks are built in. We must avoid a subversion of the process arising from its dependence on self-awareness and mutual co-operation. Consequently, there is an important role for the external facilitator. The managing process needs managing! The key point of difference from the traditional models described earlier is that the external facilitator does not come in with any predetermined view of what quality is and how it might be manifested. Nor does the external facilitator carry out the review for the school. The facilitator helps the constituent bodies set up management systems that bring out the understanding of quality that is inherent in the ability and commitment of the staff; an understanding that is informed, but not yet always fully articulated by parents, governors and the community generally.

So what does all this mean for the staff in schools, the governors and parents and LEA staff, such as advisers and inspectors? It means that any model being used to ensure quality must itself start from the work of the school itself. All too often LEAs have developed a policy for school evaluation, be it formal inspection or supported self-evaluation, and then asked schools to own it. Whilst there has been a fair measure of success when schools have seen it in their interests to make use of these processes to progress their own development plans it is noticeable that, in schools where advisers/inspectors might argue that improvement is most needed, the quality assurance process often seems to be least effective. If we are to promote the concept of managing for quality then we need to establish as a fundamental principle that the identification of quality must come from those people closest to the day to day operation of the school itself. This does not deny the role of local education authority including advisers and inspectors and other officers. The process of facilitating this identification will require very specialist expertise. The recognition by all parties concerned that such a process should apply is, in effect, the development of a whole LEA policy.

The most powerful examples of this model will involve a series of processes operating at different levels for each of the different constituent groups. Consequently, elected Members should themselves identify the quality measures that arise from their understanding of their political dogma, direct experience and the assimilation of professional advice. Each of the 'stake holders' will themselves be elements of this process and each part will be informed by, and will inform, the others. Although this sounds very complicated, the action required to make it work is far more straightforward. Schools recognise the need to produce a Development Plan. In doing so they will need to address the question 'what is quality education?'. Also they will need to address the performance measures that relate to the objectives identified. Support can be provided in order to help schools carry out this process and make them aware of the advantages of involving governors and other groups that have a legitimate view. These development plans should feed in to inform the strategic plan for the LEA. Again, the facilitating process will encourage elected members to interpret their policies in a context informed by the development plans of all of the schools. Similar processes are relevant when teams of officers and advisers/inspectors formulate their own objectives. By concentrating on this process, and the way it can be supported, we can see that the Director of Education and his/her staff will be able to provide both leadership and support by setting an example in how the service operates, producing their own development plan and sharing its understanding of what constitutes quality performance in classrooms.

This analysis does not necessarily require an organisation such as a local education authority to exist! The facilitation of the process could be provided by other agencies. In much the same way as distance learning has replaced much direct tuition, packs of resources could be used on a 'mix and match' basis. The issue then would be the validation of the organisations working locally and the accreditation of outcomes in a sufficiently rigorous manner so that the various groups can be held accountable. It seems to me that it is this validation process which holds the key to assuring quality in schools.

The processes of validation and accreditation envisaged in the model I am describing are not dissimilar to those seen in higher and further education and some aspects of industry. Central government is going to set up some kind of register of approved inspection organisations. There may well be scope for competition between different support agencies. A logical progression of this trend, particularly as traditional local authority services are passed out to the schools, could be that the residual role for LEAs will be one that concentrates on the representation of the interests of individual learners. In these circumstances it would be most practicable and appropriate for those interests not to be in conflict with the operational demands of being both an agency for accreditation and a provider of support service.

This analysis calls into question many of the assumptions that still remain concerning the LEA as the 'leading partner' in the maintained sector. It is becoming increasingly clear that the comfortable and often unchallenged relationship that has existed in the past is no longer sustainable. It is necessary to recognise that the LEA central staff, particularly officers and advisers, are not primarily in the business of the provision of learning opportunities. They are first and foremost in the 'evaluation and support' business. Once it becomes acknowledged that the schools themselves are the key people in the learning opportunities business then the relationship those schools, through their professional and lay management working in partnership, have with the other partners becomes more realistic and easier to define.

This type of model, involving the validation and accreditation of review processes is not new. The Oxford and Cambridge

Examination Authority (OCEA) has operated a scheme whereby schools could be validated against criteria that reflected a number of principles within agreed acceptable practice. Interestingly there are examples of this operating with evaluation teams including governors, parents and teachers themselves. The Technical and Vocational Education Initiative (TVEI) has also introduced some other interesting elements of review which build on the concept of accrediting process as well as product. It may well be that this idea is more easily acceptable within TVEI because the client and contractor relationship is fairly straightforward. The Training Agency (as it was then) has been providing all of the money and TVEI can be seen as a totally additional resource. Also, the emphasis on process has not been at the expense of 'going soft' on quantifiable outcomes.

The key principle here, and there is some risk that participants in the current political debate may lose sight of this, is that quality outcomes arise from quality processes. Gurus in the world of business have promoted this universal truth for many years. International leaders in management thinking like Tom Peters, and before him Demming, stress the importance of 'ownership of quality' by the front line staff. They showed, in some cases to an unbelieving group of traditional managers, that all workers must contribute in order to produce quality outcomes. This will only happen if each worker believes that he or she has a stake in the process. How can this be less valid for teachers? It is simply not true to say that more than a small minority of teachers are only interested in promoting their own value system. Teachers represent all aspects of society and the vast majority of classroom practitioners with whom I have worked wish to do a professional job effectively. They care about levels of literacy and numeracy, so berated in the popular press and want their pupils to get jobs. What they have learnt is that such qualities can not be inculcated by simplistic measures or assessed by one-off pencil and paper tests. A school that manages for quality gives the teachers a real role in providing the educational opportunities that are appreciated by the community the school serves.

So let us consider what this model means for schools themselves. I envisage a similar approach for this reviewing process as pertains for School Development Planning. There is no national 'pro-forma' for development plans but there has been a lot of guidance provided by LEAs and national bodies. Many plans have a similar structure although each has an individualised detailed format. While a number of schools have looked for some kind of standardisation, the process emerging has ensured that schools think about the issues for themselves, and devise their own solutions, without totally departing from the basic framework. Also, each School Development Plan will have a section on review and evaluation. A centrally agreed framework to the reviewing of schools will need to ensure that certain questions are asked and evidence is available to show that the school has addressed key issues and identified related criteria for evaluation. I envisage that such criteria will be drawn from a 'compulsory core' but there will be freedom to allow individual schools to identify those criteria that are most relevant to the targets identified within their own development plan.

This approach will only have credibility in the eyes of all of the partners and stake holders if it is able to be formally accredited. It may be that schools will have to submit the whole plan, including the process for self-review, to regional or national agencies. Bearing in mind the need that schools will have to draw on external agencies both to provide perspectives that will support evidence and for help in meeting targets, it might be more appropriate to have a local or regional inspectorate which could interact with schools individually.

It is necessary to review the argument being advanced in the light of the current move to inspect all schools on a four yearly cycle and to put such inspections out to tender. Whilst the details of the School's Bill currently going through parliament have still to be settled and detailed interpretations emerge (what, for instance, is a *connection* with the school which would not compromise impartiality?) it would seem to be clear that there is no going back to the previous structure of HMI and multipurpose local authority advisory services. There are many of us who believe that the system as outlined in the *Parents Charter* simply cannot work and will be revamped as quickly and ruthlessly as have the arrangements for assessment and much of the National Curriculum. However, there has been far less debate on the validity of the concept of quality control inherent within the model of inspection envisaged in the *Parents Charter* and several groups of people have been unimpressed by the Secretary of State's affirmation that by schools using delegated monies to buy in advisory support the concept of quality assurance is alive and well. Managing for quality would work in this environment, but only if school managers see the inspection as part of their own process. I am less concerned about the circumstances when the inspection team are critical than when the school is given a clear bill of health and consequently the process is, at best, irrelevant and, at most, counter-productive to the school's search for improvement.

The processes argued for in this chapter are those within and around the school as an institution – that is where young people are educated. The requirements of legislation may mean that parts of the process will have to be managed in new ways but the concept of improving effectiveness by seeing the teacher as the centre of quality assurance is fundamental. There is a view that the agency that provides the accreditation should not be associated with that providing the resources to support school development. This analysis does have shortcomings. The specific knowledge about the school, gained both by the observation of learning and long term links with pupils, teachers and governors, is such a valuable asset during both elements of the process. However, there will no doubt be a number of models developed around the concept of validation and accreditation of the review process and the most effective will prevail in due course.

To summarise my thesis: I am suggesting that the key element in improving the quality of educational provision in schools is linking the review process itself with the improvement of the effectiveness of practice. This must place the teacher and the learner, the school and its community, at the centre of the process. Quality assurance must be owned by those involved in managing the school. The government, be it national or local, must ensure that there is true accountability and consequently avoid the risk of 'professional collusion'. This can only be done in the post-Thatcher society by the establishment of a rigorous framework for review. The framework enshrines the processes involved rather than predicts the outcomes.

The degree to which other indicators of performance, such as exam and test results, truancy figures and financial measures, should be added to the core of the framework still requires resolution. However, the fundamental concept outlined is, I believe, the way maintained schools will develop strategies for improvement in the future. Only by concentrating on these essential concepts will they avoid destroying much of the effective work taking place within the current system of education. It is the development and support of quality processes in schools, not the preservation of any particular organisations, that are crucial for the future well-being of the education service in this country.

14 Improving schools: an approach to quality in Birmingham

Peter Ribbins and Elizabeth Burridge

Introduction

Ideas about how educational standards might be improved are legion, few have been carefully field tested. Since 1985 Birmingham has been engaged in the evolution of a radical approach to improving the quality of learning and teaching in its colleges. In June 1990, following months of preparation, the Education (Policy and Finance) Sub-Committee, approved the introduction of a similar approach to Quality Development (QD) in its schools. The Committee decided that: 'QD be piloted initially in a limited number of schools and evaluated fully before more extensive implementation'.

Following training of key teaching and advisory staff from each of a representative sample of 19 schools (one sixth form college, eight secondary schools, eight primary schools, one special school, one nursery school) in Autumn 1990, the pilot took place between January and December 1991. The evaluation was undertaken by a team from the Centre for Educational Management and Policy Studies (CEMPS), University of Birmingham. In January 1992 the team published its findings in *Proving, Improving and Learning in Schools: Towards Enabling a Strategic Approach to Quality*. In this chapter we report on aspects of the Birmingham experience and in doing so draw heavily on the findings of the evaluation.

Why quality development?

A paper from the Department of Trade and Industry claims:

> ... to believe that traditional quality control techniques, and the way

that they have always been used, will result in quality is wrong. Employing more inspectors, tightening up standards ... does not promise quality (DTI, 1991).

What is needed is to change:

> ... the focus of control from outside the individual to within; the objective being to make everybody accountable for their own performance, and to get them committed to attaining quality in a highly motivated fashion. The assumptions a manager must make in order to move in this direction are simply that people do not need to be coerced to perform well, [they] want to achieve, accomplish, influence activity, and challenge their abilities (*ibid*).

Similar assumptions underpin the approach to quality being developed within the LEA in Birmingham. In a report to the Education Committee, the CEO (January, 1990) expressed a desire to work with members and others:

> ... to develop a culture in which schools and colleges accept that they are responsible for the quality of the service they provide and the systems they use to develop and review their own performance.

All this suggests that worthwhile attempts to improve quality in schools entail self-evaluation.

From self-evaluation to supported self-evaluation

The idea of self-evaluation is not new. It became fashionable in the late 1970s. Elliott *et al* (1981) found more than half of all LEAs were developing self-evaluation schemes. But these schemes were by no means always successful in promoting improvement. Accordingly Birmingham has sought to develop an holistic, school based, LEA supported approach known as *supported self-evaluation*. The evaluation report is full of evidence that this approach has been successful in generating improvement. There are various reasons for this.

Firstly, staff within the pilot schools are enthusiastic about the project. They have, in effect, become partners with officers, advisers, trainers and others in encouraging other schools within the city to consider adopting the quality development approach. So successful have they been in this, that to date over 150 further schools have taken the first step in doing so.

If one reason for the success of the project has been the

enthusiasm of key staff, another has been the quality of the support they have received. This support has taken six main forms each of which is the subject of a chapter in *Improving, Proving and Learning* (Ribbins *et al*, 1992). In this chapter we shall discuss each form of support briefly.

A model for planning for quality development

The model of quality development underpinning supported self-evaluation is based upon a coherent framework of purposes, principles and working practices which has been embraced by each pilot school and interpreted to meet their particular context and quality priorities.

Supported self-evaluation has three main purposes: to improve learning and teaching (*improving*); to respond proactively to accountability demands (*proving*); to support the development of teachers as learners and of schools as learning communities (*learning*). After only one year, the Evaluation Team reported numerous examples of improvement in each of the pilot schools (*see* Ribbins *et al*, 1992, Chapter 3). Such improvements have taken place at three main levels. For pupils in learning and other outcomes including levels of attention, attendance, punctuality, behaviour, morale and commitment. For teachers individually and collectively in the nature and quality of teaching and other outcomes such as the desire and ability to work and learn together, and in levels of morale, confidence and commitment. For whole schools in the ability to innovate effectively and in an open and participatory way.

The principles informing quality development include:

(1) Building formative and summative evaluation activities into review mechanisms;
(2) A participative, collaborative way of working on monitoring and evaluation which involves all interest groups;
(3) Substantiating judgements made about worth or effectiveness by collecting evidence and setting it against open, agreed criteria;
(4) Negotiating access to information and consulting on data gathering techniques;
(5) Allocating clear roles and responsibilities for the co-ordination of monitoring and evaluation;
(6) Seeking qualitative and quantitative information;
(7) Allocating adequate resources to the monitoring and evaluation process;
(8) Identifying performance measures/indicators and inter-

preting data in context, taking into account opportunities or constraints which apply;
(9) Ensuring that the outcomes/findings of monitoring and evaluation are used – that they inform decision-making and wherever possible lead to prompt action being taken;
(10) Documenting the system and procedures developed for monitoring and evaluation (as well as the findings) and subjecting them regularly to review, preferably involving external moderation.

These principles amount to a demanding set of obligations. Even so, the evidence suggests that amongst those directly involved with the Pilot there is a high level of understanding and commitment to them.

The strategy through which the purposes and principles discussed above are to be enacted is development planning. To enable this a process model has been constructed. It offers a framework which can guide colleagues through the evaluation and development process rigorously and systematically but without inducing unduly restrictive practices. A key aspect of this process is an idea from industry of a 'quality shortfall' (or quality gap) – the gap between actual (where are we now?) and desired performance (where do we want to be?). This has been used successfully in development planning ranging from whole school to individual lesson planning.

Ideas have been drawn from the School Development Plans Project (DES, 1989, 1990, 1991). A four stage development sequence is suggested – audit (a review of strengths and weaknesses), construction (development priorities are selected and turned into specific targets), implementation (of the planned

Table 14.1: Development Planning and the Holly Model

(1) Audit, stock-taking	– 'Where are we now?'
(2) Objective setting	– 'Where do we want to get to?'
(3) Establishing Priorities, Target setting	– 'What do we need to focus on?'
(4) Identifying tasks responsibilities, roles, milestones	– 'How do we get there?'
(5) Progress review, formative evaluation	– 'How are we doing?'
(6) Success checks, final review, summative evaluation	– 'How have we done?'

priorities and targets) and evaluation (success of implementation is checked).

However, another approach, drawing on the ideas of Peter Holly (Holly, 1990), has been more influential in shaping thinking on development planning for quality during the Pilot. From his model a six stage cycle of development activity has been derived as set out in Table 14.1.

As with any evaluation activity, planners as developers must consider three main sets of questions:

— *What* information is to be collected and what criteria must be identified?
— *How* is the information to be collected and how are the criteria to be identified?
— *Who* is an appropriate source of information and/or criteria?

In diagrammatic form, these sets of considerations can be presented as in Figure 14.1

Figure 14.1: Evaluation and the generation of information
Information and criteria: three questions

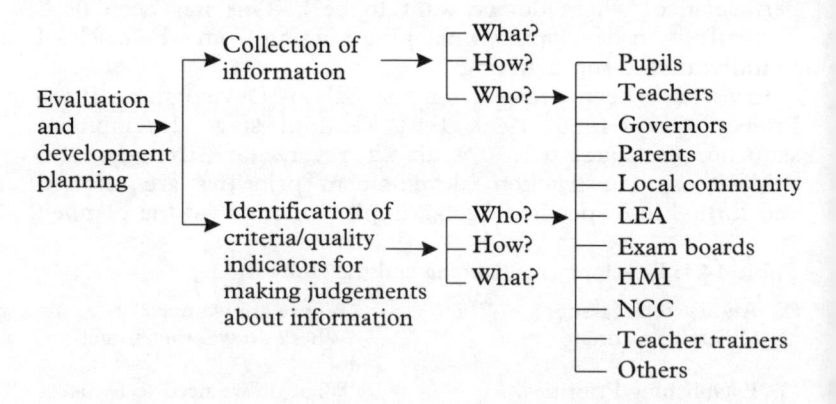

```
                    ┌─ Collection of     ─→ ┌─ What?
                    │  information          ├─ How?        ┌─ Pupils
Evaluation          │                       └─ Who? ─→     ├─ Teachers
and         ─→      ┤                                      ├─ Governors
development         │                                      ├─ Parents
planning            │                                      ├─ Local community
                    │  Identification of    ┌─ Who? ─→     ├─ LEA
                    └─ criteria/quality  ─→ ├─ How?        ├─ Exam boards
                       indicators for       └─ What?       ├─ HMI
                       making judgements                   ├─ NCC
                       about information                   ├─ Teacher trainers
                                                           └─ Others
```

If teachers are to be 'learners' and schools 'learning communities' they will need to learn to use a variety of evaluation research methods. There is evidence from the Pilot schools that this is happening and that the goal of teacher as researcher is realistic. Many who have tried express a sense of confidence in their skills and an enhanced sense of professionalism. As one put it:

Being involved in the action research has been a good experience. I found I could do it. It is some years since I have enjoyed my work quite so much.

The QD Approach entails a participative style. Pupils, parents, governors, officers, advisers, members of local communities and others can assist as sources of information, collectors of evidence, setters of criteria, interpreters of evidence, selectors of priorities and in other aspects of the development planning for quality process. As such, development planning as interpreted within the Birmingham approach should be a collaborative exercise characterised by a commitment to the participative notions of professional discourse and community involvement in which teachers and others work in partnership to enable improvement.

The notion of professional discourse entails that at each stage of the cycle of development planning, professional colleagues (teachers, advisers, officers) support one another to reflect critically and rigorously on the processes of development planning. This means they:

(1) Take collective responsibility for the task;
(2) Engage in a continuous process of reflection and analysis;
(3) Are constructively critical of practice and performance; and
(4) Are optimistic about the potential for future improvement.

These attitudes and practices apply equally whatever the educational context – whole school, curriculum or course team – in which development takes place.

The theory of community involvement envisages an open style of evaluation and planning in which teachers and many others are collectively involved and actively engaged in a continuous process of school improvement. Schools in the United Kingdom do not have a great reputation for this but several of the Pilot schools have begun to achieve a higher level of community involvement than has existed in the past. It is necessary to be realistic. In practice implementing a collaborative approach of this kind may come best in a series of stages. The Pilot also shows that as teachers become more confident in their ability to engage in effective development planning they are increasingly ready to welcome the involvement of others. Meaningful progress in this area must be carefully planned and imaginatively enacted.

The approach has other strengths. These include:

(1) Its secure foundation in the best thinking to be found in the available theoretical and practical literature on evaluation, development planning, the management of change, school effectiveness and school improvement;

(2) Its sound understanding of the practice of evaluation and development planning as this has evolved both nationally and within the colleges and schools of the city;

(3) Its commitment to the belief that evaluation and planning can be significant educational activities in their own right and properly conceived will reflect the best thinking on pedagogic practice;

(4) Its belief in an open, participative style of working;

(5) Its capacity to be useful at a variety of levels of simplicity or sophistication;

(6) Its flexibility; and

(7) Its understanding that what is required is an approach which is developmental in itself. One which is capable of future evolution.

The best test of the approach is the way it is regarded by those who have used it. As one Head, reflecting the views of many within the Pilot, commented:

> ... it offered us a model which has proved to be workable in practical terms partly because it is flexible enough to adjust to our circumstances and style of working ... the QD model can be taken and adjusted to all kinds of schools in terms of phase, size, or type. It is open but offers clear ways of working. For all these reasons staff have found it easier to grasp then some of its alternatives. Also it can be grasped at various levels and each level is useful in its own right as well as leading to the next. It is easy to grasp initially in terms of such ideas as 'Where are we now?', 'Where do we want to be?', 'What is the quality gap?', 'How do we get there?' Because you can present the thing to staff at the level they need it. They are not in any danger of being switched off by it and thinking it is not for them. It has come into the language of staff. You can be at a meeting and suddenly someone will say let's see this in terms of where are we, where do we want to be and how are we going to get there or they will say what does this mean for us if we think about proving, improving and learning. This has caught on. These catch phrases which we began by laughing at have become very important.

This framework of purposes, principles and practices has been at the heart of supported self-evaluation in Birmingham but the other five forms of support have also been important in enabling improvement. We will deal with each of these briefly.

External quality development consultancy support

The second form of support can be best described as external quality development consultancy. Staff in the pilot schools are clear they need such support. Without it schools risk becoming: 'too self-regarding and too introspective'. To avoid this they need the advice of a critical friend who knows the school well and what is happening in other schools. This role has, to date, been played by members of the local advisory service. One adviser has undertaken a careful examination of what can be involved in such support. In this study a taxonomy of 13 sub-roles are identified which include fire fighter, facilitater, negotiator, critical friend, status giver, confidence giver, comparer, enskiller, trusted confidant, celebrator, validator, critical observer and interventionist.

The evidence suggests that the role of advisers in supporting quality development within schools is complex and challenging. To carry it out effectively advisers need a good understanding of the approach and a high level of commitment to it. It should not be assumed that they can take on such a role without training and support. There is evidence from the Pilot and subsequently that those advisers who have attended pre-pilot training have tended to be the most effective external agents of support for schools taking on a quality development approach.

A comprehensive training package

If such external support for quality development, either through the advisory service or in some other way, is one keystone in the arch of supported self-evaluation, the provision of training is another. A model of training has been developed in which a tailored modular Advanced Certificate of Education course in monitoring and evaluation is at the core designed and delivered by the School of Education, University of Birmingham in association with the LEA. This course is constructed to introduce participants to the theoretical aspects of evaluation in educational contexts and of the role which such evaluation might play in facilitating effective development planning at every level of the school. It is also intended to equip teachers and advisers with the skills they require for this and an opportunity to try out their understanding as they work to introduce a quality development approach within their schools. To facilitate this the ACE is in two parts. A lead taught module in term one followed by two terms of project based work taking an action research approach with tutorial support. In the Pilot courses Heads, quality development co-ordinators and advisers from the schools were enabled to train together. There is a strong feeling among these staff that effective preparatory training is essential for staff who are expected to take a lead in introducing a QD Approach into their schools. They also believe that training together was the best way of organising this.

In the post-pilot phase, before any school comes on stream, it is entitled to have one member trained on the ACE. Given the number of schools in Birmingham, this means that 150–180 schools a year will have a member training from April 1991. To date some 200 teachers and advisers are at various stages of completion on the course.

The ACE is not the only form of training which is planned. The Evaluation Report develops ideas for a much more wide-ranging and flexible package of training which may be implemented shortly. This identifies the needs of eight groups – LEA officers, advisers, Heads and other senior staff, all teaching staff, governors and other stake-holders including parents. Such training is of four main kinds classified as intensive training, facilitating training, awareness raising and briefing. This amounts to a very ambitious and demanding programme but there is growing recognition of its importance.

Supporting networking and dissemination

Networking is assuming very considerable importance in some authorities. Dudley has been in the forefront of this. In a paper entitled 'Networking quality: the issue is quality improvement', its chief advisers argued that in educational contexts:

> The networking of quality leads to improvement and should operate ... at all levels of the organisation and within all other agencies with which it interacts. During the 1980s, Dudley ... undertook a planned programme of improvement founded upon the need to facilitate collaborative development. It created a structural framework based on networking which has permeated the whole authority ... the concept of the development network has achieved significant results not only in the areas of shared values and the quality of relationships but in the improvement of performance (Cleland, 1991).

Birmingham has taken a different path but there are many staff within the department and in schools willing to think imaginatively on such issues and to link them to the City's ideas on supporting quality development.

During the Pilot and subsequently, strenuous attempts have been made to encourage and support the development of a variety of networks amongst schools engaged in introducing QD. Many tasks have been identified for networking including stimulating and sharing ideas and experiences, creating support groups for staff leading on quality development and celebrating achievement.

As well as networking, a variety of events has been organised designed to disseminate knowledge of what has happened in the Pilot to schools which might be considering taking on a QD Approach. For example, in November 1991 three such events were held. Every one of the Pilot schools contributed and it is a mark of the growing reputation of the project within the city that teachers from almost 200 schools attended in twilight time and sometimes in foul weather.

Funding quality development

The fifth form of support for quality development has been the provision of a modest level of additional funding. This is significant for a number of reasons. Not least because it is widely felt amongst teachers and others that the LEA has something of a credibility gap to contend with in launching new initiatives. As one headteacher put it:

> It is very important that there has been a sum designated clearly as supporting the initiative. It was taken as a token that the LEA was serious about it and not just another example of trying to innovate on the cheap.

Six types of expenditure are identified – managing the project, consultancy and evaluation, training and associated cover, costs for teachers and advisers involved, an allocation of 0.2 fte (full time equivalent) staffing during the year for Pilot schools, a proposed allocation of 0.1 fte staffing for other schools during mainstream implementation. The funding allocated is specific to the project and has been used in a wide variety of ways. It is regarded as crucial to the success of the initiative in the Pilot schools:

> The extra resourcing has made a great deal of what we have tried to do possible. In a primary school we just do not have the resources to hope to fund a lot of this ourselves. I don't know what will happen when the funds dry up.

Management support for the project

Such projects need to be well managed. The small group of advisers, officers, Heads and consultants (the Quality Development Working Group) who have taken responsibility for this are highly regarded within the Pilot schools and beyond. Key staff from the Pilot schools have become partners with the QDWG in mainstreaming the project. As might be expected in a project of this complexity and size, there have been difficulties. Some have focused on the issue of which Directorate (Policy and Finance or Services) should manage the project strategically. Others have been due to inadequate professional, administrative and clerical support for the QDWG at key times.

The evaluation report stresses that the Pilot has been a success but identifies issues for the LEA to consider in thinking about how it might embed the QD approach within schools and evolve an approach to quality which builds upon but goes beyond quality development.

Embedding quality development in schools

It will take time for schools to embed an approach to quality appropriate to their circumstances. Reflecting on previous experience, learning from the Pilot and analysing the literature on change a three year, nine stage development sequence seems appropriate. Year 1 focuses on preparation.

Figure 14.2: Year 1: Preparing for quality development

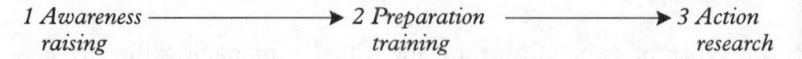

1 Awareness raising ⟶ *2 Preparation training* ⟶ *3 Action research*

The main purposes of awareness raising are to enable those concerned in schools (initially teachers but also governors and other members of the school community) to get to know what is involved in implementing a QD approach and to develop a commitment to it. Once a decision has been taken to involve the school in taking on such an approach it is necessary to determine how this is to be progressed.

A key aspect is the selection of the member of staff who will undertake preparation training in quality development. This is a critical decision since whoever attends the ACE should be expected and expect to play a major role in implementing and supporting quality development within the school in the future. Studies in the Pilot schools demonstrate how crucial the role of the Quality Development Co-ordinator (QDC) usually is. However, if the selection and training of this key role holder is crucial, the experience of the Pilot is that there are major benefits if other members of staff, and in particular Heads, have an opportunity to undertake some form of preparation training.

The purposes of preparation training include enabling course members to develop an understanding of what is involved in the quality development approach and in planning and preparing for action research. Undertaking such action research offers a critical opportunity for QDCs to try out, test and learn from the experience along with other members of the teaching staff and the wider school community. The project(s) which constitute the substance of the action research offer schools a chance to tackle an aspect (or aspects) of their practice, preferably identified as a priority in the Development Plan, which they feel they can improve. The projects need to be significant, involve as wide a range of staff and others as practicable, and demonstrate some early success.

This phase aims to increase understanding of and commitment to the approach among teachers and other members of the school community. Experience from the Pilot suggests it should not be skipped and cannot be rushed if the second stage is to be achieved.

Embedding the quality development approach is the focus of Stage 2 of the development sequence.

Figure 14.3: Year 2: Embedding quality development

4 Transition ⟶ *5 Embedding* ⟶ *6 Policy making*

Transition can take place in a variety of ways. In many of the Pilot schools this has been mediated by a dissemination of the findings of the action research project(s). It is important to be clear about what the object of such dissemination is and about how this phase of the development sequence leads to the next. If a project is not regarded as having a worthwhile outcome it may be necessary to repeat aspects of the preparation stage before continuing. What is more likely, is that the project is seen as having been successful and the need for another project identified. If undertaken by the same group of staff as before, this is unlikely to contribute much to developing a planning for quality ethos at every level in the school. One or two of the Pilot schools experienced some difficulty in making this transition because they almost got stuck in a closed project loop.

The test of embedding lies in the extent to which the approach is used by those who were not members of the initial core project group. This can be enabled by the latter in a variety of ways. They can use aspects of the approach in monitoring and evaluating their own activities or help others within the groups and teams in which they work to do so as well. In the context of the whole school the Head, the SMT and QD co-ordinator have important roles to play in embedding the approach. In its ideal form such embedding will involve teachers and other members of the school community. This has started to happen in some Pilot schools. In one case, a school has made a sustained effort to enable the development of a planning ethos amongst both staff and groups of pupils.

In the sixth phase, which is concerned with policy making, the critical decision focuses upon when a public statement of commitment to the new approach is to be made. This is not an easy decision – too early a declaration might provoke opposition or even derision, too late and momentum might be lost and confidence diminished. In most cases it is wise to have secured the prior commitment of key groups within the school's community and to be able to present evidence of effective quality development practice across a range of school activities.

Policy making may constitute a bridge between the second and third stages of the development sequence:

Figure 14.4: Year 3: Implementation and maintenance

7 Policy making ⟶ 8 Implementation across the whole school ⟶ 9 Maintenance

If the first six phases are conducted successfully then the last two should be relatively straightforward. Phase seven, implementation across whole school, entails the application of the principles, purposes, procedures and practices of QD as a routine aspect of the working life of the school. When this is achieved to describe such a school as a 'self-evaluating' institution will entail much more than this has meant in the past. Finally, to achieve such a status is one thing, to sustain it another. To achieve the latter regular review and renewal will be necessary – we may call this phase maintenance.

Such a development sequence is challenging but can be achieved by any school determined enough. Support is necessary, for some more than others. Ensuring schools get this support has important implications for the LEA.

The LEA and QD: from project to strategy

In supporting quality development in schools, the LEA is making a significant contribution to a process which has a fine chance of leading to improved standards of pupil achievement throughout

Birmingham. But important as this contribution has been, it may not be enough because:

(1) What is required is a comprehensive approach to quality integrating the best of quality assurance and quality control with quality development;
(2) It is not only schools that need to change. So too does the LEA.

Towards a comprehensive approach to quality

Three concerns are expressed about QD. Its long term orientation, its lack of a quality assurance dimension and the absence of quality control through inspection. As one officer put it:

> A difficulty I have with self-evaluation based approaches is that whilst it is crucial for improving standards, it is a long term approach taken City wide ... I am not sure it can give me an immediate audit of what standards are in Birmingham as a whole or even in individual institutions ... in the short term anyway, its gains are not for parents, pupils and communities rather they are for teachers and schools ... I support it, I welcome it, I regard it as a very good initiative. I hope that we can extend it but we do need to add an inspectorate bit as soon as possible as well to give us an audit of where we are in terms of standards.

The ILEA's penchant for undertaking general quality assurance surveys which reported on educational standards and offered templates against which the performance of the city as a whole, part of the city or an individual school could be judged was mentioned with approbation.

These are minority views, but many believe the education service needs a strategic approach to quality which builds on quality development but goes beyond it. One imaginative proposal is predicated on the belief that any acceptable approach requires careful thinking about the roles and functions of the different groups which make up the education service, the clients they serve, and their different accountabilities in respect of quality (*see* Table 14.2).

A sophisticated model for implementing such a strategic approach has been constructed (*see* Figure 14.5). It builds on the eight stage development sequence for schools outlined above and seeks to match these with appropriate operational mechanisms for support – for monitoring progress, for assuring the validity of schools' self-evaluation systems and for assuring the quality of the service as a whole.

Figure 14.5: Quality development — the development sequence

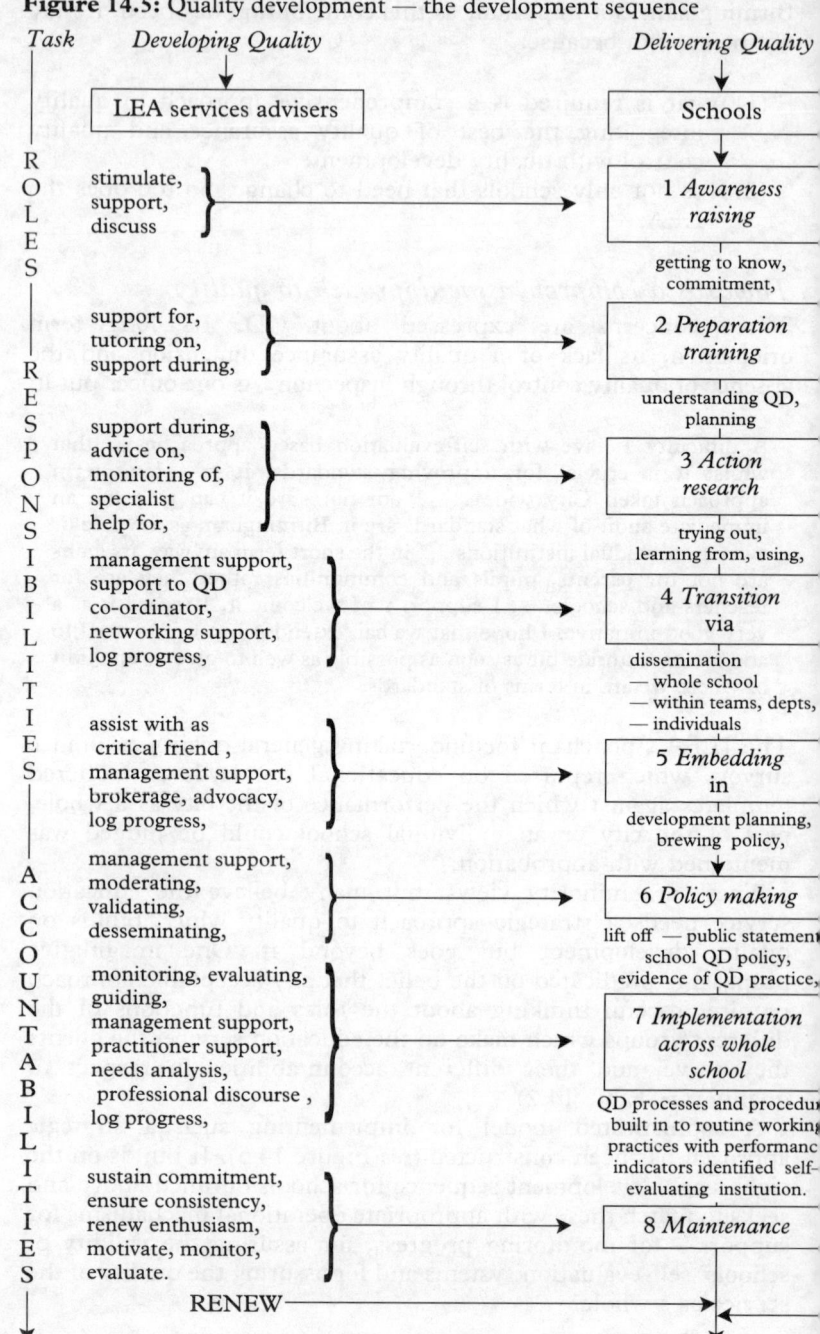

Task	Developing Quality		Delivering Quality
	LEA services advisers	→	Schools

ROLES — RESPONSIBILITIES — ACCOUNTABILITIES

LEA services advisers		Schools
stimulate, support, discuss	→	1 *Awareness raising*
		getting to know, commitment,
support for, tutoring on, support during,	→	2 *Preparation training*
		understanding QD, planning
support during, advice on, monitoring of, specialist help for,	→	3 *Action research*
		trying out, learning from, using,
management support, support to QD co-ordinator, networking support, log progress,	→	4 *Transition via*
		dissemination — whole school — within teams, depts, — individuals
assist with as critical friend, management support, brokerage, advocacy, log progress,	→	5 *Embedding in*
		development planning, brewing policy,
management support, moderating, validating, desseminating,	→	6 *Policy making*
		lift off — public statement school QD policy, evidence of QD practice,
monitoring, evaluating, guiding, management support, practitioner support, needs analysis, professional discourse, log progress,	→	7 *Implementation across whole school*
		QD processes and procedures built in to routine working practices with performance indicators identified self-evaluating institution.
sustain commitment, ensure consistency, renew enthusiasm, motivate, monitor, evaluate.	→	8 *Maintenance*
RENEW	→	

Quality and Standards

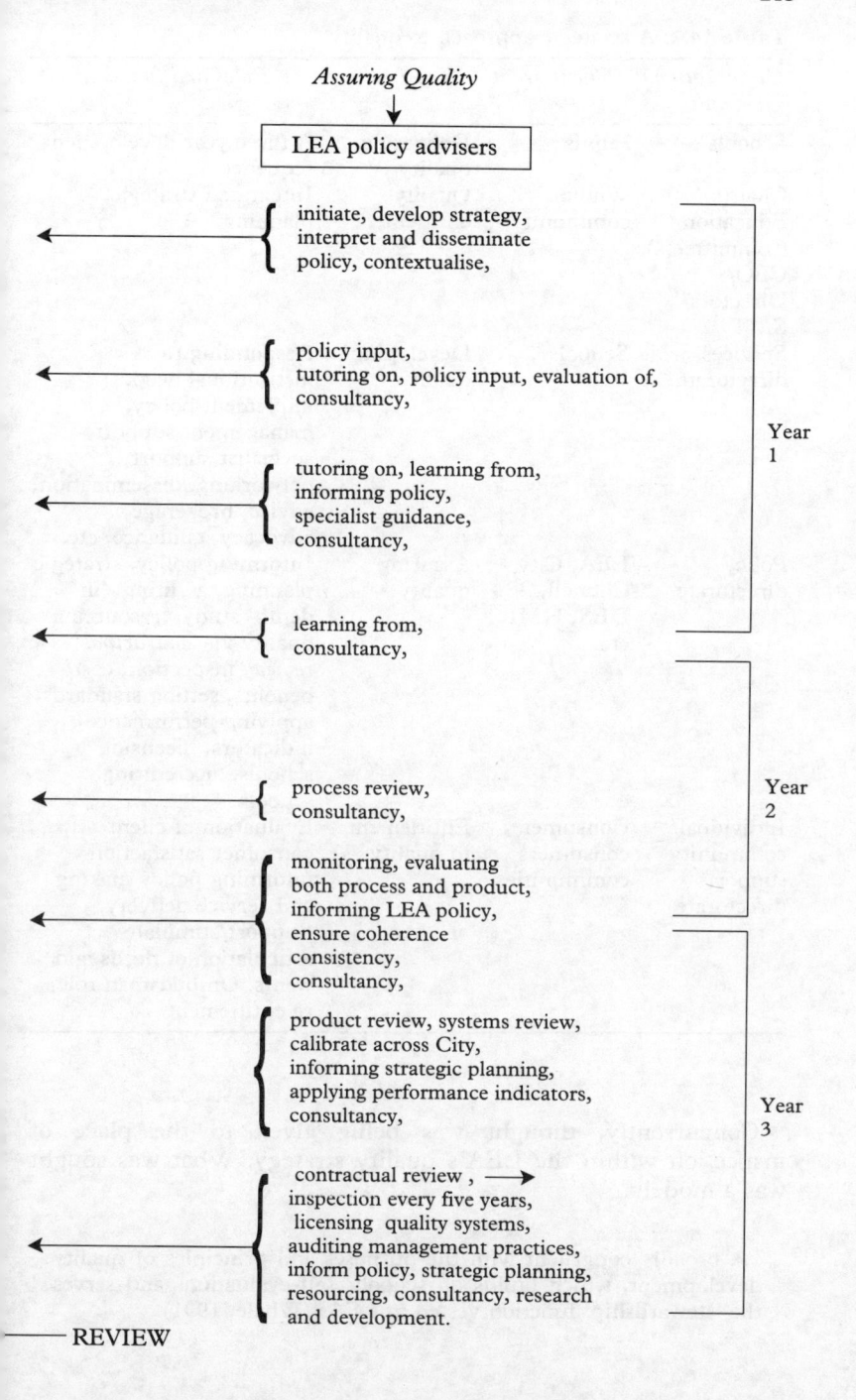

Assuring Quality
↓

LEA policy advisers

⟵ { initiate, develop strategy, interpret and disseminate policy, contextualise,

⟵ { policy input, tutoring on, policy input, evaluation of, consultancy,

⟵ { tutoring on, learning from, informing policy, specialist guidance, consultancy,

⟵ { learning from, consultancy,

} Year 1

⟵ { process review, consultancy,

⟵ { monitoring, evaluating both process and product, informing LEA policy, ensure coherence consistency, consultancy,

} Year 2

⟵ { product review, systems review, calibrate across City, informing strategic planning, applying performance indicators, consultancy,

⟵ { contractual review, ⟶ inspection every five years, licensing quality systems, auditing management practices, inform policy, strategic planning, resourcing, consultancy, research and development.

} Year 3

—— REVIEW

Table 14.2: A strategic approach to quality

Organisational unit	Client group	Key function	Roles and functions
Schools	Pupils	Delivering quality	A three year development sequence
Chair(s)/ Education Committee(s); CEO/ Directors/ SMT	Whole community	Quality entitlement	Integrated strategic planning
Services directorate	Schools	Developing quality	Responding to institutional need; implement policy, management support, specialist support, networking, dissemination, advice, brokerage, advocacy, guidance, etc.
Policy directorate	LEA, City Council, DES, HMI, etc.	Assuring quality	Informing policy, strategic planning, auditing, 'in-depth' study, 'resourcing' quality via *contractual review*, inspection, cost/benefits, setting standards, applying performance indicators, 'licensing' schools, 'accrediting' schools
Individual/ community support directorate	Consumer consumers communities	Entitlement to quality	Evaluation of client, consumer satisfaction informing policy making and service delivery. Support/stimulate articulation of needs and wants. Ombudsman role re entitlement

Concurrently, thought was being given to the place of inspection within the LEA's quality strategy. What was sought was a model:

> ... broadly congruent with the purposes and principles of quality development, which builds on schools' self-evaluations and serves the 'stewardship' function vested in LEAs (Whale, 1991).

Quality and Standards

A consultation document, *The Role and Purpose of Formal Inspection*, was disseminated. In this, an eight stage process was proposed which located inspection within a general strategy reflecting the cycle of development planning tested by the Pilot schools (*see* Figure 14.6).

Figure 14.6: Quality development — the LEA process

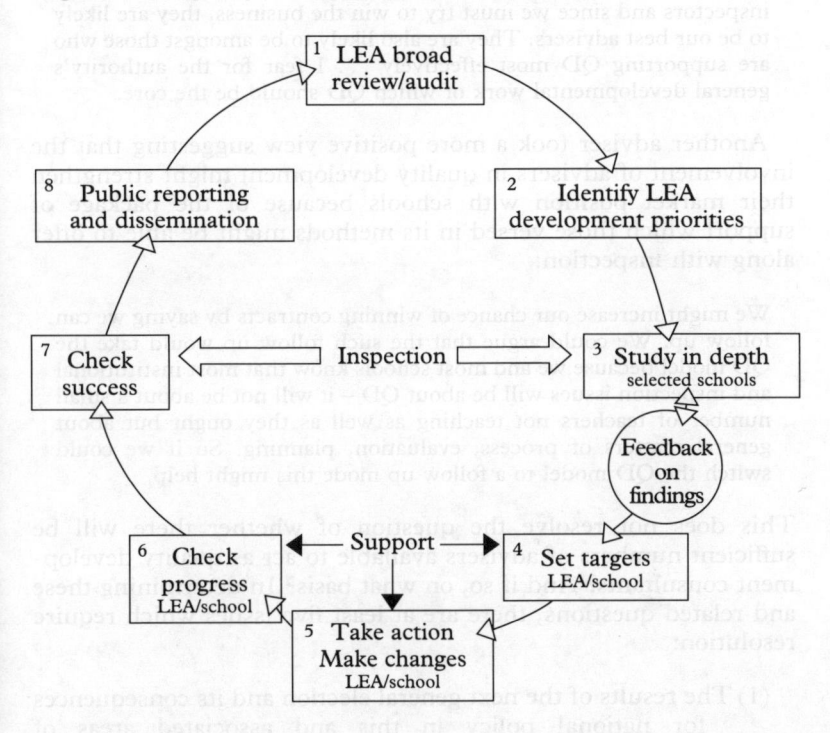

```
              1 LEA broad
                review/audit
         ↗                    ↘
8 Public reporting         2 Identify LEA
  and dissemination          development priorities
        ↑                         ↓
7 Check        ⇐ Inspection ⇒  3 Study in depth
  success                        selected schools
                                    ↓
                               Feedback
                                  on
                               findings
        ↑                         ↓
6 Check   ← Support →          4 Set targets
  progress                        LEA/school
  LEA/school    ↖           ↗
              5 Take action
                Make changes
                LEA/school
```

Four main purposes for inspection were identified:

— To facilitate essential accountabilities;
— To target action and support;
— To develop understanding of the city-wide context;
— To comply with the legislation.

Within weeks of the publication of the LEA's consultation document the Government produced its *National Parents Charter* and followed this shortly afterwards with the *Education (Schools) Bill*, 1991.

Understandably, there is confusion as to the implications such legislation might have for the LEA's proposals on inspection. Some argue it threatens the whole of the LEA's quality strategy:

> This could have enormous consequences for quality development .... It seems to me that if we do win the inspection business, and that is a big if, then most of our time will have to be spent on inspection ... I think a number (of advisers) will become full time inspectors and since we must try to win the business, they are likely to be our best advisers. They are also likely to be amongst those who are supporting QD most effectively ... I fear for the authority's general developmental work of which QD should be the core.

Another adviser took a more positive view suggesting that the involvement of advisers in quality development might strengthen their market position with schools because of the package of support which those versed in its methods might be able to offer along with inspection:

> We might increase our chance of winning contracts by saying we can follow up. We could argue that the such follow up would take the QD model because we and most schools know that most institutional and inspection issues will be about QD – it will not be about a small number of teachers not teaching as well as they ought but about general matters of process, evaluation, planning. So if we could switch the QD model to a follow up mode this might help.

This does not resolve the question of whether there will be sufficient numbers of advisers available to act as quality development consultants? And if so, on what basis? In determining these and related questions, there are at least five issues which require resolution:

(1) The results of the next general election and its consequences for national policy in this and associated areas of educational policy;
(2) The precise details of the Government's proposals in this are to date uncertain and these may not be fully resolved for months yet;
(3) The level at which the City Council is willing and able to sustain establishment within the advisory service under its existing terms of reference;
(4) The level of involvement of the advisory service in inspection and what this means in practice;
(5) The way in which this involvement is organised and what implications this may have for the ability of advisers to offer worthwhile support to schools.

Whilst there are serious criticisms which might be advanced against aspects of the inspection approach proposed within the Bill, there may still be many good reasons why the LEA may wish to register one or more inspection services. Not least amongst these is the probability that the service the LEA could offer, given the experience and quality of its advisory service, would be much superior to the great majority of likely alternatives. Furthermore, to opt out of undertaking such inspections would diminish the knowledge the LEA has of its schools and would detach inspection from advice and development support.

Quality development for the LEA

For many teachers, advisers and officers the holistic approach to quality described in this chapter is relevant not only to schools but to how the LEA itself should plan for development. Only then will a promising project in quality metamorphise into a successful strategy for improvement. As one officer put it:

> I don't see quality development as an isolated initiative or just for schools. I see little point in the authority launching off on yet another isolated initiative at a time when we desperately need to develop a coherent approach to *ERA* and subsequent legislation. I have a sense of relief that through QD the LEA seems serious about wanting to develop a coherent approach across all its activities. One which provides a unified framework, which will shape the culture for the many innovations expected of schools and the LEA.

There is growing clarity about the framework which will make this possible. At a fundamental level it entails a cultural shift at every level in the local education service and significant changes in the structure of relationships between schools and the LEA. Various attempts have been made to describe what might be required but the simplest and clearest representations we have come across was in the document setting out the LEA's proposals on inspection. This emphasised that the quality strategy implied a new partnership between the LEA and its schools along with the introduction of processes which applied to schools and the LEA and in their relationship with each other.

The difficulty of achieving a QD strategy outlined in Figure 14.7 at the level of the LEA was recognised and often forcefully expressed by officers and advisers. As one stressed, the traditional ethos of the Education Department and the attitudes of officers at every level would have to change:

> The Quality Development Initiative is about the idea that you can make things better. But if LEAs are to survive we must change the

Figure 14.7: The QD strategy towards a new partnership

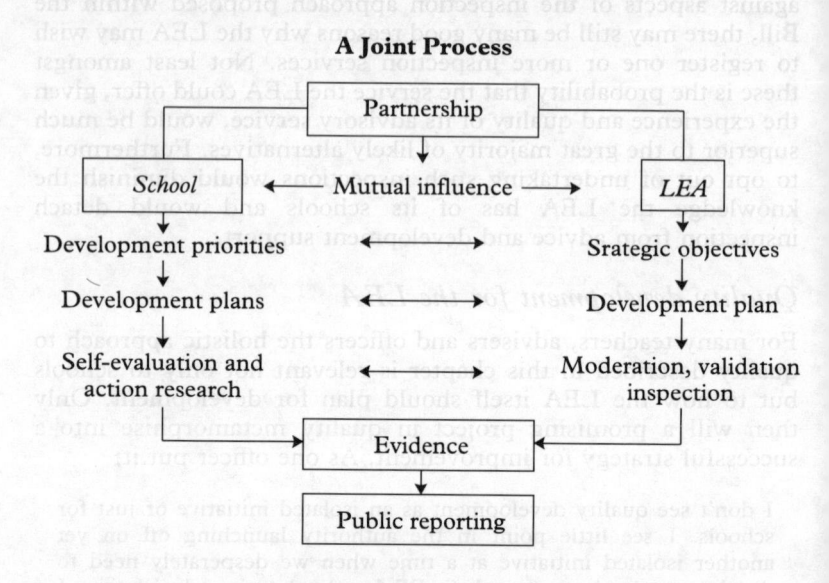

```
                    A Joint Process

                      Partnership
        ┌─────────────────┼─────────────────┐
     School  ←──── Mutual influence ────→  LEA
        │                                     │
        ↓                                     ↓
  Development priorities  ←──────→   Strategic objectives
        │                                     │
        ↓                                     ↓
  Development plans      ←──────→    Development plan
        │                                     │
        ↓                                     ↓
  Self-evaluation and    ←──────→    Moderation, validation
   action research                        inspection
        └─────────────────┬─────────────────┘
                          ↓
                       Evidence
                          │
                          ↓
                   Public reporting
```

bureaucratic culture that has characterised them in the past. This will be a devil of a job to achieve because it is so entrenched. For the LEA to make the contribution it can to the success of the QD initiative, it must change this culture of bureaucracy. If we are to survive, we must change, not only in schools but in the LEA and in every other aspect of education. This will take time and but I am not sure how much we have.

Achieving a coherent quality development driven approach across all aspects of our service is something to be looked at long term. It could be the work of a decade.

This is not to say there will be no benefits along the way. Some are already plain to see as we have tried to show. Others will come. Even so it is necessary for all involved to be patient and steady in their determination to see things through. This has been the experience of many of those who have led on the project within the Pilot schools and their experience is too important not to learn from.

Summary and conclusion

In this chapter we have sought to describe an approach to quality development in colleges and schools based upon the notion of supported self-evaluation which the LEA in Birmingham has been involved in since 1985. More recently the authority has been considering how it can extend this approach in two main ways. Firstly, by encouraging all its schools to implement the approach. Secondly, by devising a strategic approach to quality which builds on quality development but which makes the best use of ideas from quality assurance and control. This exciting vision has now been put at risk by the proposed legislation contained in *Education (Schools) Bill*, 1991. In comparing the two approaches to school improvement and standards of pupil achievement discussed above we would stress that unlike the Government's proposals for inspection, Birmingham's approach has been carefully piloted and evaluated.

References

Cleland, I, (1991) 'Networking quality: the issue is quality improvement' in Burridge, E. and Ribbins, P. (Eds) *Improving Schools: The Issue is Quality*, London: Cassell (forthcoming).

DES (1989) *Planning for School Development*; London: DES.

DES (1991) *Development Planning*, London: DES.

DTI (1991) *Total Quality Management: A Practical Approach*, London: DTI.

Elliott, G. *et al* (1981) *Self-Evaluation and the Teacher: An Annotated Bibliography and Report on Current Practice*, University of Hull/Schools Council.

Hargreaves, D. and Hopkins, D. (1991) *The Empowered School*, London: Cassell.

Holly, P. (1990) *School-Based Development in Action*, London: IMTEC.

Ribbins, P., Butterfield, S., Chitty, C., Edinborough, T. and Kirkpatrick, G. (1992) *Improving, Proving and Learning in Schools: Towards Enabling a Strategic Approach to Quality*, Birmingham: University of Birmingham.

Whale, E. (1991) 'Quality development: LEA case study' paper delivered at the *BEMAS National Conference* in Leeds.

Index

Abitur, 74
academic/vocational divide, 4, 7
activity led staffing, 24
admissions appeals, 141
Advanced Certificate of Education, 205, 206, 208
Advanced Placement, 58, 63, 64
America 2000, 58
Anderson, Eric, 114
Annual Report, 158
appeals, 113
apprenticeships, 33
Assisted Places Scheme, 35, 56, 140
Attainment Targets, 7, 92, 101, 102, 103, 119
Audit Commission, 17, 22, 23, 130
average salaries, 132
BS5750, 13, 41, 171, 172, 181
BSI, 16, 172
BTEC, 7, 36
baccalauréat, 73, 74, 79, 80
Barnett, Corelli, 2
basic skills, 54
Birmingham, 12, 198–219
Black Papers, 31, 53
British Social Attitudes Survey, 3
British Standards, 16
CBI, 37, 40, 227
CTC (City Technology College), 6, 35, 56, 125, 127, 129, 130, 135, 143, 148
COMETT, 80
Cambridgeshire, 23
capping, 133
champions, 186, 187
comparability, 112
competence, 71
competition, 79
comprehensive school (isation), 31, 138, 139
Conservative, 139, 140, 141
consumerism, 9, 11, 153
coursework, 126, 134
Criterion of Need, 99, 100
critical success factors, 181, 182, 183
customer-supplier chain, 177
Demming, W. Edwards, 174, 175, 186, 195
DTI (Department of Trade and Industry), 34, 40
Denmark, 77, 81
direct grant schools, 136, 140
EC (EEC), 13, 68, 69, 76, 84
ERASMUS, 80
Education Act 1944, 134, 136, 137, 143
Education Summit Meeting, 57
embedding, 209, 210
enterprise culture, 29, 30
entitlement, 3, 10, 120, 127, 176
equal opportunities, 8, 38, 39, 70
Examination Boards, 89–104
examination results, 26
excellence, 53, 61, 63
external facilitator, 192
FEFC, 170, 177
France (French), 72, 73, 75, 78, 79, 81, 83, 115
GMS (Grant Maintained Schools), 125, 129, 130, 131, 133, 135, 147, 192
GNVQ, 36, 40
German(y), 2, 32, 71, 74, 75, 82, 115
governing bodies, 155–165

grade boundaries, 98, 111, 112
grade inflation, 108
grammar school, 136, 137, 138, 140
Great Education Debate, 119
gymnasium, 82
HMC, 105, 108, 116, 120, 121
HMCI, 5, 121
higher education, 6, 108, 113, 115, 139, 187
human capital theory, 30
ILEA, 125
independent schools (sector), 5, 117, 120, 122, 123, 127, 129, 136, 137, 140
internal marketing, 184
International Baccalaureate, 107, 122
Investors in People, 29
JMB, 110, 111
Juran, Joseph, 174, 187
Key Results Areas, 158–164
Key Stage, 1, 95, 100, 101
Key Stage 3, 94, 95, 96
Key Stage 4, 91, 96, 97, 98, 101, 102, 103, 127
LINGUA, 80
LMS (Local Management of Schools), 6, 28, 132, 147, 164, 191
Labour Party, 138, 139, 140, 141
league tables, 11, 123
MSC, 5
Mathematics Working Party, 4
manufacturing industry, 30
mittlere Reife, 71
modular schemes, 100
multiculturalism, 55
NCC, 4, 5, 6, 8
NVQ, 7, 36, 37, 40, 170
National Council on Educational Standards and Testing, 51
national strategic plan, 141
Netherlands, 73, 75, 76, 79, 80, 81, 82
networking, 206
new vocationalism, 35
North of England Conference 1991, 98

numerical modelling, 18
nursery education, 140
OCEA, 195
open enrolment, 147
parents, 81, 147–154
Parents' Charter, 77, 196
performance indicators, 29, 70, 147, 148, 169, 187, 197, 200, 212
poll tax, 133
portfolio analysis, 60
Portugal, 74
primary schools, 6
process planning, 182
Programmes of Study, 7, 106
project methods, 10
quality assurance, 11, 12, 13, 25, 170, 171, 172, 173, 175, 191, 197, 219
quality circles, 179
quality control, 11, 25, 190, 211, 219
quality development, 11, 198–219
race question, 37
records of achievement, 128
regression analysis, 21, 24
right first time, 178
Ruskin speech, 1, 32, 35, 148
SAT (Scholastic Aptitude Test, USA), 46, 47, 48, 58, 59, 61, 62, 63
SEAC, 4, 5, 93, 94, 95, 97, 99, 110, 111, 112
SMART, 162, 163
school development plan, 157, 161, 163, 193, 195, 196
school (self) evaluation, 81, 191, 193, 199–219
Scottish Baccalaureate, 107
scrutinies, 113
secondary modern, 138, 139
sensitivity analysis, 20
Sobell, Tom, 8
Social Charter, 32
Spain, 72, 76, 81
special educational needs, 144
standard spending assessment, 132
Suffolk, 12

Index

TEC (Training and Enterprise Council), 41, 169, 170, 177
TGAT, 92
TQM, 169–185
TVEI, 35, 36, 38, 39, 143, 195
Taylor Committee, 148, 152
teacher appraisal, 3, 12, 13, 148, 151
teachers' pay and conditions dispute, 141
Thatcher, 28, 31, 56, 140, 197
Three Wise Men, 105
tracking, 160
training credits, 36, 170
UCCA, 19, 20, 22
USA, 2, 10, 45–67, 118
unions, 6
validation, 194
value added, 18, 21, 22, 23, 63, 119
vertical flexibility, 118
vouchers, 54, 55
YT, 34, 40
YTS, 39
Youth Cohort Study, 18